FERRYMAN

The life and deathwork
of Ephraim Finch

Katia Ariel

Published by Wild Dingo Press
Melbourne, Australia
books@wilddingopress.com.au
www.wilddingopress.com.au

First published by Wild Dingo Press 2025

Text copyright©Katia Ariel 2025

The moral right of the author has been asserted.

Except as permitted under the Australian Copyright Act 1968,
no part of this book may be reproduced, stored in a retrieval system,
or transmitted in any form or by any means, electronic, mechanical,
photocopying, recording, or otherwise without prior permission
of the copyright owners and the publisher of this book.

Cover designer: Alex Ross
Editors: Lenka Miklos, Paul Smitz
Printed in Australia.

Katia Ariel, 1978–
Ferryman: The life and deathwork of Ephraim Finch/Katia Ariel

A catalogue record for this book is available from the National Library of Australia

ISBN: 9781925893861 (paperback)
ISBN: 9781925893878 (ebook:pdf)
ISBN: 9781925893885 (ebook)

Wild Dingo Press works on the land of the Boon Wurrung People of the Kulin Nation. We pay our respects to their Elders past and present, and acknowledge their continuing relationship to this land.

Praise for *Ferryman: The life and deathwork of Ephraim Finch*

Tender, heartfelt and infused with deep wisdom, *Ferryman* is both a moving portrait of a remarkable man and a journey through generations of Australian Jewish history.

Katia Ariel's masterful prose gently peels back the layers of Ephraim's personal history, revealing a complex man transformed by faith who has taken upon himself to act as a living repository for a community's darkest, saddest and most life-affirming stories.

Through Ephraim we gain insights into the fragility and preciousness of life, the value of service and the restorative balm of communal belonging.

This book is for anyone who has ever thought about why we live and why we die, and it's for those of us who usually avoid such thoughts, too.

—*Kylie Moore-Gilbert*

A book full of wisdom by a writer of exquisite talent.

—*Chloe Hooper*

In her beautifully written book, Katia Ariel tells of Ephraim Finch's calling to become an undertaker with Melbourne's Jewish Burial Society. The pious, tender but disciplined care he gave to the body as he prepared it for burial was inseparable from his affirmation that each one of us is precious, unique and irreplaceable. This gave comfort to mourners, but Finch did not do it only for them: he did it for the dead person as the irreducible object of obligation, love and sorrow.

The inspired way that Finch fulfilled his vocation also revealed the importance of tradition, historically deep and poetically resonant in the ethical and spiritual life of a community when its speaks though someone like him.

Many books have been written urging us not to be in denial about death. I have read few as deep as this one. Ariel and Finch have bequeathed a gift to anyone wishing to honour their humanity by celebrating rather than lamenting our nature as essentially embodied, mortal beings.

—*Raimond Gaita*

Ferryman is a compassionate portrait of a man who has spent a lifetime in service of his community. Katia Ariel's consideration of belonging, faith, and the way we are all inextricably woven into tapestries of time, place and history—both before and after death—is beautifully written and deeply moving.

—*Hannah Kent*

Katia Ariel is a rare and beautiful writer, able to wear another's skin, look into their heart and somehow bear their pain. Her writing doesn't just bear witness, it sings back to the world.

—*Marina Benjamin*

*'I love the dark hours of my being,
for they deepen my senses;
in them as in old letters I find
my daily life already lived
in holy words, so soft and subdued.'*

— Rainer Maria Rilke, *The Book of Hours*

'Listening to a witness makes you a witness.'

— Elie Wiesel

Foreword

I am driving the familiar route on the Monash Freeway, my ageing father in the passenger seat beside me. Yet another contemporary of his has died and I ask, 'Why are you so cheerful?' 'Because it's not my funeral,' he replies.

We pull up at the cemetery, and he is there, Ephraim Finch, going about his work, on hand for a hug, a word of comfort, a quiet conversation. We make our way from the chapel to the graveside. The nearest of kin recite kaddish, the mourner's prayer. We step up one by one to shovel the earth over the coffin. Ephraim stands at a respectful distance, overseeing proceedings. An unobtrusive presence, yet fully present.

Months later it is my father's turn. He dies as he had wished, at home, in the inner-city terrace which, in the final decades of life, had become his beloved haven. Ephraim answers the call. Hours later my brothers and I are seated in his office. He is passing around the whisky and spreading his famed laminated map of Europe, locating the city of Białystok where my father was born, and Brańsk, Orły, Gródek and Bielsk, the townlets and villages where our ancestors had lived for generations.

There is love in this room, and a paradoxical lightness. Ah, the stories that have been told here, the grief that has been shared. The walls are lined with filing cabinets and books documenting the histories of old-world hamlets, cities and settlements. Yet the space feels vast. It is a Tardis in which one can travel to many worlds, a room of lamentations and revelations. Above all, a place of gentle listening.

Like thousands of others who have spent time here, we find ourselves sharing intimate details. Our father's cheeky ways, his eccentricities, his passion for Yiddish poetry. From the exchange evolves a friendship. I am one of the many who feel such a bond and sense of kinship with Ephraim. This is how it is with Finchie, as he is affectionately called. He inspires confidences.

Decades later it is Ephraim's story that is being recorded, and the map of his life that is being retraced, and it is Ephraim who is doing the telling. And in Katia Ariel he has found the ideal listener. Katia knows how to shepherd a conversation, how to sit with both words and silence. Silence creates space, and in that space a miracle of a story unfolds, as Katia writes, 'like a wave, like a melody'.

This is a beautiful, many-layered work. It deals with death, ritual and the unsung heroes who lovingly accompany the deceased on their journeys to a dignified burial. It is a love story of two Aussie teenagers who marry and embark on an extraordinary life-journey, Ephraim and his beloved partner Cas, two converts to Judaism who become the beating heart of an entire community.

Come, spend time with Finchie. Walk with him in the streets of the shtetl, where he is loved by many. After all, for thirty years he oversaw the burial of thousands. Accompany him to the cemeteries where he speaks to those who inhabit the gravesites. Sit with him in the offices of coroners, and at hospital bedsides, tending to the ill and the dying. Journey with him back to the old world as he traces generations of Jewish life.

Ephraim holds a vast history within him. He knows of his people's suffering, the tragedies they have endured, and of their joys, their celebrations. He knows the lineages of rabbinical dynasties, and their connections with those he has buried. Picture him standing in the depths of the night, where young lives have been lost, offering solace to the bereft.

Listen to the flow of his tales, the workings of his mind. Ephraim vanquishes the boundaries between the dead and the living. He walks in multiple realms. He worries about the deceased long after they have gone, speaks to them, encounters them in his dreams. 'All my life has been about connection,' he will tell you. 'With all souls, the living and the dead.'

This is an account of the life-story of a community ferryman, a tale that breaks the heart many times over, yet lifts the spirit. And this is the deepest wonder—a book about death that will inspire all who read it to live a better life.

— Arnold Zable, Melbourne, 2025

PART I: THE SHORE

Prelude

It's a cool summer morning in the last days of 1959 and a teenager is riding his bike through Sydney's Rookwood Cemetery. As he glides across the grounds, he notices the signs of dawn. The dew is melting off the grass. A fox leaps behind a bunya pine, and as if out of nowhere, a few of its cubs follow. The soil is firm beneath his tyres, and he can smell it warming, roused by the sun after a night of slumber.

Riding his Malvern Star, he is carefree. But Geoffrey William Finch, this lanky not-quite-man on his way to his carpentry job, is also careful. As he traverses the grounds, he sees the sun come up behind the headstones. Then he rounds a corner and sees the very same sun shining on an east-facing row, blazing into the engraved names of the dead.

This morning, as every weekday morning, he could circumvent the cemetery, ride along the waking bustle of Lidcombe. Instead, he lets himself in through the pedestrian gate and cuts across the field of headstones. He chooses this route because he likes the quiet. This is the interlude in which he works out his world, considers the day to come.

'And the whole time I am talking,' he tells me, some six decades later, sitting at his broad dining table in Melbourne.

'Who are you talking to, Ephraim?' I ask, because now this boy is an elderly man with a different name, a different religion, a life that he could have scarcely predicted riding through Rookwood on those dewy mornings. Ephraim and I are sitting in his front room and the sun is pouring into the space between us.

He is telling me stories. I am picturing his words as chapters, the vignettes arranging themselves between the covers of a book.

I notice that he prefers discussing his work to discussing himself. He wants to revisit his thirty years as director of a burial society—the people he comforted and held; those he ritually washed, wrapped and prayed for. But today I press him on those early years. I want to learn the soil of this man before I can describe its trees, the fruits it has borne.

'Who are you talking to, riding through Rookwood?' I repeat, lightly, as Ephraim closes his eyes, slipping into a temporal estuary.

'I am talking to God,' he says eventually, his hands resting on the table in front of him, a boyish smile now playing on his bearded face.

That Ephraim says such a lofty thing without an ounce of grandiosity, without pushing or preaching, foreshadows what I will learn about this man. This man, at once deeply religious and utterly irreverent, softly spoken but defiant, is as prone to crying as to smiling. This man, whose work deals with the body as much as the spirit, dwells easefully at their intersections. This ageing Orthodox Jew with a broad Aussie accent, this voracious archivist and beloved community figure, this working-class butcher's son who felt pulled to the Torah, is, himself, many beautiful intersections.

The notion of writing Ephraim's life has been in the ether for many years. If you were a member of Melbourne's Jewish community from the mid-1980s to 2015 you would—for better or worse—have had something to do with Ephraim Finch. Having buried over ten thousand individuals, Ephraim is—physically, emotionally, culturally and spiritually—linked to a great many lives in this unique pocket of the world.

The life and deathwork of Ephraim Finch

Not long ago, someone interviewed Ephraim with a view to writing his biography. But for one reason or another, a book did not eventuate. And so the idea made its way to my desk, via a writer who knew another writer, who approached my future publisher and asked, 'Do you know someone who could use these materials—these interview transcripts, Ephraim's journals—and shape them into a story?'

I hadn't written anything like this before, save a memoir that dealt—in its own circuitous way—with grief and loss. Well, grief and loss, but also resilience and the deep bonds of love we form in this blink of a life. So perhaps there was something.

A week after the publisher approached me, I was shown Ephraim's journal. I was struck by the language he used to chronicle his work with the dead and the dying, as well as their loved ones:

'Your heart could feel the pain of lovers separated by war.'

'How do you live a normal life? I don't know, but I feel their losses and their love for each other.'

'Sometimes you do not understand the depth of friendship until the final days.'

I noticed his empathy for all those enduring loss. The intensely personal involvement with the details of another's narrative. The reverence for forces we battle but must ultimately accept. 'He knew he was going to die and seemed to accept it. I held his hand and wished him a safe journey,' he writes in one entry. I wanted to know more about this heart-language and how a human might acquire it, become fluent in its lexicon.

Underneath this sat something else. I had my own memory of Ephraim Finch, from a death in my family almost twenty years ago. When my then-husband's mother passed away in 2006, I remember Ephraim's name being uttered; on the cusp of her death, throughout her funeral, during the rituals that coloured the subsequent weeks. I do not recall the way Ephraim looked, or even meeting him. But I will never forget the way his name resonated in that house of mourning. It was as though the name itself had a beneficent forcefield; every time my grief-stricken father-in-law would say it, he seemed calmer. 'Ephraim will know' seemed to be the answer to the questions, many of them unanswerable. Time after time, in the sheer act of saying it, something in the atmosphere would ease, even as the tears continued. When the name 'Ephraim Finch' was spoken to me again, some seventeen years later, I felt myself hurtling, with grateful awe, back into its orbit.

At our first meeting, before I have even begun to prepare myself for the flood of names and narratives, Ephraim launches into a recollection of everyone he continues to visit at Springvale Jewish Cemetery, almost ten years after retirement. 'It's my village,' he says, closing his eyes and taking me along on his imaginary tour of the place. 'I see all of them as I go around … it's like walking down the street. There is the lovely gentleman who descended from the Radomsker Rebbe, and there is Bill … Hello Bill, my dear friend! And here is Mr Cykiert, who gave me his poem just before he passed.' I continue to watch him meet them, one by one.

'And, oh.' He drops to a whisper, his fluttering hands stilling. 'Hello, dear boy.' Something subtle shifts in his facial musculature, his eyes flicker. 'You see, I buried this boy …'

In this moment, Ephraim's wife Cas, who has been sitting with us the entire time, softly interjects. 'May I tell this story, darling?' she asks, in a manner I will witness many times over the coming months. There is a concert of silent knowings between Cas and Ephraim, an instinct for each other's pauses. Intuitively, they allocate the best raconteur for the moment, illuminating and verifying one another. 'I'd like to explain why we are so connected to this boy, if I may?' Cas asks, her voice deep and low, her blue eyes cloudy. Ephraim nods.

'We were out one day with our daughter Sharona, who is now forty-two, but was then twenty. It was a hot day, but she was suddenly freezing and had a terrible headache. This went on for days and on the third night she developed a rash. On top of this, she felt like every bone in her body was breaking. Next morning, I got up at dawn to get her some Panadeine. As soon as my finger made contact with her arm, dark purple spots started to appear, spreading. And Ephraim knew exactly what it was, because he had buried this magnificent young man a few years earlier. He knew the symptoms.'

A doctor arrived not long after and administered a penicillin shot, which bought Sharona time to get to the hospital, where she would stay for three weeks. One day an infectious diseases doctor approached the Finches on the ward.

'How did you recognise the meningococcal septicaemia?' he asked Ephraim.

'Doctor, I buried a boy in 1991 …' And before Ephraim could say more the doctor named that boy, remembering the family. They stood mutely for some time, struck by the reach of tragedy. But beneath the moment was an undertow, a twist in the Finches' hearts. It was nothing as crass or numerical as a sacrifice schema—Cas and Ephraim never believed that this boy died so Sharona could live. In fact, it was an inversion of this 'lucky us' smugness—they had never forgotten that this child died while theirs had lived.

Three months after Cas tells this story, Ephraim and I will go to Springvale together, and when we reach this young man's grave, Ephraim will bend down and kiss the engraved marble. He will greet the boy and read his name out loud, along with his date of passing. He will intone the names of his mother and father. He will weep for them, while knowing the limits of his weeping. He will continue bending, head bowed, holding all the connections in all his body. And I will sense, simply by being next to this softly moving human, the shuddering proximity between us all, the near-misses, the churn of loss and the majesty of memory, the ceaseless current of our arrivals and departures.

'The most urgent part is that I was a witness,' he tells me when I ask him to help me map out the parameters of this story. Alongside his memories, Ephraim brings a bounty of archival material about his own life: interview transcripts, a video testimony he made for the Melbourne Holocaust Museum, a couple of short films on DVD, an oral testimony for the National Library of Australia. He also shows me a journal, one of several volumes he kept between the years of 2005 and 2019. This black leather-bound tome is heavy, as large as a wedding album. The pages are filled with Ephraim's distinctive hand, something that merges the printed Hebrew alphabet and the calligraphy of mid-century schoolteachers, geometric and tight.

The journal documents many of the lives and deaths that Ephraim witnessed, with an emphasis on the stories of Holocaust survivors. Over the coming months, I will see Ephraim's preoccupation with the Holocaust, namely with the details of survivors' lives—not just their birthplace, but the name of the village and its original Polish or Hungarian or Russian spelling; not just their parents' names but their siblings' and grandparents' and ex-spouses' and deceased children's. I will see scrupulous lists of internments, tattoo numbers, immigration arrival dates, names of ships. He will reiterate to me, over and over, how important it is to ask questions, to let people speak, to listen deeply.

At times, his empathy for the Jews of Eastern Europe will be so embodied, I will join Ephraim in the notion that he has somehow known their stories from the inside. In fact, there will be some astonishing crossovers between Judaism and his earlier life, before he commenced work as the director of a Jewish burial society or even found a Jewish identity.

But before we get to any of this, before he takes me to his narrow study, cluttered with binders, prayer books, novels, maps and war memorabilia, I want to go back a little. I want to know more about the adolescent Geoffrey William Finch, riding through Rookwood Cemetery on his way to the carpentry job. I want to know more about this person crossing the field of stone, innocent of the tumult, though maybe not the radiance, up ahead.

1

'I was riding my pushbike through a big intersection with my father. I must have been about fourteen. And we went through when the lights were nearly red. And I got hit by a car. I've got two beautiful scars where the headlight cut me,' he says, pointing to his leg. A few weeks have elapsed since our first interview and we are, once again, seated at Ephraim's living-room table. I have prepared a list of questions, naively thinking that we will cover, in a linear fashion, the traditional milestones of his childhood. But he wants to take it elsewhere, going with what emerges.

As he points to his scar, I notice his hands, tremulous with age and ill-health, but solid, and strikingly smooth. They resemble the hands of a master craftsman or a musician. My mind races from the bike accident to his future work, all the care these hands would go on to transmit, the steadiness they would supply to those broken or collapsing, to those waiting to cross over and those already on the other side.

He continues the story. 'So my father saw the doctor's surgery on the corner and raced in. The doctor said he'd have to stitch me immediately and my father said, "Okay, I'll hold him". There was no anaesthetic. And my father's holding me, and the doctor says,

"Are you okay, Mr Finch?" And my father says, "Yeah, I'm okay, I'm a butcher." So the doctor says, "Oh, I want to see how you do your stitches," and my father stitched me up, exactly the way that they stitched up the corned beef. And the doctor said, "You guys are very good," and that was that.'

I gesture with my hands, as though to say, 'And?', hopeful that this will instigate a deeper exploration of the father–son dynamic. But Ephraim is not interested in psychosocial banter. He is giving me a moment, a whiff of antiseptic, a portrait primed with blood and courage.

In fact, though I prod, Ephraim offers few other memories of childhood. When I ask him to tell the very beginning, he simply replies, 'I was born in 1944 in the little suburb of Ashfield, in Western Sydney, to a mother who I think didn't really know what she got into.' Ephraim recalls Gloria May Atkinson admitting her own uncertainty, her overwhelm at the demands of parenthood. She was twenty-three when she had her first child. Eighteen months later she gave birth to another boy, Richard. Like most of her friends and neighbours, Gloria May raised her children in hardship, the Finches' house built of 'Masonite ... cheap-rubbishy stuff', their kitchen table reliant on rations.

I think of the strikingly honest eulogy Ephraim gave his father James, who passed away in 2014 aged ninety-five. In it, he says, '... me being born during the war years, my father would not have known me well as he was working 100 hours a week'. This makes me wonder how Gloria May got through, what she leaned on in parenting her boys. Ephraim doesn't offer answers, adding only that on top of being absent, his father was 'a hard man'.

I do not push further into this terrain, looking instead at the memorial candles and baby photos assembled on the dining cabinet.

In fact, I notice that every available bit of space in the Finches' front room is crowded with timestamps and annotations of love: birthday cards, fading photos, oil paintings of faces and fingers and doves. Up against the wall is a record player, topped with the LP

The life and deathwork of Ephraim Finch

of Nick Cave's *The Boatman's Call*. This seems at once incongruous and perfectly aligned with this religious suburban home, with the black Hasidic hat perched at the end of the table; the engraved silver *kiddush* cups; the large, framed landscapes of ragged trees and scarlet skies. I bring myself back to the moment, even though it is tempting to fly away with these objects, holy and prosaic in equal measure.

'His customers at the butcher shop loved him because he was fair,' Ephraim says after a long pause, returning to his father. Then he tells the story of a woman from the neighbourhood who often came into the shop covered in bruises. One night, James came home with a swollen fist, prompting his twelve-year-old son to ask, 'Did you hit Mr L?' James didn't give a direct answer, simply saying, 'Mr L will never hit his wife again.'

Now I recall another passage in the eulogy, where Ephraim notes that his father 'instilled in me that you can never say "No, I can't." It always had to be "Yes, I can".' These values—fairness, a solid work ethic, tenacity—surely shaped the adult sitting before me.

Still, I wonder where the nurturance came from. Something in me refuses to believe that this man, this example of tenderness, never witnessed warmth or careful attention. Almost on cue, Ephraim says, 'See, my grandfather, Pop Finch …' Here his voice changes, regresses to something younger and more vulnerable. 'He taught me so much. When he was a boy, his father had left him and his siblings, so he had to look after the family. He'd go and deliver the milk in Pyrmont, then he'd come home and turn the mangle for his mother before going to school. He worked as a lolly-boy and he learned the violin,' he concludes, almost in tears. I must look confused at this disjointed sketch because Cas intervenes to connect the dots.

'Pop made everything a learning experience. He worked as a theatre boy, but he paid attention to the musicians—he saw Paderewski play the piano, and Menuhin playing the violin. When he became an adult, he and Nana took a great interest in their grandsons—they wanted the boys to have an education, they taught them piano and so much more.'

'I used to see Pop come home from his work at the abattoirs and he'd sit on the back veranda in his rocking chair, with a glass of whisky. And the Monopole magnum cigar and Oscar Wilde's works,' Ephraim adds. I have seen the worn hardcovers in Ephraim's study, inherited from Pop: Dickens, Hugo, the pages thin with time and use. Picturing William Robert George Finch, I see an iteration of him sitting before me: a blue-collar man with a love of scholarship.

'And of course, there was his determination to look after any woman who was left alone with children ...' Cas adds, somewhat elliptically. Ephraim explains that during the world wars, many women were left husbandless. The death notices, which were published in the local paper, listed the bereaved person's address. Pop would read the listings and organise a delivery boy to take an envelope of money to the house. For many women, this was a life-saving gesture.

'The understanding of *tzedakah*, charity, the understanding of living your life for another human being, that's what he got from Nana and Pop on his father's side,' says Cas, closing the circle.

We return to the topic of life-shaping events. Ephraim tells me that the bike accident wasn't the last encounter with his own mortality. A year later, he contracted appendicitis, which went undiagnosed and turned septic, creating a pelvic abscess that nearly took his life. 'And this specialist came in, examined me and said if they don't operate in the next twenty-four hours I won't be there,' he says, without drama but with a fracture in his voice.

'Do you remember, in the course of that experience, fearing your death?' I ask. The grandfather clock ticks in the background. I notice a tiny pomegranate lying at the centre of the table and I know it has come from the Finches' front garden. I know that Cas collected it from the ground after last night's heavy winds, gingerly giving it pride of place at this long table.

'Not leading up to it, but after the operation, yes,' Ephraim finally says. 'And in those days, it wasn't refined. They stuffed a hose down my throat to drain the rubbish out. It was about half an inch thick. And when I bent over, it would crank in the back of my throat, I couldn't breathe, and a few times I brought the tube up. And every time I did, they just said, "Don't worry, we can put it back in again!" They were rough times, tough times. Now if I get too close to a rubber hose, I sort of …' He shakes his head, indicating nausea, some terrible sense memory.

I circle back to the question of mortality. He pauses again.

'I remember lying in the hospital, and my uncle, Laurie Hall, who had emphysema, was standing by. And when the doctor gave me the twenty-four-hour prognosis, Uncle Laurie turned to my parents and said, "I hope God takes me and leaves Geoff".' It was not long after this that his uncle passed away. Again, Ephraim doesn't force interpretation, doesn't push a cosmic formula. He is not citing this example because he purports to know what happened behind the veil. He is citing it because it is the first time his own death is named directly to his face. The fright of it. The shock to a boy who had, until now, a fairly unshocking childhood. But there is something else. Ephraim is citing a good and precious thing: his uncle's grace, a memory of deep care at this time of aloneness.

'What about earlier in childhood, what had you witnessed of death, of funerals in your community?' I ask, digging for more roots to his vocation. Ephraim remembers, faintly, the death of a boy in his street. 'Fatty' Baker was twelve years old when he died from a staph infection after stepping barefoot on a nail. But even this memory lacks the traumatic imprint one would expect; the elderly man before me simply remembers the boy, remembers playing with him and enjoying their time together.

What he wants me to know is that the boys of the neighbourhood, many of whom attended Scouts, formed a guard of honour around their friend's open coffin. This—the ritual of public commemoration—seems like the salient part of the story for Ephraim.

I tell him that I grew up in Soviet Odesa in the 1980s, where street funeral processions were common; an open casket, followed by a marching band. There was always a tuba, its low tones carrying the dirge into the ears of passersby. In my childhood of hidden Jewishness and overt communism, there was no religious tradition but plenty of superstition.

He replies that he was neither superstitious nor religious, the only skerrick of either dwelling in his nightly recitation of 'As I lay me down to sleep, I pray thee Lord my soul to keep'. Still, the Anglican trinity had little purchase on his heart, while a single god, embodied in all living things, made sense.

'I always believed in the one. I couldn't believe in the three. And see, Pop, he believed in the one. My grandfather wasn't interested in religion, but to be a Freemason you have to believe in a higher power in the world,' he says. Pop introduced young Geoff into this community, fortifying two qualities that would reverberate across his life: a love of ritual and an interest in the divine, a taste for something beyond the immediately visible and immediately rewarding.

'Great Architect of the Universe, they call God. And the ritual is non-denominational. See, people need *something*,' he says, getting up to make us tea.

While he is out of the room, I consider this 'something', the essential human need for ritual. I think of myself, and my secular Jewish friends, cherry-picking customs and traditions. We grapple with notions of spirit, the possibility and texture of an omnipresent, ineffable force in our lives. Still, for the most part, it's casual Shabbat dinners with the phones on, Hannukah candles for five of the eight days, a Passover reading that we may or may not get through before everyone lunges at the chicken soup. Coming to this house, I dress more modestly than 'out there', covering my shoulders and my decorative tattoos. In other words, I am a Jew to the same extent that I am a secular humanist, a product of my agnostic world and its mixed-bag customs.

That is, until there is a great life event, namely a birth or a death. Something awesome, in the traditional sense of that word, comes into the picture, something that rattles complacency and begs contemplation.

Never have I been so grateful for the structure, the scaffolding, of ancient tradition, as when a loved one passes. Here, in the merciless hollow of fresh loss, ritual becomes everything. The quick burial, no more than a day after death. The thud of earth as it hits the coffin, fresh off the shovels of surviving family; the enforced sitting and inwardness of *shiva*; the repetitive incantation of the kaddish; the covered mirrors; the counting of the days; the mounting of the headstone. All of it is a firm grip in a measureless dark.

Ephraim returns with the tea and sits down at the head of the table, humming to himself. Cas is to my left, sewing a button onto a granddaughter's pants. I am slowly forming a portrait of his early life. But I struggle with my scant sense of his mother. I do not wish for this figure to be invisible on the page.

Although Ephraim is reluctant to confect an intimacy that was not there, he notes that his relationship with Gloria May deepened over the years, especially in her final decade. 'Towards the end of her life she came and visited. She would stay with us and the children grew to know her very well.'

When Gloria May died, in 2004, she was living in an aged-care home in Ashfield, the suburb where she was born. Ephraim had visited her there, sitting by her bedside, making sure that she was comfortable. The care facility in which she took her last breaths was about two hundred metres from Finch and Sons, the butcher shop that fed her family, had secured her livelihood and her place in the community for over five decades. Ephraim officiated at her funeral, reading the psalms, delivering the eulogy. In his farewell he recalled, with affection, swimming with her at Wylie's Baths, the wild Pacific ocean pool where she was joyful and relaxed. Then he buried his mother, 'tucking her in' for the last time.

It is after midday and Ephraim is tiring. We have been talking for three hours. Just as I am about to suggest we finish, he shuffles off to his study, saying, 'Hang on!' He returns with a small hardcover book, in faded green cloth, titled *The Observer's Book of Ships*. Published in 1953, it is inscribed in neat, antiquated hand: 'G.W. Finch. 13 Third St Ashbury, N.S.W., Australia'. I see this gangly, brown-eyed boy, assiduously adding his details to the page, perhaps hoping to show it to Pop.

'I used to love drawing boats, things from World War II,' says Ephraim. 'And you know, Ben, our eldest, also loves everything about that period in history. He knows all the *Panzer*, the German tanks, he can quote sentences in German ...'

Here is what I know about Ben Finch: he helped his father at the burial society—driving to collect the deceased, attending funerals, eventually building coffins—before he was even an adult. Now in his fifties, he is neither an Orthodox Jew nor a deathworker, sort of mirroring Ephraim's journey in reverse. I am desperate to know more about this eldest son, and about this unique hereditary apprenticeship, but I hold off. Instead, I ask Ephraim another question that has arisen, one that feels a bit risky.

'Do you think we carry things into our lives from, you know, before we come in and before we leave ... Do you think we bring things from ...' I start to trip and stumble, ignorant of the Finches' religious vocabulary, not wishing to offend.

'Past lives?' Cas asks softly, dispelling my impostor syndrome.

'Well ... yes. Do you think we bring things from other lives, things we love, things we want to hold onto?'

'Oh, we love things from another time, yes,' says Ephraim, misunderstanding my question. In due course, I will learn that both Cas and Ephraim do believe in reincarnation, and that none of that contradicts the Jewish paradigm. But right now, he takes me elsewhere, and it's just as valuable.

'That's why I love that clock. It's two hundred years old,' he continues, pointing to the grandfather clock in the corner. Its ticking has faithfully, unobtrusively, kept us company all morning. 'That's Pa's clock. It's from Scotland,' he says. Pa is George Charles Edward Atkinson, Ephraim's maternal grandfather. Earlier in our conversation Ephraim told me that his Pa had fought in WWI and had suffered terribly from the effects of mustard gas. But that was about it. We have hardly spoken about him, but now he is here. 'I feel a connection to it, I treasure old things,' says Ephraim, his voice clotting.

'I wonder if you have the soul of an archivist,' I say.

'Definitely.'

'Whereas I'm just a hoarder,' Cas pipes up, giggling.

'Maybe you enable each other?' I suggest.

'Yes, we do,' they respond in a round of echoes, 'yes, we do!'

Ephraim takes down a framed photo from the mantlepiece, a close-up portrait of his youngest daughter, Michal, on her wedding day. A veil filters her sweet, round face, her clear blue eyes looking directly at the camera. I notice that when he holds the photo, his hands stop trembling, as if the very act of touching this moment stills him. He emits a long, melodic 'Oh ...', a call that signals something I will witness time and time again—nostalgia.

It seems that while Ephraim is happy to skim over some aspects of the past, others induce a huge swell of feeling, an almost unbearable tenderness. I hope, in time, to learn which stories fall into which group, to observe what flows like water and what sits like stone, and with any luck, discern the reasons why.

Tucking these hopes into my folder, I start to pack up. I place Ephraim's photocopied journal into my bag, along with my laptop.

I turn off the recording app and move across the living room, thanking him and Cas for their time. Ephraim follows me out, but there is an incompleteness between us.

'So many stories to cover,' I say.

'I'm still trying to find … this man came in for his wife …' he replies, and I stop in the doorway. We are standing at the threshold between the dining room and a tiny library, a hallway so heavily walled with books it feels like a grove of dense forest.

'He came in to bury his wife, had his two sons with him. I asked for her name, date of birth, where she'd come from. Poland? Hungary? What year did she come here? He said 1949. Bingo, I knew I was in for a night of history.' We have moved beyond the bookshelves and are now standing at the front door.

He continues. 'I asked for her occupation. "Seamstress, machinist". "One or two marriages?" And the sons spiked up, "What are you asking that for?" I showed them the form, said, "I'm just collecting a history". Turned out she'd been married previously. We sat there, one minute, minute and a half. And my noisy brain was clicking over, click, click …'

'And no one is saying anything?'

'No. Then the father starts crying. And he looks at the boys, who are now thirty-five, forty, and he says, "I was also married before the war". I asked for his first wife's name—I want the names of the ones that perished. Wrote it down. I got the village he was born in, the year he came here, his occupation. Then I said, "Did you have a child with your first wife?" Two minutes this time. Silence, click, click. Then he looked at his boys and told them he'd had a little girl.'

Standing before me, Ephraim whispers the little girl's name. He names her exactly the way the father did all those years ago, a soft Yiddish diminutive reserved for the greatest treasures.

Sarale, not Sarah. *Rivkale*, not Rebecca. *Ruchele*, not Rochl or Rachel or Raizel. *Freidi. Shaynale. Mashenke.*

'She perished?'

'Yes. But now I had her name,' he says, as I step out of the house and proceed down the path, looking back at him. I can feel Ephraim's journal weighing down my bag, as though suddenly swollen by its own details.

'And the brothers said, "Thank you". Now they knew they had a sister,' he continues, not raising his voice. And though we are now several metres apart, with the garden wind swirling the air between us, I can hear him perfectly. My hand on the gate, I say her name. Then I step out onto the street, slowly, carefully, so as not to lose her to the onrushing present.

2

A few weeks later, I arrive at the Finches' to discover that Ephraim is absent. No one is sure where he is, but no one is worried either. So I take the opportunity to sit with Cas, who shows me a miniature crystal vase inscribed with their names. It contains two gardenias, brought by a friend. Next to the gardenias is a stem of white rosebuds, curled like newborn fists, from the Finches' front garden. 'Aren't they magnificent!' Cas exclaims, with the sincerity of someone tasting an exotic fruit for the first time.

I am starting to feel great affection for this house, with its fragrant garden and red front door, with the unconditional positive regard that greets its endless, shifting cast of visitors. Although I am writing a book about death and grief, about a life of comforting the broken, it is hard to feel heavy in this house. While I frequently shed tears during the interviews, or when reading the journals, I struggle to feel grim in the presence of the Finches.

In the hour before Ephraim arrives, I learn that Cas was born in Sydney but spent almost all her childhood in Wagga Wagga, where she would go on to meet her future husband. Just like Ephraim, while she was not raised in an emphatic religious tradition, she wondered about a bigger picture.

The life and deathwork of Ephraim Finch

'You know, as a little girl, I must have been about eight … I would be coming home from my piano lesson and I would walk down the street and somehow feel like I didn't belong,' she says. It wasn't that she had an unhappy childhood, in fact the opposite—Cas's home was replete with love, her musical and dancing talents were nurtured, she had plenty of friends. Still, there was a sense of otherness, of knowing that home was waiting elsewhere.

She is recalling this feeling when Ephraim walks through the door.

'Hello, darling!' the pair exclaim in unison.

He tells us he's been visiting an aged-cared facility nearby, something he does regularly.

'I went around the room and asked people their names. There was a gentleman, sitting next to me, born in Poland, came here in 1947. "There must be a Holocaust story in that," I said to him and asked him for his village. He doesn't say anything. Then I start to list possibilities. "You could be from Strykow, or Chęciny. Or you could be from Apta …" And now he's smiling. I asked if he wanted me to come back, to take more history, and he nodded. So I've found an entry point. It was about an hour and a quarter I spoke there. It was lovely.'

'You return something to them,' I say, thinking of our last encounter, of the perished girl whose name he retrieved. 'You give them back their history, the parts forgotten by the world.' To which Ephraim raises his eyebrows, as though to say, 'I can only try'.

Carolyn Bassett is fifteen years old at the time of the 1963 Royal Wagga Wagga Show. Late in the afternoon, on the first day of the show, she is at the Presbyterian tearoom, catching up with friends. Eventually, ready to leave, she crosses the room and goes to exit. But when she leans on the door, she feels someone pushing from the other side. The two bodies move like this, back and forth, for a few seconds. Then, having negotiated the threshold, they find themselves in the hallway.

'And, oh my goodness, I saw his face. Well, I saw his eyes. I do not remember looking below his eyes. And that was it. I don't think I thought another proper thought about it. I simply started to walk home. Walking ... thank God it was a straight road! And I only had to do one turn,' she says, her voice catching.

When Cas gets home, she begins to get ready for the barbecue at her friend Cheryl Baikie's house. Minutes—how many?—pass, as she moves about in a daze. At some point the doorbell rings. She can hear her father's footfalls down the hall, his confident stride.

'And who are you?' comes the voice of Alonza Leo Bassett.

'My name is Geoffrey Finch and I'm staying at the Baikies'. They asked me to drive around and pick up everyone who's going to the barbecue. I'm here to collect your daughter.'

At this, Carolyn starts to walk down the hallway. When she gets to the door, she looks at the young man and the words fall from her, as though it was just a matter of time, as if her heart is beating with recognition rather than surprise. 'Oh, it's you!' she says, and they depart.

It's a warm October night, and young people are coming and going, some clustered around the bonfire in the yard, some inside dancing. But Carolyn and Geoffrey find it hard to stay apart. She introduces him to her friends, they make small talk. And then, tired of milling about, of making chit-chat with others, they go outside and take a seat on the stile. Through the smoky night sky, they catch echoes of 'I Will Follow Him' and 'Cry to Me', the music wafting between their faces, their timid smiles.

I picture them sitting on the stile under the dark cape of night, sheltered by stars, finally able to speak freely.

'Did you make small talk or go deep?' I ask.

'We went deep straight away,' says Ephraim.

'We spoke about how many children we were going to have,' adds Cas.

'And she said, "I'm an only child, I'm not having just one",' he recalls, laughing. 'We're having more than two. Because two get judged between one another.' And they left that night saying they'd have five. (They would go on to have six children and, in due course, seventeen grandchildren.)

I ask Ephraim to circle back to seeing Carolyn Bassett for the first time. What did he perceive when he looked in her powder-blue eyes?

'It's hard to be minimalistic about what I saw,' he says, smiling distantly, channelling that teenager on the threshold of everything. 'But I knew.' A few moments pass before he adds, 'I said to my mother one day, not long before meeting Cassie, "Mum, I don't think I will ever get married because no one will love me". And it was a beautiful thing she said to me ... "When the right person comes along, that'll be it". Mum didn't have many words of wisdom when I was growing up. But then she said that.'

Sitting on the stile, the teenagers continue to speak. Geoffrey—slender, nineteen years of age, deeply brown-eyed, slightly hunched—shares an image with his new acquaintance. He describes a field of golden wheat. He speaks of having his feet in the soil, looking out at this field, the field where the source of all life dwells.

'And it was actually nighttime by then, so everything was dark,' says Cas. 'But because I could imagine it, the reality was ...'

I suggest that this itself reveals their compatibility, because another kind of girl might have said, 'Oh, don't be silly, what are you talking about? I can't picture that!' But Cas had run with his image, imbibing it wholeheartedly.

'Yes, yes,' she hurries to confirm. They disclose to each other their feeling that the divine is everywhere and that in this omnipresence, every being is important. We let this moment hover between us, and again, I notice how unprescriptive they are in their cosmology. The

Finches have been deeply religious for five decades. I am a cultural Jew whose life is, functionally, miles away from their Orthodox neck of the woods. And yet they have never assessed my place in the community, never suggested I do as they do, as a condition of entry into their lives. And here, on the cusp of their journey into Judaism, I see this same phenomenon; their faith is a current that passes between them, a self-evident thing that they embody, that needs no signatories or validators.

The weekend of the Wagga Show is the last public holiday of the year, which means they won't see each other for a few months. So Geoff promises to write. And write he does, sending her a letter every day until their reunion the following Easter. He sends Carolyn a record player, and a sequence of 7-inch records. Roy Orbison, The Beatles. All his gestures comfort her, as do the many hours she spends talking to him in her head. These months flow into their engagement, then their marriage, on 11 June 1966. By now they are living in Sydney, where Carolyn is studying nursing. Geoffrey has finished his apprenticeship and is working as an estimator. He has learned all the key trades of construction, is ready to be a master builder. He remembers this work as 'beautiful'.

'When you work on building, it's creation. It's a person working to bind everything together,' he tells me. Thinking about his future work, I like this image very much. I picture Ephraim measuring beams for doorways, appraising the depth of a roof cavity. The consideration of warmth, the drift of natural light, the height of a ceiling, the stability of a window frame. I see the same man sanding coffins, lining them with a sheet and a pillow; the simplest shelter. The wrapping of the shroud around a deceased body, the pressing of the hands of the bereaved, the sealing of the body's final, wooden home under forty inches of soil, the smoothing of the transitional moments with a psalm. All of these will become his daily work, a labour of binding.

After a brief stint living above the butcher shop, the Finches buy their first home, in Strathfield. The young couple, hoping for a baby, trialling their new life together, love this green suburb. Their backyard has a firepit, which Geoff has surrounded with seating made of railway sleepers. Their kitchen is fitted out with sandstock bricks, western red cedar and a triple sink that he has designed especially for their budding family. Their life feels, in its way, replete. This is the setting in which two extraordinary things happen.

The first is a trip Cas takes to the newsagent on Paramatta Road, Enfield, to buy a book on Russian history. She walks to the shop and reaches for what she thinks is the history text. Instead, she pulls out *This Is My God* by Herman Wouk. She knows nothing about this author or this book, which—to this day—is regarded as one of the simplest and most engaging guides to Modern Orthodox Judaism. She starts to flick through it and is immediately drawn in.

Cas is struck by Wouk's warmth, his desire to unlock an ancient tradition for his modern reader. He ventures to convey 'the Hebrew idea of the Creator' as it is constellated in daily life—the tenets of Jewish faith, its three-thousand-year-old origins and its enshrinement in the Torah. She is particularly taken by the descriptions of the holidays and the rituals of keeping a Jewish home.

There are many passages that delight and awaken her, like the bells of multiple towers across one city, chiming at the same time. She is especially moved by the description of Judaism's paradoxical heart, its tight knot of obligation and privilege. 'Tradition says the Creator gave our folk the task of bearing witness to his moral law on earth,' writes Wouk. 'This is what the battered phrase "the chosen people" means. Our history ... is in the main a melancholy account of our failure to live up to this high election, and the catastrophes that came from our failure. But the election stands, the mission remains.'

Standing in the newsagent, oblivious to the surrounding action, Cas is reading, and the whole time, she is thinking, 'This is us. This is us.' She loses track of time. Then she remembers herself, pays for the book and rushes home, where she shows it to her husband. Over the coming days, they take turns reading, anxiously awaiting their moment with the book. They read passages out loud to each other, hearing a resonance they can't ignore. It dawns on them that not only do the traditions make perfect sense, but nothing else feels as warm, as deep. They find themselves talking about the rituals, contemplating what it must be like to worship in just this way. 'Time on earth is a pattern of wheels within wheels,' writes Wouk, '—the day, the week, the seasons, the year—and on each of the wheels Judaism has its stamp.'

A few weeks after Cas brings the book home, the second remarkable thing happens. A family moves in next door. These are the Israels; Ian, Pam and their young daughter Deborah, who have come from England. 'They must be Jewish, with a surname like "Israel",' the Finches think. The next Friday evening, as Cas and Geoff are standing in their kitchen, they look over the fence, peering into their neighbours' window. And they see Pam lighting Shabbat candles, a scarf over her head, challah on the table. Looking on, yearning spikes them, again.

The next day, they knock on the Israels' door and are invited in. A neighbourly friendship ensues.

'And never once did we say we wanted to become Jewish,' Cas remarks. 'Now I have no idea why not. Do you?' she throws to Ephraim. He shakes his head. I wonder if perhaps they didn't feel qualified, that they doubted their right to this tradition.

'And then you moved to Canberra,' I prompt, having done some pre-reading.

'Yes. In 1969 we had Benny, then Sarah was born in 1971. Mummy was in Canberra, and so it made sense,' Cas says. I note that aside from Cas's mother, they would have had nobody in Canberra; they were starting from scratch.

'But every time we went for a drive,' Cas picks up, 'Ephraim would go around the National Jewish Centre. And one day I said, "Look, if you don't go in, I just won't ever come in the car with you again!"' At this all three of us laugh, though it's not a simple laugh. Each of us can see the pathos in the comedy of this couple circling, quite physically pulled by longing.

'We were afraid,' Cas finally says. 'To be so close to something you've wanted so much ... you either run towards it quickly or you become very, very timid.'

Only there is something else, a third remarkable thing. This vignette, which has unsettled my heart, upset the neat trajectory I have been plotting for this book, Ephraim had told me at our first meeting. I have not known where to put it, rotating it internally as the weeks slip by. And yet its home is surely here, in this chapter on thresholds and wanting, on dreams projected and words withheld.

One day, not long after the Finches' move to Canberra, Ephraim called in on his father at the butcher shop. Nana Irene was there, hoping to catch up with her grandson. This was the Nana Irene who, alongside her husband, gave young Geoff his first music lessons, showed him the value of scholarship. Irene had kept a polite distance from his Jewish customs, though not a cold one. She seemed to be observing him.

Standing at the counter, Geoff looked over the large glass cabinet at his father, who was preparing a cut of meat. Then, seemingly out of nowhere, wiping his palms on his apron, James spoke. 'You know, son, my mother's got Jewish blood.'

The shop was empty, the white tiles gleaming in the morning sunlight. Geoff didn't say anything, perhaps unable to assimilate this statement and its tone of brusque indifference, the way his father continued to work the slab of meat, his gaze withdrawn. He took a moment, gathered his thoughts. Then he turned to

Nana and asked her point-blank: 'Are you Jewish?' Her reply, as he now recollects it, was 'very vague'. But he persevered, asking if she had family in Germany, to which she nodded. He had heard the words 'Altona Hamburg' mentioned in previous years. He knew that Nana's father, whose surname was Behrmann, hailed from there. He asked for names. She shrugged, giving only one morsel, a phrase that would yield its dark substance way down the track, when he was besieged by other griefs and least expected it. 'They lived happily ever after,' Nana said, closing the conversation by the counter at Finch and Sons, the esteemed butcher shop of Summer Hill.

'I was the construction manager at Stocks and Holdings in the centre of Canberra, and I'm at work one day and everybody starts talking ... "Oh, there's a director coming down, he's a Jew, you know",' Ephraim tells me, as we continue to cobble the chronology. He recalls listening to this, infuriated by the derogatory tone but also excited, because he feels compelled to speak to this man.

'So, five o'clock comes and everybody is going home. And I've built up enough courage, so I approach him: "Mr Fisher, I'm wondering, could I have a word? My wife and I would like to become Jewish".' To this, Jack Fisher says, 'I think we'll go downstairs to the Greek tavern, what do you think?' And so the two men proceed to the restaurant, where the director of Stocks and Holdings says to the waiter, 'My friend will have a double whisky and I'll have one with him.'

I can only imagine the warmth flooding young Geoff's heart in this moment. And indeed, his eyes sparkle as he recounts this episode, not just because something so foundational is shifting, but because he is finally visible, his deepest dream beheld.

And so Jack Fisher takes Geoff under his wing, inviting him on site visits so the two men can talk freely. He tells Geoff about the Beth Din, the ecclesiastical court that presides over matters such as conversion, located in Sydney's Kings Cross. Then he helps him draft a letter to the five rabbis who comprise the court, asking for an appointment.

A few weeks later, Cas and Geoff receive a phone call from the Beth Din. The rabbis are inviting them to their headquarters. It is now 1972. The Finches have been idling in anticipation for five years.

'We go down there and open this heavy door and start walking up five flights of stairs,' says Ephraim. Beneath them is the graphic mayhem of Kings Cross; drug deals, people sleeping rough, the odd brawl. 'And we go into this room, and it's dark.' And when their eyes adjust they realise they are standing in front of five rabbis, virtually hidden behind a very tall wooden bench. Each is bearded and grey, in a yarmulke and black suit.

A voice invites them to sit down. Later, they will learn that this is the voice of Rabbi Abramson, the head of the Beth Din.

'And which one of you is not Jewish?' the voice demands, soaked in the Ashkenazi tones of its homeland.

'Neither of us is Jewish,' Cas replies, weak at the knees.

Despite its intimidating beginnings, the interview goes well. Cas and Ephraim now don't recall what else they were asked, but they do remember Rabbi Porush peering over the imposing bench, delivering the verdict: 'We are impressed by your sincerity. We advise you to go away and read more. Then come back.'

After the first meeting with the Beth Din, the couple are appointed teachers, Nehama and Chaim Rieder. This elderly husband-and-wife team instruct Cas and Geoff on the finer points of Torah law. Each Finch goes to a Rieder of the matching gender, their lessons quickly deepening to something beyond scripture, to a sharing of hearts. Nehama, who has lost much of her family in the Holocaust, shows Cas her dark disorientation. Chaim gives Geoff advice not just on kosher cutlery but the very path of life. To this day, Ephraim recalls a parable shared by the elderly man.

King Solomon was at a festival when the Angel of Death showed up. And Solomon, being able to see such figures, spoke to him. He asked the presence why it was there and the Angel of Death pointed to two of Solomon's servants. Solomon urged his servants to run to the city of refuge, where they would be protected. And so they ran. But after days of running they were exhausted and stopped at a cave to rest for the night. And who is in the cave? The Angel of Death, of course.

'I took this to mean that no matter where you go, no matter what you do, no matter what strategies you put in place, there is only so much you can do when it comes to death,' Cas says, and Ephraim nods in agreement. This strikes me as a huge statement, which prompts another delicate question. I pause to consider my phrasing.

'Are you afraid of death?' I ask eventually, addressing them both.

'I'm not afraid of death,' Cas replies. Her face, however, scrunches with ambivalence. The sentence is not complete, or not fully unfurled.

'I'm not afraid of death, but I don't want you to go, darling,' she says, turning away from me and towards Ephraim, who is sitting across the wide white table. At this, tears cloud his eyes. He continues to sit for a moment. Then he gets up and begins to walk slowly around the table, to the tip of its oval. As he does this, Cas walks towards him. They meet in the middle, backgrounded by an empty fireplace and a crowded mantlepiece. They embrace each other, standing in a knot for a good many breaths. And although I cannot see it, I hear Ephraim weeping quietly, his tears soft as dew on Cas's shoulder.

When the moment finally comes, the Finches receive a phone call from Rabbi Apple.

'Mr Finch, the Beth Din thinks you should come up to Sydney because you're ready,' the great rabbi says.

'Rabbi, I don't think we are,' Geoff replies. 'I don't think we know enough. Can we call you when we are ready?'

A month later Rabbi Apple calls back, this time with some sternness in his voice. 'Mr Finch, the Beth Din has decided you are to come up.' By now they have three children, having welcomed their second daughter Shoshi in 1975. They contemplate the trip up to Sydney, the physical and metaphorical borders they are about to cross with these three small humans.

They are not briefed about the ceremony at all, only that they will be immersed in the *mikveh*, a ritual bath containing naturally gathered water. The family will be separated by sex, each member having to immerse fully and say a blessing. The rabbis will be in an adjacent room, peering around the corner for the moment of complete submergence.

After years of learning, of practical application, of rules and questions, the immersion brings something else: a moment free of thinking, of pure embodiment. The limbs let go, the eyes must close. The fall, the fleeting withdrawal from the world above, the naked re-emergence from an amniotic embrace—all of this is familiar to the human body, but on this day, for this family, it is utterly new.

However, first, the family must come before the full bench. Rabbi Abramson poses a question to the father of this growing family, to the man who is minutes away from shedding 'Geoff' and becoming 'Ephraim'. Rabbi Abramson is, of course, across all the recent prevarications; the Finches' uncertainty, the multiple calls from Rabbi Apple. No doubt, he can also sense this man's trepidation, bound up in the force of his yearning.

'Mr Finch, do you know enough about Judaism?' he asks, his voice imposing.

'Rabbi Abramson, I will never know enough about Judaism,' replies the man politely but surely. 'As long as I live, I will never know enough.'

'You're ready,' says the rabbi.

And so Geoff and Carolyn receive their Hebrew names: Ephraim, Carmella. 'Ephraim' comes by way of Rabbi Abramson, who notices the 'ef' in 'Geoff' and builds on it. It means 'a fruitful field', which goes beautifully with 'Carmella', a 'garden' or 'orchard'. When it comes to the children, there is nothing to change: Benjamin, Sarah and Shoshannah. Undeniably archetypal, these names speak of an early instinct for ancient music, a prescience in their parents' hearts.

3

Ephraim goes to the kitchen to make tea. He comes back without the tea but with a palm-sized ceramic bowl, painted with a delicate frieze of blue and yellow flowers. The bowl holds the cherry tomatoes I had brought to the Finches' door earlier in the week. It has been an uncommonly wet summer, and this is the meagre crop I gleaned from my garden. It was a very strong impulse, perhaps not entirely professional, but the one thing I wanted to do was share this 'harvest' with these two people, these people I find myself thinking about more and more when we are apart.

I stood on the doorstep wondering what exactly I was doing with the tomatoes, yet somehow unable to walk away. Greeting me with his sing-song voice, Ephraim opened the door and ushered me in. He took the tomatoes as if they were diamonds, telling me how excited Cas would be to receive them as he placed them on the kitchen bench. Now they are between us on the dining table, their shiny redness tingling with neighbourly affection, of new bonds formed.

I shepherd the conversation to Sydney in the early 1980s.

Over the past fortnight Ephraim has told me about his and Cas's second wedding, a *chuppah* under the star-speckled ceiling of the Great Synagogue in Sydney. Then the family's move from Canberra to Sydney, by way of Israel. The ten months the Finches spend in Israel, in 1978—studying in Jerusalem, working the land on a kibbutz—will crystallise as one of their most precious experiences. Cas recalls the children acquiring the language 'just as if they were drinking it', Ephraim knowing 'the air and the soil' like it was his first and last home. Then, due to a concert of family obligations, and with heavy hearts, they return to Australia. The Finches fly back across the planet, this time settling in Bondi Junction, the Hasidic heartland of Sydney.

As they become immersed in the community, Ephraim finds himself drawn to the elderly Orthodox men, most of them from his synagogue. He watches the way they pack their satchel; first the *tefillin*, the black leather phylacteries; then, the *tallit*, the prayer shawl. Always in the same order, always with the same steady hand. He listens to their stories of perished families, the prayers sung in mourning.

Some of these men perform *tahara*, the ritual of preparing the body for burial, and Ephraim asks them about it.

'It was just a natural progression, it just folded,' he says, describing his earliest steps towards deathwork.

I love this image so much, the course of Ephraim's life folding itself in front of him, like a wave, like a melody. In fact, how he 'got there' is itself a sort of temporal folding, parts of his past and present layering into each other with the softest synchronicity. He asks if I remember Rabbi Abramson, one of the five on the Beth Din who had sanctified the Finches' conversion. It was Rabbi Abramson who asked Ephraim if he knew enough to become Jewish. Rabbi Abramson who watched the young Geoffrey in the *mikveh*, giving him and his wife their Hebrew names. Down the track, Rabbi Abramson would delve into the intricacies of Torah with the adolescent Ben, bonding with the boy but also bonding the boy to spiritual enquiry.

So it reads like yet another thread in the shawl of Ephraim's story, woven through and alongside and forward into a new stretch of fabric, that Rabbi Osher Abramson's body is the one Ephraim fetches as his first ever task for the burial society, the Sydney Chevra Kadisha, in November 1981.

'Rabbi Abramson,' Ephraim says, 'I prayed in front of him ... I used to look at him, on the top area near the Sefer Torah. And this one Shabbat, I notice his bag is there, but he isn't. In the midst of the afternoon, we hear that he's passed away. And I'm in the front row, where only the converts or the mad ones pray. So the other rabbi turns to me and says, "Ephraim, go and pick up Rabbi Abramson from the hospital". After Shabbat ends, Ephraim goes to the *mikveh* to prepare himself for the holy tasks ahead. Then he drives to the hospital to meet the Chevra Kadisha workers, who have brought the hearse. I ask what it was like to see this precious man deceased.

'He had tired eyes,' says Ephraim.

This detail is so precise, so sensitive, I leave it in the air between us.

'Now, when I go to Rookwood, his grave ... it's my favourite spot,' Ephraim eventually says. Another silence, an unspoken eulogy. 'And after that, I approached the Chevra Kadisha and said I wanted to become a member.'

'When you go in it's unknown,' he says. I have asked Ephraim to close his eyes and conjure his earliest memories of entering the Chevra Kadisha.

'It's about five or six in the morning. It's a quiet hour, it's dark outside. You ring the buzzer and the *shomer*, the guard, lets you in,' he says. The *shomer* is another volunteer, whose sole job is to sit by the body, reciting psalms. According to tradition, from the moment of death until burial, the body of the deceased must not be left unaccompanied.

'Then you go down the stairs, into the bowels of the earth. And it doesn't ever leave you, the feeling that you are doing something very special. You never take it for granted.' As he says this, Ephraim unspools in a way I have not yet seen. Rather than pushing through, he stops the moment entirely. Letting the tears stream down his bearded face, he flutters his fingers in front of his chest. 'The trouble is, I have people coming, talking …' he says. Cas, sitting to my left, leans in and whispers to me that this happens sometimes, that Ephraim sees 'his' people. She advises that it's just a matter of allowing it, of granting him the time to dwell in that realm, to reconnect with those whom he has let go but not forgotten. I watch him, tears streaming down my own cheeks. Then, just as swiftly as he unravelled, he re-ravels, back into the dawn shift at the Chevra, greeting his fellow volunteers.

'And then it's "Good morning, how are you?" Wash your hands, put the gear on and your gloves and then you check the person's name.'

I ask Ephraim who mentored him and he lists three Ashkenazi men's names, saying, 'Men do the men, women do the women'.

'Mr S was an island of calm,' says Cas about one of the elderly gentlemen she came to know. Cas and Ephraim use the men's full names, but I am reluctant to include them given I cannot ask for their permission. In addition, most *tahara* volunteers prefer to keep their status private. Like all *mitzvot* (voluntary good deeds), *tahara* is not something to show off about, to trumpet to the community. It is a silent giving, a gesture of humility.

'They were the best of the best,' she continues. 'Older. Men from the world that no longer exists. And they went through hell on earth. And they were …' she pauses, searching for the perfect wording, '… the heaven on earth, really'.

'They were the pillars of the community,' Ephraim adds. 'And quiet.'

'Yes, so quiet,' Cas echoes.

I ask if doing *tahara* was shifting his sense of his place in the world; did it, right from the start, recalibrate him as a parent, as a human, as a spiritual being? I imagine him as a young father, beholden to a whole world of 'above ground'. There would have been sunshine and crayons and shoes and books, all of it somehow opposite to the chilled stillness of a mortuary, to the energy of ending rather than beginning.

'You are not as free,' replies Ephraim. 'You realise continually that things can happen.'

'The fragility of things?' I ask.

'Yes. Life is so fragile.'

'And were you more protective of your children and your wife, from doing this work?'

'I was vigilant, but I wasn't superstitious,' he replies.

'Did you feel at one with the physical aspect of the work, right from the start?'

'Yes, I think so,' he says, after a pause. 'Because you believe totally in the love for another human being, love for your fellow man.'

These words chime through me, especially since I have been listening to the reflections of other *tahara* volunteers. My hope has been to find a common thread to their intention: what draws them to this work? Moreover, I want to know *tahara*'s deepest imprint, on their heart, their very way of being in the world.

The answers have been surprising. First, there seem to be as many motivations as there are volunteers: a wish to return something to the community, participation in a holy process, a pull to the work of cycles—not just birth and death, but *tikun olam*, the healing of the world through positive gesture. One volunteer, who comes from a very small community, has shared that he does it because 'it needs to be done'. As a doctor, he feels comfortable in the realm of bodies—the way they age, fall to pieces, expire. As a Jew in a tiny population, he feels responsible.

And the imprint? This seems universal. Every volunteer—regardless of age, gender, location or level of religiosity—speaks of a sort of alertness that descends upon them in the course of preparing the body. They do not speak of fear or shock, though sometimes there is distress. Rather, each and every person describes something akin to being awoken, to emerging from the bowels of the building crisper, more grateful, possessed of a wider lens.

One volunteer describes the 'minute and a half' when he is sitting in his car waiting to re-enter traffic, feeling complete focus on the sublime gravity of being alive. He notes a fullness of presence, a complete availability to the world.

Another volunteer recalls a similar expansiveness, which settles on her with clockwork regularity, as she exits the Chevra grounds. As she waits for the slow-moving gate to issue her from one world into another, she is stilled by a sense of participating in 'something profound'. Having just helped another being move across their own threshold, she is focused on how to inhabit the day ahead. There is no point in road rage, she thinks. There is no benefit in shouting at the kids for being late to school. There is a larger story at play.

I see that for Ephraim, these crystalline insights are not occasional; they are embodied in his very being, as though thirty years of this work have changed his very physicality. His whole kinetic presence—the way he holds his fountain pen, the way he serves Cas a piece of cake, the tone he uses when speaking to a stranger—conveys this constant, mindful cherishing. It has been years since he performed *tahara* as a daily task, but the way Ephraim handles the living seems deeply infused with how he handled the dead.

Listening to him describe his early years I am reminded of Ralph Waldo Emerson's words: 'Adopt the pace of nature. Her secret is patience.' I see why Ephraim would have felt drawn to this quiet, pre-dawn world, a world free of chatter and rushing and mindless resentments, free of all the habits that exile us from each other's love. In this place, both time and nature reveal their truest form. For what is more natural, what is more certain, than the death of our bodies? And what is purer than forgetting oneself in the act of giving, more sacred than love given freely?

In 1984 the family moves to Melbourne. Cas and Ephraim want to be on the ground with Ben, who has been learning at the Melbourne Yeshivah; they also see better educational opportunities

The life and deathwork of Ephraim Finch

for their other kids. By now, they have been joined by Sharona and Mishi, bringing the tally to five. They have a good feeling about Melbourne. This, they hope, will be their final destination.

The night that they drive across the Victorian border and into Melbourne, it is torrentially rainy. Cas is thirty-four weeks pregnant with her sixth and final child, Michal. The car is loaded with precious human cargo and many of their possessions. They do the trip almost in one go, stopping only so that Ephraim can rest a little between his 'long blinks' down the Hume Highway.

Upon arrival, Ephraim mounts two horses simultaneously: he starts a full-time job in construction and he enlists as a volunteer at the Chevra Kadisha. His day begins at the local synagogue, where he prays in the earliest session, with the other working-class men, 'the factory workers, not the businessmen'. He is back from morning prayer by 5.45 am, but in that twilight hour he has lain *tefillin* and has spoken to his fellow 'villagers', often over a quick whisky and piece of herring. They discuss the rabbi's words and notify each other about important events of the community—births, weddings, consecrations. Sometimes a call comes through to the synagogue, informing the rabbi of a death. In this case Ephraim rushes down to the Chevra to prepare the body.

Ephraim describes this as we bridge out of his construction phase and into the deathwork, a transition that feels both inevitable and unique. He is, on any given day, descending into the Chevra's depths, then emerging to supervise a concrete mixer or the laying of tiles. In fact, the first time he shows up to do *tahara*, he is dressed in his work clothes. 'He still looked great,' defends Cas. 'He had his singlet, his vest, his *tzitzit*, his shirt and black pants.' This was not considered formal enough by some of the members, and Ephraim was told as such. 'It was not *kovedik* enough,' he says, throwing his hands up in surrender. It twists my heart to learn that *kovedik* means 'honourable'. Nonetheless, he prioritises being at the Chevra on time, attending to the body as soon as possible; 'you race to get there, to get the *tahara* done'. Which means sometimes he comes straight from a worksite.

One of Ephraim's earliest Chevra mentors, an elderly Hungarian man who has lost his wife and children in the Holocaust, reinforces this duty of punctuality. 'He always had a very stern face. Bald head. And we did a lot of *tahara* together,' says Ephraim. 'And one morning I came in ten minutes late because Cas had just had Michal. I had just gotten back from the hospital. So, I came in and I said, "I'm sorry, sir. My wife just had a baby". And he says to me, "Well, the dead person has been waiting".'

These stories speak to the vertiginous contrast of Ephraim's life at this juncture, to the collage of noise and reverence, of cement dust and sterilised surfaces. There is a cacophony of blue-collar labour above ground and the ancient motions of ritualised gentleness below.

Still, this configuration does not last long, a couple of months perhaps. Because one day, a Chevra colleague suggests Ephraim take on other tasks. While his building work puts food on the table, the family are living very modestly. Five of the kids share the front room, while the baby is in the bedroom with her parents. There is an outside toilet, the house has no workable bathroom and the cornices are peeling. So, the colleague's timing is good when she suggests to Mr Kantor, the president of the Chevra Kadisha, that Ephraim drive the hearse. Ephraim is immediately hired.

Around this time, another fortuitous event occurs. Rabbi Michael Mandel, the executive director of the Chevra Kadisha, announces that he is moving to a large suburban synagogue to become its rabbi. He recommends Ephraim to Mr Kantor as his replacement. Mr Kantor seems interested but tells Ephraim they will be advertising Australia-wide for the position. It might take three or four months, he says. Undeterred, Ephraim collects references from members of his village, letters vouching for his decent character and community-mindedness. Discreetly, Mr Kantor tells him that while a lot of rabbis have applied, he 'would like to have a more practical man'.

And so it is that in February 1986, this practical man, this enmeshed community member and devoted Yeshivah attendee, is appointed to the position of executive director of the Melbourne Chevra Kadisha. He is told there will be a three-month trial ('I think they were trying to keep their muskets loaded, so that if I did something wrong, they could get rid of me,' he says, a cheeky glint in his eyes). He suspects there might be dissenters on the board, that he may be in over his head with this position, but he knows in his bones that this is his life's work. I ask him to locate the source of this insistence, to identify why *tahara* wasn't enough.

'I wanted to absorb the community. I wanted to be there for the people.'

'You wanted to work with the living and the dying, not just the dead,' I suggest. To which he nods, looking down at the table.

I ask if he can remember what the position description said. 'Oh, run the Chevra. Do whatever was necessary to be done,' he replies. 'But once I got in the saddle, it was gonna go in one direction.'

I enquire as to what direction that was, knowing already that Ephraim was gunning, above all, for inclusivity. One of the first things I had learned about Ephraim Finch, before I even met him, was that he reintroduced the *mikveh* as an active procedure at Melbourne's Chevra. Arriving on Day One as director, he asked why the bath was dry. 'We only use it for the very religious,' he was told, meaning only those deemed sufficiently pious were bathed immersively before burial. 'With all due respect, that ends with me,' he replied, refusing to accept that some deceased are more worthy than others.

'He wanted people to feel that they could come and speak to him, to feel that the Chevra was a communal body,' says Cas. Here her voice rises and she shifts, mid-flight to second person: 'That it was for you, the community! Something that's open! Let the air in, let it be something that people aren't afraid of.' Cas's torso heaves with the momentum of this wish, this offering. 'Death, I mean,' she clarifies, referring to the thing most of us fear the most. Ephraim nods in agreement as her voice lowers and lands on the solid teak table between us, leaving only light, only silence.

4

In *The Wild Edge of Sorrow*, grief psychotherapist Francis Weller writes on the role of community in times of mourning, the vital influence of belonging in one's encounter with deepest loss. He posits that being seen, understood and accepted is an essential 'medicine' for the human heart, that community heals body and soul. According to Weller, 'We need to create circles of welcome in our lives in order to keep leaning into the world; to keep moving grief through our psyches and bodies, so we can taste the sweetness of life'.

Weller cites a longitudinal study conducted in the Italian-American mining community of Roseto, Pennsylvania. Researchers examined the death certificates of its residents from 1935 to 1985, noticing that in the first thirty years, Roseto locals had notably lower rates of heart disease than their neighbours. Interested in the possible reasons for this, they looked at smoking rates, exercise patterns, diet, access to medical services and the genetics of the residents. None of these variables seemed to be causally related to the good health, but what they did find was that between 1965 and 1985, the structures of communal living—which had hitherto characterised the borough—were dissolving. Weller notes that

'Rather than living in multigenerational homes, where sharing life and meals, rituals and traditions was the norm, people opted for single-family dwellings on the outskirts of town. As the bonds of connection frayed, so too did the protective effects for the heart. Disease rates actually became higher than those of neighbouring communities. The only thing that originally protected these people from heart disease was belonging.'

Max Dzienciol does not recall exactly when his family met Cas and Ephraim, only that their friendship goes back to the mid-1980s, when the Finches first settled in Melbourne.

I have asked him to join us this morning to tell me about his beloved son Nathan, who died in 1990, aged seven. I know that the Finches bore intimate witness to this time and am interested in Max's memory of this, namely how the community held him, his wife Estelle and their three surviving sons. So, we start there, with community.

'There was a time when it was all one place,' Max says, meaning the village of schools, shops and synagogues at the heart of the neighbourhood. He is a softly spoken man with extremely dark eyes. Although I estimate that he is approximately Ephraim's age, he seems younger, perhaps because he does not have a long grey beard and is dressed more casually than his friend, who is always in a shirt and jacket. By way of warming into the conversation, Max and Ephraim reminisce about a man who treated everyone with unconditional hospitality, who ran a grocery store that routinely gave credit to its poorer customers to the detriment of the vendor himself. All three of them—Cas, Ephraim and Max—repeat over and over that he was 'a true *chossed*'. I ask each of them to tell me what this word means to them.

'A *chossed*, from my late-coming into Judaism, is a person who is totally committed. But they have warmth ...' Ephraim says.

'And joy,' Cas adds. 'They are *leibedik*, which means loving life.'

The life and deathwork of Ephraim Finch

'Some people are just religious in themselves, but they don't spread it around,' says Max. Conversely, this man would 'give you the shirt off his back'.

'I'm glad you came,' Ephraim suddenly says to Max, his voice faltering. He is visibly transported back to this time and Cas reinforces this with her words: 'You know, we were lucky that we came to see all of that. Those people … they brought the old country here.' She says 'old country' with such conviction that for a moment I forget that it is not first-hand familiar to her.

I ask Max to tell me about Nathan and he replies that just this week, someone brought him a memory. Apparently, even in early primary school, Nathan would go up to the rabbi and say, 'I want to learn.' Unprompted, he would ask to learn the Talmud. Max and Estelle knew nothing about this at the time but discovering it three decades later makes other memories fall into place. 'And he'd stand there and he'd …'—here Max imitates his son singing the words of the Torah portion—'and he'd keep going on and on and on. He had a knack for learning. So much so that he used to hide under his blankets with a torch and read.' I picture Nathan's parents hovering at the doorframe, watching their boy sneak some extra reading time, unable to interrupt him for the pride in their chests.

'And the headmistress used to say to us that he would go up to kids, if he saw that they were alone, and play with them. "Nathan" in Hebrew means to give, so he gave.' Max speaks quietly, his dark eyes deepening. There is a long pause, as we make space for what needs to come. 'He was a good soul, he really was a good kid,' Max says, before I ask him to describe the day of Nathan's passing.

'Well, we used to live on Hotham Street, just fifty metres from the corner. And he was going to the 7-Eleven across the road to get a Slurpee. It was a very hot day, a Sunday evening. And he was very, very … he knew the rules. He would never cross without it going green. He was a pretty responsible little kid,' Max says.

'It was the *driver* who was irresponsible,' Ephraim cuts in, his voice curling like a fist.

The driver who fatally hit Nathan Dzienciol on 4 March 1990 was going ninety-five kilometres per hour in a residential area. Max retrieves this detail as he recalls the 'horrendous' day in the Coroners Court. He remembers Ephraim holding his hand. Then he tells us that a few years ago, he and Estelle joined a Jewish bereaved parents' group. He says it has been a great source of respite. 'Some of the men have really opened up,' he notes, citing the empathy among its members. 'I mean, I'm the oldest, I'm sort of the vintage one … I think I cope pretty well.'

'Of course you do, mate,' Ephraim responds, holding his friend's gaze as though it is his hand, once again.

I am interested in the bereaved parents' group, in its specific comfort. Max tells us that the greatest gift of this group is 'comradeship', but also the cultural webbing. He compares this to a non-denominational group that he and Estelle attended years ago. 'And you'd go and you'd sit in a big circle and they'd say, "How do you cope?" And people would say, "Well, I went to the pub," or "I went to chop some wood". So I said, "Well, we had a *shiva*. We had a *shloshim*. And we have *yortzheit*".' I notice how even the naming of these ancient rites—the seven days of house-bound mourning, the thirty days of slow return to the world, the consecration—gives Max something solid to hold on to all these years later.

'Because you have the ritual, there's a method in the madness,' he says, articulating my thoughts.

'It's an interesting group, the parents' bereavement group,' he continues. 'One of the questions, one time, was, "How has the death affected your religious beliefs?" One guy said, "I don't want to talk about it". And another one said, "Look, I used to go to synagogue, but I don't go anymore. My wife still goes and I go with her sometimes but I don't really believe." And this one says, "I still believe". And so I said, "Look, I've never stopped believing. But I can tell you now that the time in the hospital, when my son was lying on the table, I lost a lot".' The room is still as Max sheds soundless tears. He closes his eyes and runs his palm across his forehead. Sighs. Goes on. 'The thing is that every day you hear about car accidents. You know, you just think about it, I think about it every day. We get on with our life, but it's difficult.'

I ask if he remembers the funeral. He recalls being driven to the cemetery, the car wending its way through his neighbourhood, past Nathan's school. He pauses, his breath slows.

'And all the children, the teachers with their classes, were walking up Balaclava Road, to acknowledge,' adds Cas. 'We are meant to escort the dead, it tells us in our morning prayers. So we walked up a section of the road and that was considered part of the burial. And the hearse, driven by Ephraim, was slowly going past so that everyone was able to honour Nathan.' At the time, Cas was teaching in the preschool at Beth Rivkah, the sister school to the Yeshivah that Nathan attended, both campuses a stone's throw from each other and from the intersection where he died.

'And then we gave Nathan a good send-off,' adds Ephraim.

'I do remember,' Max says, 'at the cemetery my mother kept saying, "Take me, take me". And she died nine months later. I think she died from a broken heart.' There is another very long pause, Max's anguish sitting beneath us all like an enormous slow-breathing creature.

I had learned of the Dzienciol family, the special place they held in the Finches' heart, months earlier, when Cas recalled the closeness of the community in the 1990s. Now I ask her to retell the day as she remembers it. She looks to Max, as though for permission, ever mindful of encroaching on another's moment, tangling their thread to the deceased. Max invites her to go ahead and she tells us of driving through the neighbourhood that Sunday, approaching the intersection that she had been through thousands of times. Only this time there was an ambulance, so she parked her car and walked to the crossing, to find a friend of both families holding Nathan. Just moments earlier, she had seen Max drive by, unaware of what had just occurred. Everything seemed to be happening at once, swirling and shapeless.

'She told me that Nathan had passed away and I thought, "Oh my God, they have no idea". So, I threw my shoes off, into the gutter, and started to run,' Cas says. As she ran up the main road, another friend was driving past and slowed down to pick her up. The two women drove to yet another friend, one who was very close to the Dzienciols. When the third woman opened the door, Cas told her that Nathan had been hit by a car, that someone needed to urgently drive down to the Children's Hospital, where the family would be seeing their boy for the final time. 'I wanted someone to be there for Max and Estelle,' she says, looking again to Max. He nods and picks up the story.

When the accident happened, Max was driving along Hotham Street. At the same time, Myer Herszberg, who knew Max and would—astonishingly—go on to become the president of the Chevra Kadisha, was driving in the opposite direction. He had seen the accident and knew that Nathan had been hit. So he doubled back to Max to deliver the terrible news.

'And he said, "Hop in",' Max recalls. 'He said, "There's been an accident". I asked, "Who?" He said, "Nathan". I asked if he was alive. He didn't say anything.' Max pauses again. Folds and unfolds his hands. Ephraim is sitting directly opposite his friend, Cas is sitting next to Max and I am at the top of the table, completing this distended circle. The moment feels torn, porous, and there is nothing for it but the sitting.

'We'll never forget Nathan's bright face,' says Cas eventually. 'The eyes alight, the smile, the intelligence.' Nathan's sweet smile comes to me in that moment, gleaned only from a photo, but insistently radiant in my mind's eye. We are rounding the corner in our hours-long conversation, as the morning shifts to afternoon.

'How have you made meaning from Nathan's passing over the past thirty-three years?' I ask, hoping to get a deeper sense of what Max meant earlier on, when he said he was 'doing pretty well'.

'Well, in Yiddish you say, *"Der mensch tracht un Gott lacht"*,' he replies. 'Man plans and God laughs.' In other words, he has developed a certain amount of trust in a bigger picture. He goes on to reiterate that being part of a cultural tradition certainly helps.

Listening, I sense that there is something else, something that is fed by the tradition but also sits apart. Throughout our conversation Max has been naming all the ways in which his community has continuously honoured his son's memory. When he cites these examples, he is not pointing to orthodoxy or scripture but to names and gestures, to the hands and faces of those who knew and loved Nathan and who love him still. Two of his grandsons have the middle name Nathan. For three decades Estelle has organised a women's Torah learning circle in honour of her son. A former schoolteacher has written a poem about Nathan that now hangs, framed, in the Dzienciols' living room.

Max mentions the boys who were in Nathan's class, all of whom are now, of course, grown.

'One of their mothers said to me the other night that she remembers Nathan as a sweet kid. And she said all the boys still remember him very vividly. And they're all forty, forty-one now. You just wonder what life would have been, you know … You see all those guys around with families …' he trails off, and the comforting memory once again reveals its inextricable braiding with the loss.

Still, there is a rabbi who teaches school kids pieces of the Mishna (the oral law encoded in the Talmud) in Nathan's memory. 'The kids are learning millions and millions of lines. And it's not a matter of "off by heart", they've got to know what they're saying. I mean, these kids are learning a whole novel. I wish I could do that!' Max says. The air lightens, as though a breeze has come through.

'Everyone has a little *pekel*, you know?' Max continues, using beloved Yiddish idiom to indicate that everyone has their bundle of adversity in this life, that no one is immune to suffering or misfortune. It is a deeply humble statement, especially coming from someone who has endured the greatest anguish of them all.

Perhaps the most magnificent tribute is the Torah scroll made specifically for a synagogue in Nathan's name. It is difficult to overstate the significance of a Torah in the Jewish tradition—it is not just a record of our rules and stories, it is the very hinge to the Mosaic faith, bestowed on the Jews at the same moment as our identity. Its year-long cycle governs the structure of weekly Shabbat services; it is a font of guidance but also mystery; its language is kaleidoscopic, crafted in a way that nurtures questions and revelations and endless contemplation. The Torah is considered so holy that when we congregate, we do not merely read it—we sing, and every portion has its own unique musical composition. It is this melody, along with Aramaic and Hebrew script, that a child learns for their bar mitzvah. In this vein, an encounter with the Torah is considered so joyous, a person in mourning is not permitted to read from it. When the yearly cycle is complete, we dance with it, circling it like a bride. The examples—of veneration, of adoration—go on and on. So, to donate a Torah scroll to a community is an immense gesture, both for the family and for the recipients.

Nathan's Torah is wrapped in royal-blue velvet, embroidered in gold. It says his name, the names of his parents, how dearly beloved he is, the fact of his death and its date and, like all Hebrew references to the deceased, it blesses his memory.

'I just think having a Sefer Torah in somebody's name is a beautiful thing,' says Max. 'It uplifts their soul, you know, keeping the person's name. It's not a matter of having their name in lights or anything, but that person's memory living on forever.'

'It's like a memorial not in a cemetery,' adds Ephraim.

'A living memorial,' says Max, their sentences holding each other up.

The life and deathwork of Ephraim Finch

In June of the year that would have been Nathan's bar mitzvah, the Torah was carried across the intersection where he died. The Dzienciols' closest people then carried it to the synagogue, where it was ceremonially added to the other scrolls.

'I remember the first time we carried it.' Ephraim tells the story now. 'We were walking from Willy's house, up Hotham Street, and when we got to the intersection, I think Nigel was holding it.' He is using people's first names as though this was three days ago, not twenty-eight years, and this too seems like a comfort to Max. I observe Max remotely observing this procession, listening to Ephraim for crossovers between his own memory and that of a witness. The passage of time is, for a moment, softened, some continuity restored amid decades of rupture. 'And I said to Nigel, "Give the scroll to Max",' Ephraim says, once again dissolving into visible anguish. '"Let him carry his boy across the intersection."' The moment is tender, the centre holds, while Ephraim carries Max and Max carries his son.

I ask Max if he remembers Ephraim's presence on the day of the funeral. 'Absolutely, one hundred per cent. Ephraim is just the person who's there without you knowing,' he replies. I consider this quality of being there for a person in distress without them knowing, the fine line between visibility and intrusion.

'The thing is that Ephraim was, is, an unbelievable person. He is a real *chossed*,' Max says. 'I don't know if it's because he came into the community ... I don't know what it is, but he just has that heart for it. With my case with Nathan, we were, we are, like family even though we don't see each other. I can say that we're like blood brothers.'

I know that Ephraim will baulk at me including Max's praise here. He is not great with compliments and on several occasions has asked that I don't make him 'too good' on the page. I have generally taken this on board, but in this instance, I find it hard to disregard

Max's language, for there it is again, that word that kicked off the conversation, *chossed*: that special sort of person who is devoted but joyful, who gives of themselves unconditionally, who is a master of kindness and generosity.

In fact, *chossed* is root-joined to *chesed*, the Hebrew word for—among other things—kindness. *Chesed* variously encompasses love, compassion, the altruistic goodness of one's gestures. Like love, it crosses the material-etheric divide and moves in multiple directions; it can be felt by one human towards another or by a human towards the divine. It is also conceptualised as God's mercy towards humanity. It shares qualities with the Greek *agape*, or humanistic love.

It is not, however, just a nebulous emotional experience, a feel-good aspiration. It is a foundational ethical virtue and is explicitly embedded in the Torah's commandments. The word *chesed* appears in the Old Testament several hundred times. This makes it something atomic—a set of discrete deeds to fulfil, a catalogue of actions—but also synergistic, greater than the sum of its parts. *Chesed* is a way of existing, a quality of enacting one's life.

Max did not visit his son's body at the Chevra Kadisha, but he remembers Ephraim being involved in the *tahara* and is visibly soothed by the memory. In turn, Ephraim closes his eyes to return to the task, takes a moment to honour 'that beautiful little boy', whose name means 'given' and 'gave' and 'gift from God'.

As I prepare to say goodbye to Max, I notice more interplay between the words of mourning. *Tahara* is also known '*chesed shel emet*', the truest giving. This gift, of ritual preparation ahead of burial, is the highest form of generosity because it cannot be reciprocated—the deceased individual will never thank their final carer. To attend to them lovingly, devotedly, without public recognition or private acknowledgment, is an end in itself, binding the deceased in time as they are released from place. Caring for the dead, caring for those left behind—these are the spaces where love and sorrow meet. This is the holy joinery; the bonds of belonging, the circles of welcome.

PART II: THE CROSSING

5

The day I meet Ben Finch in Sydney, it is extravagantly muggy and I am struggling to find shade while waiting for him outside the Lindfield train station. I am not uncomfortable for long though, because a minute later he materialises in his van, waving at me through the window. 'Jump in!' he calls out, clearing the passenger seat as I get in. He adjusts the air-conditioner, the volume of the music, asks about my flight to Sydney. He is immediately, naturally, attentive.

He is also immediately familiar. I recognise his father's solid shoulders and his mother's deep voice, I see a warmth and a complexity in his blue-grey eyes. Most of all, I am drawn into the babbling brook of chatter that has become a hallmark of my Finch interactions. Even as I'm buckling in my seatbelt, we peel off into multiple conversations, layering over each other's backstories and answering questions with questions. We spend less than ten minutes driving along the undulating roads of his suburb, but we cover much ground, from politics to *The Matrix* to Ben's travels in Japan. He doesn't need to tell me that he has moved away from Orthodox Judaism, because he is dressed like an ordinary secular bloke, and I can see that the studious Yeshivah boy is a historical presence. He asks about my writing work and tells me that he loves his work repairing commercial coffee machines. I learn that he is on the road a lot, that he meets people every day. I also learn that he collects rocks, which is a topic I reintroduce when we arrive at his apartment.

'We were in Jerusalem, in 1978,' recounts Ben. The family was driving past a construction site where a hill was being bulldozed, the rockface edged by mounds of earth. 'And we're driving along, and I yelled at my dad to stop. And I got out of the car and bounded up this hill and picked up this piece of Jerusalem limestone which had an ammonite fossil in it,' he says. (Ammonite is an extinct marine cephalopod that last lived on our planet some sixty-six million years ago.)

We are sitting in his small kitchen, in the modest apartment where he lives alone. There are art supplies in the hallway and an array of petrified wood on the windowsill. In the corner of the tiny dining area, an easel holds an acrylic painting, about one-by-two metres in size, filled with blue and yellow geometrics, an eye in a cloud. Ben's artworks also line the hallway, brightening the space and giving the mind something bold, almost psychedelic, to play with.

'I had to climb this embankment to get to the stone. All the stone looks the same because it's all just rubble from limestone that has been blasted,' he says.

'You just felt called to pick it up?' I ask.

'Yeah … and I've had it ever since,' he says.

He describes the fossil as a bit of an anchoring presence, something he looks at regularly. 'It speaks to me,' he says, 'and that ties in very interestingly with the whole funeral thing, particularly with memorial headstones. The whole idea that a stone is like a slice of memory.' I am relieved when Ben arrives at the topic of Jewish burial because this is why I have come to see him—to get a fuller sense of Ephraim through his child, with whom he worked so closely for so long.

The life and deathwork of Ephraim Finch

I have known for some time that not long after he started working at the Chevra Kadisha, Ephraim enlisted Ben, who was in Year Eleven, to help him. First it was to pick up bodies, then to drive the hearse. In time, Ben would perform *tahara*, assist at funerals and even build coffins. There are so many rich topics here, topics that drill into the nature of the father–son relationship, of family obligation, of the multi-faceted demands of deathwork. But all of it feels delicate, which is why I'm pleased that Ben has raised it himself.

I ask him to elaborate on this beautiful image, 'a slice of memory', how it relates to Jewish tradition.

'It's the idea of memory because it's a transformation of the earth's properties into something different,' he says.

'Into something that lasts?'

'Exactly.'

We discuss another application of stone in Jewish burial, the custom of placing pebbles on a grave. I'd always believed that memory was the rationale behind placing stones (rather than flowers) on the grave, that stones speak to something eternal rather than ephemeral. Like death—and life, for that matter—stones have gravity. Ben doesn't refute this but suspects the origin of both the headstone and the small rocks is more prosaic. He points to the desert environment, where many of these Jewish practices would have formed, and the difficulty of digging and maintaining a grave. He is referring to a cairn, a pile of stones placed atop the corpse so that it can decompose without being threatened by wildlife or the elements. He also points to cairns as a way of caring for your ancestor, 'so that if the earth subsided, or they fell, you could go and put the stones back on top'.

'A bit like the way we tidy a grave these days,' I say. 'We go back and give it a little wipe, pull out any weeds …'

'Absolutely,' Ben replies. 'And all the cultures have, if not ancestor worship, then some reverence for ancestors.' I mention that recently I came across yet another interpretation of the stone-placing tradition, that the rock or pebble acts as a grounding force, to stop a soul from becoming lost and homeless.

'That sounds scary to me,' he replies. 'I would want to actually fly away.' And when he says this, I suddenly agree. It does seem like a strange notion to tether an etheric entity to this physical plane.

'Well, maybe the idea is that it can go where it needs to, but it can also come home,' I suggest.

'*Da miayin bata ule-an atah holech*,' Ben says in effortless Hebrew. This will be the first time of many in our conversation where he seamlessly quotes from the Torah, grabbing the essence of a moment and filtering it through a theological lens.

'Know from whence you have come and where you are going,' he translates casually, responding to my face of incomprehension.

When Ben tells me about his childhood, I see how his recollection braids into that of his parents', but also has its own dimensions, its own pockets of darkness and uncertainty. While he was indeed a studious boy, his childhood at Yeshivah was not an easy one. He tells me that he was often oppositional in class, that he found the institution's singular focus on the mind oppressive, and the estrangement from the body unnatural.

'You could never play competitive sport, or if you did play sport, you worried about your yarmulke coming off. I was told that you can't sweat too much and get your *tzitzit* sweaty,' he says. He wondered, over those years, about distant Aussie relatives who had been sheep farmers, who lived on the land and made their livelihood with their hands. He tells me, with submerged sadness, that had he had more 'kinship with the land', he 'could have gone hunting, and had been in my body, and gone swimming instead of sitting and being told that I wasn't allowed to go to the beach because I'd see naked women'.

He loved reading, but as a child, the words that drew him were of J.R.R. Tolkien and Robert Heinlein, not the weekly Torah portion.

Eventually, he circled back to find beauty in the Jewish texts. 'It was very interesting, intellectually interesting, to learn some Aramaic, and learn the old stories. It was always the old Midrashic stories I was most fascinated by,' he says. This squares with the critically thinking and curious person I am getting to know—the Midrash is an interpretive process, a commentary that uses allegory, intertextual dialogue and even wordplay as a way of parsing the Torah. To this day, the Midrash is an interface between the literal wording of the scripture, the archaic Jewish laws and the practical world. Both colourful and cerebral, it forms a bridge out of an arcane canon and into our daily concerns.

Friendship was also sparse and, outside his family, Ben had few people to reality-check with. 'You know, we were taught, very specifically, you have the *Shulchan Aruch*, which describes everything you do from when you wake up to when you go to bed. And there was one period of time, around thirteen, fourteen, where I was told that the only place that God couldn't see you was in the bathroom. And I used to get undressed and dressed under my sheets for a while.'

He sought solace in the wider world.

'There were two people, two shops, in Bondi Junction. One was the music shop. The other one was the comic shop. The music shop, I must have looked like a complete freak, because nobody who looked like me would have gone in there. And I got friendly with the man who owned it. He used to tell me about music. And I would collect the old Top Forty chart that was printed out on an A4 sheet. I've still got a whole lot of them.'

Ben's parents did not police the cultural items that he brought into the home, which gave him some room to breathe.

'... and the comic book shop, I would go in there and buy these war comics and the lady was just really decent. She treated me normally. She didn't look at me like I was a freak. That was the big thing.'

He saw what Judaism had given to his parents, respected the nourishing bonds of community, but also felt divided. 'I was a child of two worlds ... I was this blond-haired, blue-eyed child, didn't look Jewish at all. But then I had a big yarmulke and *tzitzit* hanging out, and *payot*. So I wasn't fully in the Jewish world and I definitely wasn't in the non-Jewish world. I was a child of nowhere.'

Ben had absorbed the years of formal learning—he spoke fluent Hebrew; his dress and gesture and daily rhythm enacted the laws and prohibitions of the Torah. He believed in a source of life, but not necessarily as articulated in Genesis. He instinctively respected the virtues of compassion and charity, but struggled with a mighty, wrathful presence watching his every move.

Given all of this, I am surprised to hear how little resistance Ben had to working at the Chevra Kadisha with his father. True, the Finch children grew up with death as a natural phenomenon, as a part of life. People would phone the Finches' landline and the children knew to say, 'I'm sorry for your loss,' before getting their father. Distressed mourners would knock on Cas and Ephraim's bedroom window at all hours of the night, asking if Ephraim could collect a deceased family member. However, it is a whole other level of involvement to participate in the work directly. And Ben seems to have had remarkable equanimity about his father's request, one day, to drive with him and collect a body.

'I was sixteen. My first body that I went to pick up with my dad, I was in my school uniform. The woman had been dead for a couple of days in the heat of summer.' I contemplate the sensory assault of this experience on Ben's young body, not to mention the emotional learning curve. But Ben does not speak of this experience as especially harrowing; he explains that helping his father was a matter of necessity and stepping up was not something he questioned.

'First, my dad was doing *tahara*. That was out of the goodness of his heart ... He wanted to do good. The picking up of the bodies, that was something you got paid to do. Not very much, mind you, but that was a way of earning a bit of extra income. So I went with him so we could do it together,' he explains. I know from speaking to Ephraim that the handling of a dead body is physically demanding; even with two able-bodied workers, even with an average-sized adult, it is cumbersome, especially the sliding of a sheet beneath the body and the transfer onto a gurney.

'It's nigh on impossible,' confirms Ben.

While the reason for needing help is clear, I wonder, out loud to Ben, why Ephraim chose to enlist his son rather than ask the Chevra for an assistant. Ben looks across the kitchen table, past me. The fan is whirring in the background, meekly moving the humid Sydney air around our faces. He answers carefully, slowly.

'I've always been ... through different things ... an extension of him. There is another Hebrew saying, "*Shluch ato shel adam k'moto*",' he replies. 'The emissary of somebody is like him.' I am not familiar with this phrase, so Ben explains.

'If you are an envoy for somebody, then you are in their place. So you have the power. But also tying into my name, Ben, "Son of my right hand", it's the helping sort of thing. I think for him we were on this whole journey together.'

I add that perhaps there is also something in it about the first-born, and the first-born son, the archetypal properties of this role in the Judeo-Christian tradition.

'Yeah, yeah ... he would always tell me stories of when he was a child or a teenager, helping his grandfather, so it's this continuation of things.' I think about the formative influence of Pop Finch on Ephraim, the way he taught him not only the etiquette of living but the ethics of labour, of making a living.

'He comes from a line of hereditary traineeship,' I say, thinking of Finch and Sons, of Ephraim driving around to the abattoirs with his father and grandfather, unloading carcasses; and later, as an adult, driving around the outer suburbs of Sydney to collect payments from the butchers. From the age of ten, Geoff and his brother Richard would do the accounts for Finch and Sons ('check everything, pounds, shillings, pence and halfpennies, no calculator, just adding it all up!'); when the adolescent Geoff told his Pop he 'wanted' to buy a car, Pop's reply was, 'No you don't'. There's a difference between want and need, he told his grandson. 'If you'd have told me "I need that car", I'd have helped you buy it.'

'So Pop taught him how to be a mensch, but also about responsibility. And I suppose he intuitively projected that onto you, because these things go down the line,' I say.

Ben nods.

I suggest that perhaps his father was also initiating him into a cycle of *mitzvot*, bringing him deeper into the tradition of selflessness.

'I don't know,' Ben says. 'And it doesn't really matter.' I am surprised by this response, so I ask him to unfurl it.

'To me, it doesn't matter if he thought he was opening me up to *mitzvot*. I don't even think that necessarily came into it. He needed someone to help him. I was capable of doing it. So I did it. I was there. *"Hineni muchan u'mezuman"*—"Here I am, ready and willing,"' he says, once again, interlacing the holy with the hands-on.

Ben and I have been sitting together for hours, though it feels like we are just warming up. He has continued to be solicitous, bringing out cheese and crackers, offering me tea. The air around us grows muggier by the minute, and somewhere in the distance I hear thunder. When we do go outside for him to smoke a cigarette, he says, 'Oh, let's not stand at this side of the building. This apartment has a shiftworker living in it, and she's on nights. I don't want to talk outside her window.' I am moved by his consideration for others, and of course, see it as a trait shared with his father. He tells me that the work of caring, and of good listening, is something he learned from being around the bereaved, and that he uses to this day.

'That's how I see him in the work I do now. I get people talking to me, I know about their families. It's more than just fixing their coffee machine. But I really had to learn those skills,' Ben says, finishing his cigarette, the clouds above us gathering. 'It's quite a baptism of fire,' he adds, 'to sit with people who have just lost a family member.'

'Are you talking about the work of comforting?' I ask.

'Is it comforting or is it just being with people? I wouldn't even put a term to it. It's just being around them,' he says. 'There is a big difference between making small talk and an open listening. So you allow them space, you allow the silence, so that they can talk if they want to.'

I ask him what he believes people need most in that moment of acute mourning.

'See, some of these things I haven't actually put into words ... It's something that you try to embody. It's almost, what's the word I'm looking for?' he says, stubbing out the cigarette and carefully dropping it into the council bin. 'Instinctive,' he finally says, looking at me, then at the sky, then at me again.

Back inside I ask him what he thought Ephraim did well, what he observed and admired in his father as a funeral director.

'He made people feel ... I was going to say comfortable, but that's not the word. *Comforted* is probably a better way of saying it.' I'm struck by the synchronicity of this statement because it references, verbatim, a conversation I had with Ephraim just days earlier. He'd told me about visiting a family who had lost their beloved matriarch. Tradition dictates that we do not speak to the mourner until they speak to us—they must initiate the conversation. But as we take our leave, we say, 'I wish you long life,' or 'May you have no more suffering'. Ephraim has never been able to come at the latter, knowing that it is impossible. When he farewelled the late woman's granddaughter, he paused to consider his words. 'May you be comforted,' he said to her, feeling that this was the warmest wish one could bestow in this coldest of moments.

'What did he actually do?' I press Ben, hoping he will flesh this recollection, give me a granular portrait of his unique skillset.

'The look on his face, his posture,' Ben says.

'His voice?'

'Yeah, his voice. Because I actually knew him before he honed his skills, so ...'

'Of course! You knew him as your dad! And then you see him in this professional realm. So what's the through-line? What do you know as continuous about his character?' I ask, thrilled at Ben's willingness to help me understand his father.

'See, you can be interested in people. But if you are interested in their stories, I think that is something that is ...' he says, closing his eyes, steepling his fingers at his forehead, 'if you are interested in their history, that makes people feel valued. It's like letting people know that they are not alone, that they are a part of a string.'

When the Melbourne Chevra Kadisha takes a deceased person for burial, it is standard procedure to furnish the mourners with a copy of Maurice Lamm's *The Jewish Way in Death and Mourning*. This book, first published in 1969 and reissued in 2000, takes the reader through the key aspects of the mourning observances, as well as rites and protocols of caring for the immediately deceased body, including *tahara*, interment and the funeral service. It is a compendium of customs and requirements, as well as a practical guide to the first year after a death.

'As there is a Jewish way of life, so there is a Jewish way of death,' says Lamm by way of introduction, astutely noting that 'the study of mourning observances is not likely to be undertaken before it becomes absolutely necessary, and when it is necessary, mourners will be in no mood to do so'.

One of the things that Lamm describes best is the bewildering period between death and interment, known in Hebrew as the *aninut*. 'At the moment of death, there is severe disorientation. We are perplexed not only by the large questions of life and death, but also by the problems of how to feel and how to conduct ourselves properly,' he writes. 'The golden chain of the family link is broken and swings wildly before our eyes.'

It is in this short but intense phase that the *onen* (mourner) is thrown into an uncomfortable paradox: shock and distress cripple their organisational capacity, yet they must also make practical arrangements, as well as notifying family and friends. There may be medical or forensic issues, as well as legal ones. 'Practically, the *onen* must make immediate and significant decisions based on the reality of death. Psychologically, however, he has not yet assimilated the death, or perhaps not accepted it,' writes Lamm.

The book also delineates between the purpose of the burial procedure and the purpose of the mourning laws. While the former is 'devoted to the respect, honor and endearment of the deceased', the latter focus on consoling the living, 'devoted to the mitigating of intense grief, the slow disentanglement from the web of ... rebellion that enshrouds the mind of the mourner'. According to Lamm, who references the Sages, comfort from friends and family is of limited value to the acutely bereaved 'while their dead lie before them'. Until the body has been buried and the funeral rites completed, the honour and integrity of the deceased must remain the focus. Lamm is not suggesting that the mourner be ignored or neglected; of course, it is appropriate to offer verbal acknowledgement, practical assistance, an open heart. The point he is making is that whoever is accompanying the mourner immediately after death must be conscious of their own limitations in providing solace. It is 'psychologically futile to effect reconciliation between the mourner and his fate at this time', Lamm maintains, pointing to the great humility, the standard of restraint required of those caring for the freshly bereaved.

It is in this space that the members of the Chevra Kadisha must operate as they arrange the burial and orient the bereaved in the funeral procedure. Ephraim would have listened to the weeping of blindsided family while collecting information for a eulogy. Getting the body to the Chevra Kadisha, ensuring a swift burial, working with the restrictions of Shabbat and other holy days—all these things would have taken high-level competence under pressure. He would need to liaise with a large range of personalities, to be efficient with bureaucracy and the rules of a secular state, while honouring ancient tradition. And the whole time, while in the presence of the bereaved, he would be providing that atmospheric support, the invisible hand-holding that Max Dzienciol described when he said Ephraim was there 'without you knowing'.

These are the balances to be struck above ground. But of course, there is a whole other plane on which this phase is operating—while the practical arrangements and emotional currents are churning in the world of the living, there is the body of the deceased, awaiting burial. As the Chevra Kadisha prepares the body for the coffin, and eventually its final home in the earth, it is performing the holiest tasks of all. (This is perhaps most starkly reflected in the fact that the very term 'Chevra Kadisha' translates to 'holy society', and that one of the first things a Jewish community does when it settles in a new location is establish a such a group.)

The emphasis on the body as a sacred vessel is paramount. 'A human being is equated with a Torah scroll that is impaired and can no longer be used at religious services. While the ancient scroll no longer serves any useful ritual purpose, it is revered for the exalted function it once filled,' says Lamm. This notion is not just metaphorically beautiful, it points to an exquisite cornerstone of much religious tradition: the notion of treating others with dignity, in death as in life.

Tahara customs, while ancient, are orally transmitted; as such, they bend according to regional requirements and the cultural fabric of a community. For instance, a volunteer I interviewed at the Melbourne Chevra Kadisha believes that she was trained in customs hailing from Jerusalem, while the men have inherited protocols from Eastern Europe. Similarly, Ephraim told me that when he first started at the Melbourne Chevra, the men held a *chuppah* over the dead body, 'so it wasn't exposed to the heavens'. This means four separate people were required to hold the posts, as well as men to do the washing and dressing of the deceased. As Ephraim revived the use of the *mikveh*, this custom faded, the water acting as the symbolic intermediary between the mortal and the divine.

Nonetheless, some customs are performed almost universally.

Upon arrival, the volunteers prepare the *tahara* room, filling buckets with warm soapy water, ensuring that there are plenty of towels, that the shrouds are laid out and the packets of Jerusalem soil (to be sprinkled on the body) are at the ready. For the men, there would be a *tallit* ready for final wrapping. The casket should already be in the room, with the name of the deceased stamped into a soft plaque, doweled to the coffin. If there is a *mikveh*, the volunteers check that the water is clear. At this point, they wash their hands using the ancient method of pouring three times on each palm from a cup. They robe up and put on gloves. It is only then, once they are completely ready to receive the body, that it is wheeled out of the fridge and transferred onto the washing table. All of this is done in silence.

Before the body is washed, the volunteers stand by the deceased and say a prayer, which is over a thousand years old.

In the washing, there is to be no doubling back. Reverence for the body must underpin every motion. In the words of Lamm, 'The sanctity adheres to the body even after the soul has left.'

Then it is time to immerse the body in the *mikveh*. This is the cornerstone of the purification ritual, the moment where the deceased is symbolically presented before God. The attendants lower the body into the water, while the word *tahara* is repeated three times. 'Purify, purify, purify,' goes the incantation, recalling the untouched state of the body before it had begun the current life cycle.

For communities without a *mikveh*, this ritual is performed with buckets of water poured over the body in a continuous stream.

Finally, it is time to dress the body in shrouds, which must be made of unbleached linen, hand-sewn with white linen thread. If linen is unavailable, cotton is permitted. But in all cases, the fabric should be simple and uniform—the underlying principle is that there is no hierarchy, that a pauper is afforded the same dress as a prince. In fact, there is a great emphasis on equality in this stage, the cusp of crossing over; the deceased is to mirror their state upon arrival, unadorned, free of class and status and privilege. This is also reflected in the fact that every Jew is buried in the same style of coffin: a simple casket made of untreated pine. There is to be no embellishment or decoration, no special materials used to finish the lid; it is a perfectly compostable and perfectly egalitarian container.

The shrouds must be free of seams and pockets, and the garments are to be tied (almost exclusively) with slipknots. One female volunteer described to me the delicacy of the process, the level of attention that must be given to every moment: 'we are twisting, twisting, twisting, then folding it on itself and then pulling. And if it turns into a full knot, you've got to undo it and redo it'. The volunteers work in a continuous loop, waiting for one person to finish tying before another picks up the cloth. This silent choreography will unravel if even one of the participants drops their focus.

Now, some sand or soil from Jerusalem is sprinkled on the face and heart. The body is then wrapped for the final time and transferred to the coffin.

Before the coffin is closed, each member of the *tahara* team intones a silent invocation, as well as the name of the deceased. The intention behind this, as it was related to me by a volunteer, is to 'make the person feel comfortable moving on, letting them know that you are grateful to have had the opportunity' to take care of their body. They are uttering an apology for having inadvertently wronged the deceased, either by improper handling or the causing of embarrassment. The words are said in a circular sequence, like a one-person choral round. It is a chain of humble entreaty, by its structure trance-like and deeply introspective. As Lamm eloquently puts it, 'At the end of their holy service, the chevra kadisha asks forgiveness of the deceased because it may not have performed to perfection, and also because handling a person's body under these circumstances requires exquisite sensitivity and a devotional talent that even the best of us do not always possess'.

'Who taught you to do *tahara*?' I ask Ben, now into the third hour of our conversation.

'My dad. And whoever else might have been there,' he replies. He concedes that initially the process—despite its calm, reverent cadence—was challenging. It was physically demanding and at times emotionally confronting. There is a lull in conversation as we let the intensity of memory settle. Then Ben speaks again, just as the rain is coming. The downpour is suddenly deafening, changing the air between us, electrifying the tiny kitchen.

'When you are doing this to the person, you can almost feel it as if it is happening to you. How would you like to be treated? If someone was washing your body, you would want them to treat you with care. And you say you are sorry to them, if you bump them, or anything like that. Years ago, there was this show called *Six Feet Under* and people used to say to me, "Ben, you should watch this, the guy talks to dead bodies". And I would go, "Yeah, of course they do". I didn't watch it. I didn't need to. None of what people would describe to me, none of that was strange.'

Before I leave Ben's apartment, we discuss his experience of making coffins, a task he did for an inordinately long time. Between the ages of twenty-two and thirty-eight, even throughout his move interstate, his getting married and making a family in another city, Ben Finch made coffins for the Melbourne Chevra Kadisha. After he left Melbourne to study at Sydney University, he would periodically come back down, for a fortnight or so, and make over a hundred caskets, working from morning until late at night. At the same time, he would help his father with the sorrowful work of collecting bodies from the arms of the bereaved. Sometimes this meant the collection of a young body; a baby from a hospital ward, or a child from its home. I can see unease crossing his eyes when he remembers this time.

'What did you do to cope? What did you do outside the work hours to centre yourself?' I ask.

'I would dissociate,' he says, startling me with his honesty. Then he says something even more astonishing. He describes where his mind went when he switched off.

'It was like a clearing,' he says. 'It was nowhere, but there were trees. And tall grass.'

'What colour?'

'Wheaty sort of colour,' he says, conjuring his father's vision of a field of gold, the image Ephraim has clung to since seeing it the night he and Cas met.

'There was a breeze blowing,' Ben adds, tracking my baffled face.

'Do you know about your father's vision of a field of wheat?' I ask.

'I don't know ... I've never heard him talk about any ...' he shakes his head slowly, digging for memory. We smile at each other, a non-verbal appreciation for this moment of synchronicity, these invisible bridges across time and space. Then he grabs his car keys and we walk through his apartment, out to the communal hallway. The rain is now a full-blown tempest, fragrant and intrusive, as loud as our voices in the tiny corridor.

'This just used to be a place that I would go to,' he says, coming back to the field of tall grass.

'And you felt calm there?'

'Yeah, yeah. And then I'd come back into my body.'

The night I leave Ben's apartment I go for dinner with one of my oldest friends, whom I met on my first day at school in Australia, aged ten. Because I did not grow up in Australia, and due to the rupture of migration, I have no friends that predate this age. In fact, the only people who have known me across my lifetime, and who are still in my world, are my parents. When I arrived at primary school in 1988, without a word of English, baffled by the pecking order of the playground, this friend was my cultural interpreter. She explained the rules of four-square; she did not laugh at me singing 'Home among the Gumtrees' with an accent at our Friday music lessons; she lent me her Baby-Sitters Club books, which I only dimly understood. We also finished at the same high school, sharing a love of literature and imaginings of world travel. Then she moved overseas and we spent our entire adult lives—meeting spouses, making children, finding and changing work—apart. But still our bond held. So when I meet her for dinner after an epic afternoon with Ben, I am thankful that it is her; I know I can be raw, a bit shaky, and it will be okay.

My friend and I meet at a square in Chinatown and walk around for an hour in the rain looking for somewhere to eat. The streets are packed with bodies and it is impossible to get a table. Stumbling from awning to awning, we catch up on each other's years. We find ourselves taking great, incredulous gulps of air as we recount illnesses, heartbreak, the impossible predicaments of parenthood. At some point a giant flag comes off a pole, carried by cataclysmic wind. The square keeps buzzing. We wait in a ramen queue and laugh at the absurdity of life's temper. We laugh with the same maniacal edge we had as children.

When we finally get a table, I tell her about this book, about the seemingly endless resonance of Ephraim's work. She listens to my grappling. It is only once we have finished eating, once our beers have grown tepid, that we raise the achy topic sitting beneath the surface of both our hearts. This friend and I knew a child who was fatally hit by a speeding car, the sibling of a mutual friend in high school. As teenagers, we witnessed the agony of it for the family at close range, standing by silent and incompetent. I tell my friend that Ephraim remembers this family, remembers the dear girl he buried. I ask her if she thinks it would be appropriate for me to contact the family. Might it agitate them, cause them more pain? She has no answers. But I leave the restaurant, once we have hugged for too long, and promised to find each other sooner next time, thinking about our mutual high school friend and her sister's untimely death.

I sit on the train, a pause in the rain's operatic outpouring, wondering where my old friend's heart is after all these years, wondering how she has managed the passage of time without her sibling on this earth. I think about her parents, remembering their tear-smudged faces at the *minyan*, their scant presence. Then I realise that along with our school community, and the family's other circles of support, I would have trailed behind Ephraim on the afternoon of this girl's funeral, all of us droplets in the current that accompanied her on that cloudy day in 1998.

I spend the next day reading and writing in the apartment in Rose Bay where I am staying with yet another friend. We have a slow morning, chatting and drinking coffee on her balcony. The sky is a flawless expanse of powder blue, the rains of Saturday having well and truly gone. Native hibiscus rings the marina below, dropping its citrine blossoms onto the paths. Gulls swoop and stalk the bay.

Again, I feel immense gratitude for the elemental gifts of this moment; the way nature is boldly carrying on its summer dance at our feet, the good food my friend has prepared for me this morning, the richness of her intellect and our conversation. All of it accentuates the life in my cells, a life I sprint through, a miracle that too often slips through my busy fingers, my frenetic mind.

My friend, let's call her Paula, is especially drawn to the stories of Holocaust survivors. Paula is a South African Jew of Hungarian descent, and a journalist. She tells me that in the mid-1990s she participated in the Twelfth Hour Project. The program, managed

The life and deathwork of Ephraim Finch

by The Australian Institute of Holocaust Studies, spent thirteen years collecting the oral histories of Holocaust survivors who migrated to Australia. Today the collection is housed in the State Library of New South Wales, as well at the US Holocaust Memorial Museum in Washington DC.

The survivor Paula recalls most powerfully was a woman from Eastern Europe whose children were taken by the Nazis and never returned. I ask how on earth this woman could recount such a fact, what sort of process enabled survivors to access and speak their stories.

Paula explains that the Twelfth Hour Project was one of several attempts—emerging in the 1980s and 1990s—to chronicle the Holocaust via first-hand audiovisual storytelling. The frontrunner in this wave was Claude Lanzmann's nine-and-a-half-hour film *Shoah*, released in 1985. The film collated twelve years of interviews with survivors, perpetrators, academics and non-Jewish eyewitnesses, providing the most comprehensive account of the events to date.

This project was also unique in its methodology, and what Paula recalls is that 'Lanzmann would ask a question that would be translated into the subject's language. The subject would speak and then their testimony would be translated back into English, all on camera. It was completely unedited. And it was long and laborious and emotionally wrenching. And you would hear the minute details ... and they hadn't joined the dots. Some of it hadn't got fully into their consciousness, but you understood that they knew. In any case, you could form your own opinion. You were in the room with the witness.'

'There was no extrapolation forced on the viewer?' I ask.

'No extrapolation, no prompting. The ummmms, the aaaahs, the expressions, the looking away wasn't edited out,' she says.

This format lay the foundation for the Twelfth Hour Project, where interviewers were encouraged to spend unstructured time with the subject in order to create a safe space for recall. The imperative was to allow the story to come in its own time, to allow the portal to open to the emotional experience, often locked away behind the protective wall of pat memory. I had not heard this term before, and Paula explains that pat memory is a fixed narrative, firmly grounded in fact rather than feeling, which covers the unbearable emotion of an experience. 'On this day this happened', 'we went there', 'the trains came at six o'clock'—these are classic examples of pat memory statements, often uttered in the same order, with no variation. Many of the subjects 'have the raw memory inside, but they've enclosed it in the story. And that surface story is true, it's factual. And it dispenses with everybody asking questions,' Paula explains.

What's interesting about pat memory is that it functions like a door—it blocks the feeling, but it is also the way in. Before Paula interviewed her, the woman had refused to speak about the Holocaust. Her children, the ones she had given birth to upon leaving Europe and settling in Australia, knew only that their siblings had been taken by the Nazis.

'I spent twenty hours with her,' Paula says of her subject. 'And the first five or six hours we didn't record a word. I had to build up an enormous amount of trust. I went there and I had barley soup ten times. And I had kashke, buckwheat porridge. And I sat there, in the lounge room, and we had tea. And we had these long silences. And I said to her all the way through, "You can pull out at any moment. This is your story and these are the tapes and if you want to put them in the garbage, you can do so".'

There were many pauses in the story, many times when the woman would come to an emotional precipice, then pull back, reiterating place names and train timetables. Paula does not recall the pivotal question, but one day, after many cul-de-sacs and retractions, 'the wall broke and an avalanche came out, of raw, unbearable sadness, the granular detail of what happened'.

When Paula played the cassettes to the woman's children, they heard a person they did not recognise. They learned that their

The life and deathwork of Ephraim Finch

siblings had been shot in a nearby forest, that their parents had the option to go with them when the Gestapo first burst in but made a snap decision not to. They were told the children were going somewhere safer, better.

'They said their mother's voice was different,' says Paula. 'The sensitivity, the concern, the emotional nuance, the depth was different. It was a person they "did not know".'

We discuss Steven Spielberg's Shoah Foundation, which filmed some fifty-two thousand Holocaust survivor and witness testimonies between 1994 and 2001. The foundation trained interviewers worldwide, with a similar hands-off method to Lanzmann's. The interviewer, who has collected basic biographical information ahead of the session, asks the occasional guiding question. These fit into the three-part template of the interview: early life, conflict/genocide experience, post-genocide to the present. Beyond that, the interview—which averages two, three hours—is driven by the subject, who delivers their story as they wish. Silences, cul-de-sacs, digressions become the account. The Shoah Foundation took these reels and archived them, undoctored.

Paula recalls that sometime in the late 1970s, it felt like 'the Holocaust taboo was broken, and people started talking about this'. This aligns with a fact I recently learned, which is that the term 'Holocaust' didn't come into usage until decades after the war. The term, which comes from the Greek *holokauston*, means a sacrifice by fire, or a thing wholly burnt. It started to appear in academic writings in the 1960s but only entered the popular lexicon in 1978, after the TV series *Holocaust*, starring Meryl Streep. Until then, it was variously referred to as World War II, or The Chorban (a Yiddish word meaning 'destruction').

'And how was the Steven Spielberg project related to the Twelfth Hour Project?' I ask.

'It wasn't. The through-line is the approach,' says Paula. 'And this desire, so many years later, to capture the living experience before people die off and it all becomes historic and deniable.'

When Ephraim stepped into the role of executive director at the Chevra, documentation of the deceased was perfunctory. The person who had previously kept the records ('he was a sort of bookkeeper, accountant, historian') completed the Victorian Government Notification of Death Certificate but did not 'pursue the history of the family'.

Ephraim noted that the deceased person's name was anglicised, transliterated in a way that disposed of original diacritics; there was an erasure of geographical nuance and hence regional accuracy. So Sztark became Stark, Fischer became Fisher.

Ephraim created a second form, to supplement the government one, naming it the 'Family History Data Form'. This noted the burial compartment, row and grave number; the deceased's English and Hebrew names; date and place of birth; transport to Australia and arrival date; parents' names (including maiden name); occupation; marriage details. The bottom of the sheet provided for 'Holocaust Details'; this was not itemised but gave space for internments, escape routes and tattoo numbers. He invited families to bring in birth certificates, family trees, *ketubot* (religious marriage contracts, written in Aramaic), conversion certificates. 'I'd be writing as much as I could,' he once told me, speaking with the urgency of a paramedic or firefighter.

The interviews often relied on props. First, he would pull out a laminated map of Europe, a metre wide and cross-hatched by the names of hamlets and rivers and mountain ranges. Unfurling it across his desk, he would sit back and let the person roam. Then he'd proffer his trusty copy of *A Dictionary of Jewish Surnames from the Kingdom of Poland* by Alexander Beider. Time after time, people surprised themselves with a shocking or poignant memory—the name of a village where they hid out, the last place they saw their disappeared spouse, the surname of the gentile family that fed them as they fled over a border. 'Opening out the map, I gave them a vehicle by which they could travel to the past,' he said to me once.

The life and deathwork of Ephraim Finch

Paula and I discuss this perilous process of excavation, the huge responsibility that comes with shepherding an individual through repressed terrain, and I think of Ephraim as interview subject. I think about the way he too has patterns of pat narration, how often he will relay the same set of facts about a person and the scaffolds that obstruct parts of the story. And yet, I have also noticed that his barriers are soft, even porous. I think of how often he will tear up spontaneously, the way he pendulates between repeating explicit detail and welcoming the spirit of the remembered, opening to a flood of feeling.

'It really is, to this day, a very corporeal experience for him,' I tell my friend. 'And the way he conducted his burial work was very corporeal. He took care of people's bodies so beautifully, he attended to their vessel as much as their legacy.' Of course, Ephraim took care of the living in an embodied way too, sometimes disregarding rigid orthodoxy to provide solace in extreme grief. I think of a woman he's mentioned, who comes to his shul, who lost a baby not long ago. 'She comes in and makes a beeline for me, and I give her a cuddle,' he tells me. This is not in line with the Hasidic rules of physical separation between men and women, but Ephraim makes the call that, in this instance, the mother's heart takes priority.

I think, too, about Ben, and how self-aware he is of his coping mechanisms around grief. I think about his field of golden wheat and his admission that so often there is nothing to say to the bereaved, that some circumstances are so devastating they leave no room for words. 'It's hard to tether it to something verbal,' Ben had said to me about the constant intimacy with people in profound pain.

I'm struck by the way he kept it together for our entire conversation, stayed present and available to all the stories, for a good three-and-a-half hours. But something catches me, a moment during our last ten minutes together, once we were in the car on the way back to the train station, once I had switched off my recording device and the official interview was over. Ben remembered a woman who had died of a long-term illness, whose body he came to collect. For years, he had carried, in his mind's eye, the wildly disparate responses of each of her children. While the older child wept, 'a dark cloud of grief above her head', the younger one became intensely hyperactive, seemingly leaving his body. As Ben described these children, each blindsided in their own way, his voice began to shake. He recalled leaving their house, realising that the entire front of his suit was saturated with his own tears. 'As my father and I were trying to move the mother's body with the utmost care in front of the children, I was moving in the gulf between them.' Perhaps he was crying the tears that the younger child couldn't cry. Perhaps something in the polarities ruptured—or, in fact, fused, the personal and the professional collapsing.

Ben's knuckles had gripped the steering wheel as tears inflected his speech, his words pooling and circling. 'I don't know … I don't know what it was about her, but that has really stayed with me,' he kept repeating. This broad-shouldered, solid man was suddenly soft with sorrow. I did not know how to comfort him in this flood, or if it was even appropriate. So I thanked him for his generosity, feeling my own damp face, and stepped out into the driving rain.

On my last day in Sydney, Paula and I take a walk. As we round her building, she says, 'Look, here is my Kotel,' referring to the Wailing Wall in Jerusalem. I squat down and see, in among the large sandstone bricks, a plaque that reads, 'This wall holds sacred texts. As you walk by you may wish to wish upon them.' Paula has embedded excerpts from various holy writings inside the wall: text from the Kabbalah, prayers from her mother's funeral, a snippet from the Bible.

'People come by and leave prayers, and candles, and flowers in the wall,' she says, filling my heart with warmth for the hopefulness of human nature, and for ritual, the way in which just a little opening can house our delicate, precious inner selves.

The life and deathwork of Ephraim Finch

The last thing I do before leaving Sydney is visit the ocean pool at McIver's Ladies Baths in Coogee. I let the fierce Pacific waves hold and rock my body, pull it to the cliffs then out towards the horizon. To my right are Wylie's Baths, where Ephraim picnicked and swam as a boy with his mum. I let the stories of the past week churn, knowing that to call them mere stories is a disservice, a flattening of something dynamic and still living. These words that Ben and Paula and Ephraim have shared with me are the living resonance of their subjects, of lives that have been given a proper send-off, an honouring of what they have meant. I say hello and goodbye to each of them before heading home to my children, whom I suddenly, desperately, need to see with my own eyes and hold in my own arms.

6

I have wanted to visit Springvale Cemetery with Ephraim for many months and finally our day has arrived. But before we leave—even though I am shuffling foot to foot with a backpack full of snacks and water, even though Ephraim has put on his labourer's boots and his Akubra—he and Cas want to know all about my visit with Ben.

I tell them that Ben's account of his childhood and adolescence showed me new things about this family, that it sits on top of their account but not squarely.

'He stepped up, he did what was expected,' Ephraim says with a sadness he perhaps couldn't have felt in the heat of the moment, deep in the energy of service. Ephraim often startles me with his contrition, throwing a diagonal line across an otherwise straight portrait of a sure-footed individual, a man of unswerving conviction. Over these months I have met a man who works with confidence, who prays with unshakeable faith, who fights with passion. But in moments like this—and this is not the first time I have seen him do it—Ephraim exposes a faultline of doubt in his own instinct, in what may have seemed utterly predetermined at another time.

I tell them that Ben was generous, erudite, that he had some beautiful memories of working with his father. They seem momentarily soothed. In the way of any parents living in a different city from their child, they want to know more.

'He said to ask you about George,' I tell Ephraim.

'Ah, George, what a lovely man,' he responds, ushering me to the back of the house as though George himself might be sitting there, awaiting us. I know a story is coming, so I put down my backpack. We approach a corner of the living room that has visibly been given over to the grandchildren. There are plastic and fabric animals, craft activities and board games. And in the corner of the corner, there is a glossy, chestnut-coloured rocking horse. It is strapped into a black saddle with gold trim, and on its frame is a plaque that reads: 'Presented to Ephraim Finch in appreciation of his generosity to the Berwick District Woodworkers, 02/12/07'. And, of course, there is a story, which is that George, aside from being the man who taught Ben how to make coffins, also ran the Men's Shed in Berwick. Throughout the 1990s, the Chevra would donate its unused pine to this not-for-profit initiative, which has chapters all over Australia.

Next to the rocking horse I see a glossy wooden aeroplane and Ephraim explains its shared provenance with the horse. Both are made from untreated pine that was surfeit to the Chevra's requirements once the larger planks had been used for coffins, repurposed by volunteers at the Men's Shed. Members of the Men's Shed mentor each other as they work on community projects—restoring bicycles for a local school, fixing furniture, making Christmas gifts for underprivileged children.

'Isn't it beautiful to think about everything that tree would go on to give people?' I think out loud.

'And to think that it was the final house for people on earth, that little tree,' says Cas. 'And then, the leftover things that might have been just burned, becoming toys that mothers were able to give their children at Christmas,' she adds.

The sun is shining through the large window, on the glossy black eye of the rocking horse.

Ephraim describes driving out to Berwick with George. Of the men he met, he says, 'They were all over fifty, and the women, when they came in said, "You don't realise you keep my husband off the street!"'

'He was a beekeeper too,' Ephraim says. Even though he wasn't Jewish, George would usher in the Jewish New Year with the Yeshivah and Beth Rivkah kids by bringing them honey.

'And when George died,' Ephraim continues, looking out across the yard, 'the family wanted me to do part of the service'.

'And did you?' I ask.

'I had to!' he replies, equal parts grateful and proud.

Eventually we get on the road. As we pull out of his street and head east I absently ask Ephraim if he knows the best way to the cemetery. The look he gives me is so full of disbelief and held-back laughter, I wish I could bottle it. I feel idiotic, but only for a moment, because just as quickly he says, 'Of course, dear, I'll show you,' disappearing my shame like waving steam off a hot cup of tea.

Earlier this morning, my friend Paula called from Sydney. 'I'm going out the cemetery with Ephraim today,' I told her. 'Ah,' the village of the dead,' she said. There was just one beat before she spoke again. 'No,' she course-corrected, 'it's the village of the remembered'. I share this with Ephraim, and he smiles deeply as we head out of our shtetl and onto the highway.

Driving in, we carve a line through the cemetery and park up the top, beneath some towering gum trees. Dragonflies flit between us as we proceed down the central path to the bottom of the hill, where Ephraim wants to share some of his most precious stories. The fenceline is bordered with a fine-leaved shrub, and Ephraim tells me that he planted those with a mother who'd lost a child.

The life and deathwork of Ephraim Finch

He says this sotto voce, because he didn't exactly have the Chevra board's approval, and again I see him bending rules in order to hold a heart. In fact, he doesn't need to lower his voice, as the cemetery is deserted. Aside from a distant figure in a high-vis vest pushing a wheelbarrow, we appear to be the only people here. It is cold but blazingly sunny. It is also ferociously windy, and Ephraim frequently holds on to his hat.

The black marble headstones, thousands of them in neat rows, all facing east, absorb the sun, glinting with intensity. The mynas swoop, their metallic song bouncing repetitively, like trampoline springs. This, together with the intermittent rumble of a whipper-snipper in the distance, is dizzying. The wind dances between the rows of headstones, stern in their geometry, thousands of gilded names refracting back and back again, in layers. The atmosphere is, somehow, both still and wild.

As we walk down the hill, towards the Browns Road entrance, Ephraim greets numerous people out loud, just as he did the first time we met and he was describing this place to me. His voice changes according to the person he is addressing, as does his diction. 'How are you, mate?' he says to certain individuals, his song rising with nostalgia, while others get a sombre, 'Hello, dear Mrs So-and-so,' or an adoring, 'Oh, hello, Rabbi!'

Finally, we get to the row of headstones Ephraim has been wanting to show me. He recaps the astonishing story behind four adjacent graves. I am focused on Regina Goldman, the woman at the centre of the row. I am thinking of her descendants, including her niece Sally, who holds the silken thread to the past. As Ephraim and I apprehend these headstones, this soil holding bones from a field in rural Poland, I say a quick agnostic prayer to the gods of time and remembrance so that I may gather it all.

'You know, things have changed because I grow older, and I live in the past now,' says Sally Felzen when we meet on the deck of her aged-care home. The day is sharply sunny, almost blinding, and Sally is asking her daughter Sharon to make her comfortable. She is almost ninety-four years old and incredibly beautiful; not just along classic measures of youthful skin and lovely posture, but in the openness of her face, the bright kindness of her eyes, all of her somehow luminous despite the sadness I know she carries.

'And my auntie was a big part of my past,' she adds, referring to Regina Goldman. I ask her to give me some basic family history, so that I can understand their connection and eventually the connection to Ephraim. Between Sally's memories, my own research, and the information offered by two of Sally's daughters (Sharon and Belinda), I construct something of a portrait.

Sally was born Sala Peczenik, in 1929, on the outskirts of Złoczów, Poland. Sally had a sister, Mela, who was three years younger, and the girls grew up in an idyllic farm setting. Their parents, Leon and Klara, ran a dairy. Sally's father was the love of her heart, so much so that she was known as his 'shadow'.

Sally had a happy childhood. She attended a local school, where her favourite teacher was a Catholic Ukrainian woman, and she 'ran in the fields' with the other local kids. Later, Sally would see the locals setting their dogs on her family and dobbing them in to the Gestapo. But in childhood, anti-Semitism was the furthest thing from Sally's mind. In the school holidays, Sally would visit their aunty Regina, who lived in Złoczów and whom she adored. 'We really loved each other,' she tells me, in lieu of describing how they spent their time together.

What all three women do tell me is that Regina was quite a force. They recount the story of Geoffrey, Regina's much-longed-for son, whom she had after a series of miscarriages. Perhaps this long road of loss made Regina extra protective of Geoffrey, because at some point after the Germans invaded, she gave him for safekeeping to a local woman. As the war drew to a close, Regina went back to the woman to collect her child. But the woman had absconded. And when Regina finally found her, she was reluctant to give Geoffrey back. More distressingly, Geoffrey refused to return to his mother, having formed a bond with his caretaker. Regina managed to reclaim her child, but not without a battle.

Even while Geoffrey was missing, she managed to focus on the survival of those around her. As the war escalated, Regina negotiated with local farmers to hide Jews, including her own family.

I learn two more details that help me grasp the eager drive of its protagonist: Regina and her husband Lonek were, in Belinda's words, 'madly in love'. Meanwhile, Klara and Leon were also ensconced in a romance that was 'quite revolutionary'. Klara fell so quickly and deeply in love with Leon, she broke off a pre-existing engagement, an act of unheard-of defiance for this time.

I notice that despite such details, there is a tragic lack of specificity in these anecdotes; Sally's children aren't in fact sure if she was born in Złoczów or the satellite village of Snowicz. Her year of birth is also uncertain; maybe it was 1928, not 1929. Her birth certificate cannot be found, or perhaps does not even exist. The various accounts constellate around one narrative: at some point circa 1943 Sally was sent to live with a forester's family. The time estimate would make her approximately fourteen years of age. Over the months that she spent with the forester's family, Sally pretended to be their relative. She changed her name to Nastusha. She took on farming tasks and went to church on Sundays. She learned Catholic prayers and crossed herself in public.

One day, when the family was out, she spotted a goose-down doona that belonged to her parents, understanding that a trade had been made for her safety. But not all was safe at this harbour, as the forester's teenage neighbour started to make advances towards her. Sally does not say how long she bore this, and what it entailed, but I can see that this horrific time was made worse by her obligation to stay. She had to stay for her survival, but it seems she was also paralysed by shame. As she recalls the period, tears come to her already shimmering eyes. 'Before I left for the forester's house, my father told me not to shame the family,' she recalls, pointing to the sense of disgrace she carried, while at the same time enduring trespass. Still, at some point, she resolved to leave, spurred on by the forester's growing nervousness about sheltering a Jew.

The day she left, the forester's wife had packed her a small bundle of food. She also had a note from her family, roughly identifying their whereabouts. She stepped out of the forester's house, seeing the ground and trees covered in snow, everything looking 'the same in every direction'. She picked a direction, as though guided by an invisible force, and walked for several miles to the mill where she hoped her family were hiding.

When Sally finally arrived at the mill, the miller's wife slammed the door in her face. The woman shouted at her, threatening to call the police. 'They were worried that she was an informant,' says Belinda. 'Nobody trusted anybody at the time.' Eventually, softened by Sally's insistent weeping, her frantic, repeated knocking, and perhaps her young age, the woman took pity. She opened the door and allowed Sally to speak. Sally's descriptions of her family members matched the faces of the Jews hiding under the pigsty on the miller's property.

The miller, who had been listening, told his wife to let Sally in. Inside, he fed her and let her warm her bones. Then he led her down to the barn, where he opened a trapdoor covered by straw. 'I saw a crack in the door,' she recalls, 'and a candle, and then my mother's face. I did not see my father.'

Upon reuniting with her family, Sally learned of what had come to pass. While Sally was with the forester's family, her father and her uncle Lonek had been shot. The family had been hiding in the forest, surviving on foraged scraps. One night, they made a fire, inadvertently alerting the Nazis to their location. Then there were dogs, and SS officers. The men and women scattered. Gunshots rang out, bodies falling. This was the last that Regina would see of her beloved Lonek, and Klara of her Leon. Leon was forty-two years old, while Lonek was a mere thirty-two.

The life and deathwork of Ephraim Finch

When the Nazis had come to the forest, they went straight for the men. As Klara, Mela and Regina ran for their lives, they saw the men falling, then a Gestapo officer 'coming to finish them off'. Leon was shot in the head. After hiding in long grass all day, Klara and Mela wandered the forest, searching for their men, fruitlessly calling their names. Meanwhile, Regina returned to the site of the shooting and found fresh graves that the locals verified as being Leon and Lonek's. She made a mark on a nearby sapling with a stone, vowing to come back for their remains, to one day give them a proper burial.

Over the coming months, the surviving family members continued to hide in the forest. Having lost Leon, Klara completely fell apart, becoming virtually catatonic. The children would pour water into her supine body just to keep her alive, but her will to live had dwindled. Meanwhile, Regina doubled down, making deals between locals and displaced Jews seeking shelter, and ensuring that her family was included in the arrangements.

When the family came out of hiding, they returned to Złoczów, where they survived by selling baked goods and diluted alcohol to the Russian soldiers returning from the front. About a year later, Klara paid a smuggler to take them across the border to Czechoslovakia; they ended up in the Foerhenwald Displaced Persons Camp southwest of Munich. Meanwhile, Regina and her mother Berta were sent to Neu Freimann, a DP camp in the Munich district. There are many stories inside these stories, and Sally has a muddy recall of who went where when. But there is an immigration record confirming Sally and Klara's arrival in Adelaide on the cargo ship *S.S. Oxfordshire* on 25 May 1949. Regina had already arrived in Australia with her mother Berta, Geoffrey, and the man she had met and married at Neu Freimann.

How the women rebuilt their lives is yet another multi-volume story. But the essential fact is that through it all Regina continued to be a determined and exceptionally intuitive character. I learn that at some point in the sixties, Geoffrey left for Europe and went AWOL in Paris. Regina, in a heart-cracking reprise of an earlier separation, somehow found him, using a combination of clues and instinct.

With similar resolve, Regina maintained a decades-long correspondence with the villagers who were there when Lonek and Leon died. She had been sending them gifts and money, making sure that they kept an eye on the graves of her husband and brother-in-law. As the years went by and the villagers died off, she corresponded with their children.

None of Regina's descendants know why the lightning bolt struck when it did, but they all remember her suddenly leaving for Poland in 1989, declaring that she was returning for the bones. She was missing for approximately three months, and no one knew how to reach her. When she did eventually make contact, it was via a telegram to Sally, asking her to secure a plot for Leon and Lonek's bones and to be ready to pick her up from the airport. Regina had found the makeshift graves, paying a local man to dig them up. Two facts confirmed the accuracy of her search: a bullet hole and a silver tooth in Lonek's skull, and a mark on a nearby tree, which was no longer a sapling—it was an established tree, perhaps an oak, towering over her as she stood guard over the digging of the soil.

Regina arrived at Tullamarine Airport with a suitcase containing the bones, somehow clearing it through customs. Her great-nieces both tell me, through giggles of disbelief, that she also forgot the suitcase on the baggage carousel and had to return for it once she'd gone through security.

Here, the story threads into what Ephraim has told me, as we pored over his records. Sally Felzen approached Ephraim Finch in late 1989, with a request. She wanted to buy a plot for the recovered bones of her uncle and father.

'I will do what I can to help you,' said Ephraim. 'But first, tell me about your family.' So Sally 'unwinds her family history', as Ephraim's journal lyrically notes.

Some weeks later, Regina Goldman marched into his office, leather bag in hand, exclaiming, 'I want Kaver Israel for my bones!' Kaver, or Kevurah Israel, refers to a Jewish burial, the fulfilment of a promise she made some forty-five years earlier. Ephraim's journal reads, 'We put the large suitcase on my desk and she opened it and sitting in the midst of her clothing was a sealed tin trunk. Approximate size of 900 millimetres squared. It was very heavy. I said I would have to take the box to the Chevra president. She was not worried and said to me, "The one with the bullet hole in the forehead and silver fillings is my husband."'

Ephraim arranged a meeting with Mr Kantor, who enquired as to the provenance of the bones. In the course of the meeting, Regina said: 'I got the man to dig and found the two bodies lying together.' The Chevra made a decision to bury the men's remains in one plot.

In fact, Sally had made another request when she first visited the Chevra. She wanted the bodies of her mother and grandmother to be exhumed from Fawkner Cemetery (in Melbourne's north) and brought to Springvale, so that all the family could be laid to rest together. Ephraim completed the government exhumation forms. He was also treating this reburial as though it was a first, with the same fidelity to ritual. 'I had to bury her mother as quickly as possible,' his journal says.

The journal entry contains these poignant words, where Ephraim acknowledges the ethical gravity of exhumation, and the momentous nature of this story: 'I know there must have been a tumult in heaven, but I am sure all the souls are happy to be united once again, with their families around them. On Sunday, we had a service and buried all of them together. In 1997, Mrs Regina Goldman was laid to rest next to her mother and husband.'

He describes the family gathering at Springvale: 'After I had lowered the coffin, all of the family came and knelt down. And cried. Then we filled the grave so she could be at peace again.' The filling of the grave with hand-shovelled soil is a specific aspect of the Kevurah that Regina had fought so hard for. 'Showing' the back of the shovel to the casket as it is being covered in earth demonstrates the reluctance of the act, the heart that wants to deny such a sorrowful reality.

And that is the end of the entry, which I read to Sally and Sharon at our meeting on that glary day, sitting on the deck of the aged-care home. As I am reading, Sally weeps, the posture of a hunched child holding something close to her chest. 'We sat *shiva* for our dead,' she says, putting another close on this story of many endings. 'I want this to be in the *Jewish News*, will you put it in the *Jewish News*?' she pleads. I tell her I will write it into a book. 'Thank you,' she says through quiet sobs. Her crying is young too, heart-wrenchingly fragile, and in this moment, she is not just the elegant elderly lady, but a girl hiding her body, a broken daughter leaving her father behind, a hopeful young woman moving across the world to repair and start afresh, a sapling, an oak.

Ephraim and I stand by Regina Goldman's grave for some time before moving on. I take a breath, I follow his footsteps. He is calm, but he is also in a zone of sorts, not entirely reachable. He leads the walk and the conversation, much of it not with me.

We move down the path only a few metres before coming to a bronze sculpture. Approximately three metres in height, it looks like a vertical scroll of paper, or a thin cone of rising smoke. It is split coarsely down the middle, like a canyon or a scar. Ephraim explains that this is a memorial to those who perished in the Holocaust, as we read, out loud, the plaque at the sculpture's base: 'Interred are ashes from Auschwitz, soil from Riga-Rumbuli forest and fragments of bones from Chelmno and plant matter, given by a parent of a child who was killed in the Holocaust.' Later research will tell me that this sculpture, titled *Tomb*, sits atop a grave; the ashes and soil and bone were collected from Auschwitz in the late 1980s and officially interred in 2004. The significance is not just that these deaths were memorialised, but that these bodies—immolated as they were by the furnaces of Auschwitz—were given a Jewish burial. As the burial took place, many of the Holocaust survivors in attendance shovelled earth into the grave. Even those unfamiliar with *halacha* (Jewish law) tend to know that it forbids cremation. This monument offers reparation on many levels.

The piece was created by Melbourne artist Andrew Rogers, who at the time of installation was one of approximately thirty thousand Melbournians who had lost relatives in the Holocaust. Rabbi Philip Heilbrunn, who officiated the interment of the ashes, said, 'It is vital for us, in these unique circumstances, where we are able, to bring these sacred bones and ashes to a proper Yiddishe kevurah—Jewish burial.'

I think of Regina Goldman, the way she used these exact words when she fronted up to the Chevra with her precious suitcase. By the time she got to Poland, to the field that held her family members, she was in her eighties. Ephraim's records also state that she was sick with cancer. I think of her insistence on closing the circle, on the human need to keep our loved ones close. It seems that the need for community and belonging transcends our living bodies, that the notion of home transcends death.

As we move on from the memorial, I ask Ephraim how many people are buried at Springvale Jewish Cemetery and he estimates twenty thousand. My brain swirls with the numbers, which are of course not just numbers. Each of these twenty thousand is a being as intricate and precious as anyone I have ever known, or ever loved. The Melbourne Chevra Kadisha has been burying its people here since the 1960s. More figures come at me as I contemplate the fact that Melbourne has the highest per-capita population of Holocaust survivors outside Israel.

I take in the sea of black marble, growing light-headed. I close my eyes. When I open them, I see the wordless man standing next to me, just one human, with one outline. His beard is moving with the breeze. Otherwise, he is still as an anchor, dropped here long, long ago.

More hours slip by. Ephraim and I have been alone all day, our solitude perforated only once, by a woman, who appeared around lunchtime. She materialised in the innermost rows, looking disoriented. When he spotted her, Ephraim looked at her for a long time. Then he took a step towards her, and I could see he was struggling to leave her lost, unattended. He moved towards her like the solicitous owner of a store, or a kindly teacher noticing a new child in the schoolyard. Then, for reasons he did not share, he stopped. We left the woman to her search and kept moving.

Now my senses are faltering and the thousands of names are starting to bend before my eyes. Names and numbers, so many numbers. Names of people I know, truncating my breath. Golden text in Russian, Hebrew, Yiddish, Georgian. Nicknames in quote marks. Every familial role under the sun: mother, father, son, daughter, niece, grandmother, son-in-law, uncle, great-grandfather, wife, sister. So many Beloveds. So many Never to be forgottens. Too many Gone too soons. The occasional candle, river stones and pebbles of every shade. Periodically there is a photo encased in plastic, embedded in the stone. This seems to be more common with children, and Ephraim tells me that although photographs are 'not encouraged' he always found it hard to refuse parents this request.

There are two more sections that I want to visit before we leave. The first is the Spare Parts section, which despite its glib title reveals a great reverence for the preciousness of the human body. Jewish law requires that if limbs are severed while a person is alive, they are to be interred. Organs do not classify; only body parts with a bone require burial. There are two exceptions to this: blood and the womb. Blood is considered sacred, a carrier of life-force, and is to be collected and buried with the individual where possible. The womb, as the seat of creation, demands equal honour. And so, Springvale Cemetery has an area, perhaps ten by three metres in size, specially dedicated to these remains. There are no stones here,

The life and deathwork of Ephraim Finch

no inscriptions. But it feels extraordinarily special, a small zone of concentrated reverence.

One of the first times I ever sat with Ephraim, he told me about the Spare Parts section and the women who had requested womb burial after a hysterectomy. The hushed awe with which he mouthed the phrase 'seat of creation' cracked me a little, and I found myself suddenly weeping, sharing the story of my daughter's placenta, which was taken after her emergency caesarean and thrown in the hazardous-waste bin once the doctors were done examining it. Even in my heavily sedated state, I found this gesture shocking. This dense, potent organ had been her source of food and oxygen, her pillow, her direct link to my body, for months. 'It was neither hazardous, nor waste,' I said to Ephraim through tears. He didn't reply, but nodded, while Cas silently took my hand.

Eventually, we turn around and head down the path. We are finally, blessedly, heading to an area of the cemetery that houses something other than mourning. In fact, quite the opposite. We are heading to a final resting place of the most unusual kind, a subterranean repository of sacred thoughts and sacred things.

On many occasions, I have arrived at Ephraim's house to find him humming joyously about a book he has just acquired. Often, this book will have come from the Chevra; he would have salvaged it, at the last minute, from disposal. Often, it is a book waning in contemporary appeal, such as *Memories of My Life in a Polish Village, 1930–1949* by Toby Knobel Fluek. This strange but beautiful volume is a sort of picture book for adults, featuring acrylic paintings of a bygone era. He's shown me a slim hardcover volume titled *The Bridge of Life; Life as a Bridge between Past and Future* by Rabbi Tucazinsky. This book, published in Jerusalem in 1983, is a theological treatise covering topics such as 'Longing for the Source' and 'Life Caught between Conflicting Types of Energy'. In fact, Ephraim does not usually keep these books for himself; often, he passes them on to the Melbourne Holocaust Museum, which adds them to its library collection.

'How do these books end up at the Chevra?' I ask.

'People drop them off,' he answers.

'And would these go to the tip if you hadn't taken them?'

'Well, no. They would go to the *shaimos*.'

And this is where we find ourselves now, as the sun approaches the horizon, drawing the curtain on a very long day. *Shaimos* is another word for *shemot*, or holy objects. These include books, prayer shawls, *mezuzahs*, any part of a Torah scroll and even homework that has the name of God written in it. (The word 'Shem' translates to 'Name'.) In the case of books, the first port of call is to see if it can be restored and hence reused—a book's primary aim is to educate the living. Where possible, a book should be donated to a library, school or synagogue. Burial is the last resort, not only because it takes the text out of circulation but because it uses up consecrated space.

In this way, damaged or unusable books are apprehended similarly to deceased bodies—as holy objects that once performed holy tasks, and hence deserve a proper burial. While practice seems to vary around the world, the Melbourne Chevra Kadisha first places the objects in clay pipes. These are sealed with concrete and interred in a single, large plot. This use of clay—an organic substance—is in line with the requirement for natural burial materials; no metal or plastic is to encase the Torah. Springvale's *shaimos* area spans about four metres squared, while the newer cemetery at Lyndhurst has a larger section, housing the youngest batch of thoughts and prayers.

As we walk back to the car, I feel the weight of today's visit in my body. I struggle to fathom how one person, with just one heart and just two hands, did this work, day after day for thirty years. I wonder where he put the aggregate heartache, how he continued to stay empathic and clear-sighted and available to his families. There must have been deaths (and lives) so tragic that they lodged in him, derailing his faith and impairing his stamina. I do not ask him. We climb into the car and sit mutely, the late-afternoon sun warming us through the windscreen. It feels wonderful to close my eyes.

I unzip my backpack and retrieve the picnic I have packed. We share kosher pastries from Cas's favourite cafe, munching in companionable silence, crumbs falling down our fronts. I feel very grateful to be feeding my body in this moment, to be in the cosy car, to be sitting not walking. I think about the way that deathwork is deeply spiritual but also very bodily, how the body, like life itself, can be both confronting and glorious, sometimes in the one moment.

In its exhaustion, my mind reels back to Ephraim's childhood, inchoate images of him as a butcher's son, observing the preciousness of blood, the handling of flesh, the sudden movement of life-force out of a living thing. I wonder if this, in part, explains his ease around the body and its states. I wonder also if it laid the foundation for his expansiveness, the knowing that each moment contains its own end, that life is fleeting. I know Ephraim has a rare gift for embracing paradox. Often, I have seen him laugh and cry with mere seconds in-between, and noticed how strangely freeing it is to be in the presence of that.

I put the car into gear and we start to reverse out of the cemetery. I look at the row where we began, so many hours ago. Before we took off on our walk through the headstones, Ephraim showed me his and Cas's plot. I did not expect this to shock me so much; after all, we were at a cemetery, we had spent months talking about death, contemplating its many dimensions. Perhaps over these months, in the calm and equanimous company of the Finches, I had lulled myself into a false sense of ease with it all. But seeing a tangible signifier of Ephraim's passing was suddenly too much to bear. Rattled by the intensity of my sadness, I turned away from him. Then I wiped my eyes and turned back to face him, the wind leaping between us like an irritating toddler.

'I don't want to think about you dying,' I heard myself saying, the words spilling involuntarily. He smiled mildly, almost peacefully, remaining at a distance.

'Ah, it's all gonna come,' he said.

'I've been bragging about how much I've grown and made peace with all this, and then I think about you and I don't want you to go.'

'Don't worry, don't worry,' he replied. There was a pause, the mynas of the morning absent. Then he added, 'But you do wake up in the morning and say, "I wonder …"'

This scene catches in my throat as we exit the gates and head up Browns Road. Of course, he is right: none of us knows how long we have. Not only that, but preparation can only take us so far. Ritual holds us, community catches us in the fall. But loss is loss—by definition it will leave a hole. And while it may give us comfort to imagine our beloved's spirit by our side, it is really the body we miss. It is the hair we will never brush off their forehead, the cheek we will never kiss or wipe or press against. It is the reason people keep their deceased's clothes, tightly knotted garbage bags holding their mother's smell. It is the reason people can't wipe and recycle a phone that had their sibling's outgoing message on it, or change the sheets after their partner has passed. It is the mother's longing for the child's tiny ribcage and all the growth it will not know. It is the longing for bones, the need for things that we can hold.

With this in mind, I take a good look at the person sitting next to me as we wait at the lights. I notice his hands folded neatly on his black undertaker's satchel. I listen to his voice, its ageing tenor. Then I pass him the final pastry, thankful that I get to have this drive with him, that both he and I have families to return to, that I do not have to worry because he knows the way home.

7

The light on this coast is mild. Caramel sun streams through the spinifex, while moonah and tea-tree contour the saltmarsh like an elaborate necklace. Pink succulents push through the swampy soil as black swans traverse the creek in formation. Pelicans and egrets dot the bank, as do the tiny blue wrens and grey fantails that like to feed in the dunes. As you curve around the estuary, the beach opens out proper, and suddenly you are faced with the roaring majesty of the ocean, churning, immense. I have been here in every season, and unlike the light, the water is never mild. It is a roiling run of timpani, untameable, wed to its own furious logic.

This is where I come to write this story, this story of soil and breath. I come to think and dream, to walk these Wadawurrung sands and waterways. This conversation of marsh and sea, these endangered hooded plovers nesting in the dunes, make the space both delicate and powerful.

My dog is never so happy as when we come to this stretch of Victoria's surf coast. Here, she runs for hours through the salty spray, bolts to the ocean's edge, then stops short for reasons I will never know. She follows me off the beach, up the one-street village that terminates in a caravan park. We go upstairs, I sit down at the dining table, covered in boxes of transcripts and books, in the unoccupied beach house of a generous friend. I open my laptop. The dog snoozes at my feet while I sift the past.

On this occasion, having just been to Springvale with Ephraim, I am returning to the notion that the physical matters, both in terms of our bodies but also the land that we bury into, and how we bury. It seems terribly important—even to the most secular of us—that we don't bury arbitrarily and without custom. Even those who may not prize ritual in life seem to demand it for life's end. As I unpack the documents, then get up and warm some soup on the stove, then sit down again, slurping the borsht I have brought with me, I think about roots. It occurs to me that many people do not know their roots, or do not wish to access them. Perhaps they are not curious, or perhaps it is the opposite—they are confronted by a history, by something they do not wish to feel. But like so many self-evident, invisible things—like air, like breath, like love—our roots are there, soundlessly deepening, whether we look at them or not.

Ephraim has worked hard to ensure people are woven into their history, buried alongside their own. He has also been on hand in the days and hours prior to a person's passing, gathering stories, offering ritual. He has nurtured a culture of reverence and even homecoming around what is traditionally viewed as an ordeal, an experience most of us avoid thinking about.

'No one actually taught him,' Cas tells me. 'It was him developing his version of the process, putting his love into it.'

'You mean the record-keeping?' I ask.

'Yes, but not only. I mean being with people, going to the hospitals, speaking at events, attending meetings with the government.' The last detail refers to the advocacy Ephraim undertook on behalf of the Chevra in 1996, when the *Cemeteries Act* was up for review.

The life and deathwork of Ephraim Finch

Ephraim was concerned about the community's ongoing right to conduct burials according to Jewish law if Victorian cemeteries were privatised. In addition, there was a greater threat: the government was proposing a twenty-five-year tenure on graves. After this, it could inter new coffins over the existing remains. Together with a range of synagogues and other Jewish organisations, the Chevra made a written submission to the review committee. Subsequently, the government scrapped the twenty-five-year limit, assuring community members that Jewish graves would be held in perpetuity and that all Jewish burial law would be respected.

'He was doing everything,' Cas continues. 'And by that I mean Jews die everywhere, they're not just all in Caulfield!' She is rounding a narrative corner, moving from the political to the practical, from one facet of Ephraim to another. I am myself interested in this functional aspect of the deathwork, having often pictured the sheer amount of driving Ephraim would have done, some of it to unfamiliar areas, much of it at night.

Cas describes what this was like in the era before mobile phones, when Ephraim would find himself rushing to collect a body in an unknown part of town, sometimes losing his bearings: '... the number of times in the dead of night, or early hours of the morning, he would have to knock on people's doors and ask to use their phones. And how often they didn't want to do it. They were frightened'. Eventually the Chevra got him a mobile phone, which came in a case with a handle. And it would sit next to him in the hearse, in the passenger seat, like a dark and comical apprentice.

'He had to know every hospital, every back door, how you can get in on the Shabbos,' Cas goes on. Of course, bodies would have to sometimes be collected on Shabbat; hospital wards or aged-care facilities might urgently need the bed, or a body might need collecting from the site of an accident. And in this case, the Chevra used a non-Jewish driver to perform the task. But wherever possible, Ephraim would ensure that he could be there for both the deceased and the bereaved.

He tells me many stories that illustrate this.

One time, in what he describes as 'the early days', a phone call came through to the Chevra at five o'clock in the afternoon. Ephraim was in his office, finishing up some paperwork. He heard another staff member answer the phone.

'And I heard him say, "You want to report a death, interstate? Look, our office is closed now. Could you ring back in the morning?"' Then Ephraim heard his colleague taking the bereaved person's number and hanging up. Something in Ephraim bristled at this dismissal of the caller, even though he knew it was past closing time. He shuffled papers for a minute, while his colleague packed up for the day. Ephraim waited to hear him closing the back door, get in his car. When he heard the car engine starting, Ephraim walked into the office and dialled the number scribbled on the memo pad.

'I knew you'd call back,' said the female voice on the end of the phone, ragged with distress but also relief. It took just a few seconds to establish that she knew Ephraim from a bereavement group, where both had volunteered. She had suffered another terrible loss prior to this one and had seen Ephraim's care at close range.

'Can you imagine, having to be told to wait till the morning?' he says to me, still indignant, heartbroken, all these years later. 'So I said to her, "Please tell me what's happened". She said, "My son was killed in a car accident this afternoon. I just want to get everything organised".' He assured her the body would be collected immediately and driven down to Melbourne. Then he asked, 'When are you coming back, my dear one?' The woman told him she was flying back to Melbourne at midnight and that she would be alone.

'So I picked her up at the airport and I drove her home,' he says, the image crumpling his face, its anguish still fresh.

'The Chevra wouldn't have liked to know that you went out at midnight,' I venture.

At this, Ephraim flicks his hands up in a familiar gesture, a blend of 'who cares' and 'it couldn't have been any other way'.

The life and deathwork of Ephraim Finch

I think of the many other instances where he physically went the distance to comfort the bereaved, to give the deceased a community burial. There is a persistent imperative to bring everyone together, to make sure no body—or spirit—is left uncommemorated, unaccounted for. One day Ephraim tells me about compiling an electronic database of all the Jews buried across the various cemeteries of Melbourne since 1843. He collected names from the major cemeteries, such as Springvale, Fawkner and Carlton, as well as from historical locations, such as the Jewish section in the cemetery beneath what is now Queen Victoria Market. He tells me that between 1920 and 1922, when the Old Melbourne Cemetery was repurposed as a market, the Jewish bodies were exhumed and relocated.

'And where did they go?' I ask.

'Fawkner Cemetery, Pioneer D section,' he says without pausing. 'And then I'd go around to different parts of the state … Rutherglen, Distillery Lane, turn left into the cemetery …' he says, drifting with the memory. Cas adds that, for many years, it was impossible to go for a drive in the country without Ephraim veering off the highway to explore the local graveyard, to lay eyes on any Jewish headstones and check on their condition. He would also take down the details and add them to the database.

'And you could see the effort that people went to, to have the tombstones brought up from Melbourne, cut with the Hebrew. The amount of effort!' he says, admiring and satisfied.

I ask if the land needed to be sanctified in order to be deemed a 'Jewish section'.

The answer is not straightforward. Ephraim explains that when a new piece of land is purchased for a cemetery, it must be consecrated by a rabbi. However, in non-denominational cemeteries, in remote places where there is no community and no Jewish cemetery per se, the section of earth where a Jew is interred is rarely officially sanctified. Still, a sort of informal sanctification occurs. Thinking of all the isolated Jewish plots he has sighted in country Victoria,

Ephraim says, 'Once a Jew gets buried in that ground, that ground is holy for our purposes'.

This reminds me of something he said earlier this year, when I'd come with a personal question. A few days before my grandfather's one-year death anniversary, my mother was struggling to reach the rabbi. Being secular Jews, we felt unsure of the ritual and my mum asked me to ask Ephraim. We knew the headstone went up after twelve months, that prayers needed to be said, but little else. What were the prayers? Did we need a *minyan*, a quorum of ten? Must it be made entirely of men? What happens if we don't read Hebrew? How do we conduct the ceremony without a rabbi? This last question was most pressing for my mum, whose father we were consecrating, and who loved his rabbi.

'You don't need a rabbi to do something Jewish,' Ephraim said to me over the phone the day before the event. 'What do you mean?' I replied, flustered.

'You don't need a rabbi to do something Jewish,' he repeated. 'You just need Jews.'

Ephraim would periodically enquire with the Cemeteries and Crematoria Association of Victoria as to Jewish burials, adding them to the database. He learned of one burial in a rural pocket of Victoria, of a woman with three sons, all of whom had married out of the faith. This would mean the end of the line for her Jewish heritage, but adding her to the database would ameliorate its disappearance.

Another time, a woman came into the Chevra to arrange her mother's burial. She told Ephraim that she would be cremating her mother, 'so then I can take mum with me' to regional Victoria, where she herself intended to be buried. Ephraim asked, if given the chance, would she like to have her mother buried alongside her. The woman said yes, of course. So he contacted the cemetery and organised a plot. When the time came, he buried the elderly lady in

The life and deathwork of Ephraim Finch

the non-denominational section, next to where her daughter would one day rest.

He tells me about a friend and community member phoning him in utter devastation at his son's drowning. When he took the call, Ephraim was in Katoomba visiting his aunt. Without any deliberation, he got in his car and drove, through the hairpin turns of the Blue Mountains, the traffic of inner-city Sydney, down the Hume Highway and back to Melbourne, in one go. Fatigue, and perhaps reason, fell away, as he hurtled towards this man's inconsolable voice.

As he tells me these stories, I can see Ephraim is itching with regret for what was not done, for all the times he was restricted by formality, the instances where there was not enough time, or too many voices, the occasions when bureaucracy trumped compassion.

'I suppose at some point in your life, you just have to make peace with what you've done. And that it's enough,' I suggest.

'Yes,' replies Cas, 'and to let people know that you're available. Whenever they have questions.'

This notion of having not done enough seems to trail Ephraim's working history, and I see how fixated he is not just on narratives of good gesture, but good gesture curtailed. I am unsurprised to learn that he regularly rewatches *Schindler's List*, that he holds in his mind the 1200 or so that Oskar Schindler rescued and the thousands he could not. One day he tells me that he has a personal link to the story. At the end of the war, Schindler received a gold ring from the Jewish workers he had saved in his plastics factory. The model for this ring travelled all the way to Australia and remained in the ring-maker's workshop until the late 1990s.

'Well, I buried the man who made that ring,' Ephraim tells me.

Jozef Gross had made the golden ring famously handed to Liam Neeson by Ben Kingsley at the end of the Spielberg film. Now the ring model resides at the Melbourne Holocaust Museum, whose website quotes Louis Gross, Jozef's son: '[My father] made a model out of lead pipe, used cuttlefish to make the mould, with a channel to pour the molten gold into the cuttlefish'. The ring was inscribed with the Talmudic words 'Whoever saves one life saves the world entire'. Although the ring itself was lost after the war, Jozef kept the model and shared the ring-making process with his business partner in Melbourne.

Louis expresses that his father was a very private person and spoke with few about his war experiences. In fact, the ring model was only found by Louis after his father's passing in 1997. 'My father was a bit ambivalent about Schindler,' he says on the Melbourne Holocaust Museum website. 'He had seven brothers and sisters, most married with children, he was married with a child, and no one survived other than my father. That was very traumatic, so he had trouble saying [Schindler] was a German who deserved praise.'

Indeed, the ring was a complicated object, both in its provenance and in its legacy. 'That ring, made from gold taken from people's mouths!' exclaims Cas, referring to the fact that the metal was sourced from prisoners' teeth. 'Where had they been, what words had been spoken?' she pleads rhetorically, into the void.

I have my own question, one that shadows me week after week as I learn the life of Ephraim: how much of his sadness over people lost, histories truncated, informs his colossal energy for this work of preservation? In other words, to what degree is he driven by something missing, something unfinished? And underneath that, what are the limits of restoration and how do we care for wounds that can never be healed?

I see over and over how sentimental Ephraim is, how attached he is not just to objects and stories but relationships. One afternoon, I come by his place so we can call his old friend and colleague Sister Cletus. As Ephraim dials her landline number, he says, 'Let's get

The life and deathwork of Ephraim Finch

this young lady on the phone,' referring to the eighty-seven-year-old nun of the Brigidine order, now living in Echuca. He has told me about this 'young lady' many times before, always with a cheeky lining to his voice, his dimples deepening at her memory. Today he shows me a handwritten letter he's just received from her, alongside a parcel of fifteen books she is gifting him and a miniature photo album of their times working in pastoral care in the 1980s and 1990s.

'Thank you for the books,' he says to her, 'they're beautiful. I'll keep them and make my library bigger.' Stroking the photo album, he says, 'I love it, I love it. It's very special. I'll treasure it. And I love how you made that Jewish pastoral care ...' By this he means that Sister Cletus, in her role as head of pastoral care at Bethlehem Hospital in Caulfield, brought him in especially to care for the Jewish patients.

'Well, that was important!' she says loudly down the line, her crisp diction resonating through the speakerphone. 'I had the cheek to just say to the head nun, "I wish Mr Finch to be made a pastoral carer".'

At this, Ephraim giggles in delight.

'"He doesn't just come here and take the people away after they've gone," she continues, recalling how she insisted on Ephraim joining the team. "Do you realise he spends time with a lot of them before they go?" And I looked her in the eye and she couldn't say no,' she tells us.

Sister Catherine Cletus worked at the Catholic-run Bethlehem Hospital for seventeen years and for several of those years she did not meet Ephraim, even though he had regularly attended her ward.

'He used to come generally in the night, to take away the Jewish people who had died. And the staff were waffling on about him and saying how wonderful he was.' One day Sister Cletus finally laid eyes on Ephraim Finch, watching on as he chatted to a patient. She was struck by the peace this brought the dying individual: 'I could see how they needed a person of their own faith to help them before they died. I said, "He should be here not just when it's all over but before".'

At the time of Sister Cletus's tenure, Bethlehem Hospital had fifty beds for short-term terminal cases. Generally, the longest admission was eleven days. Most people passed away within a week, many within a day or two. 'And because the hospital was situated in Caulfield, out of the fifty beds they would have eleven or twelve Jewish patients … it was in their area. And they must have spread the good news that we loved having them,' she says.

The palliative care unit received ministers from various faiths—Anglican, Greek Orthodox—but not a rabbi. 'We ordained Mr Finch ourselves,' says Sister Cletus. At this, Ephraim laughs with unhindered joy, an ease I have yet to see in him. He laughs right from the belly, his lungs seeming larger than usual. And I understand why—this scenario contains all his favourite things: ordinary people taking charge, anti-hierarchical action, the pulling of strings so that basic humanity may prevail. Of course, Sister Cletus is being facetious; Ephraim was 'ordained' only in spirit. So there is that too: a little naughtiness, a gentle 'stuff you' to the establishment and the reins of bureaucracy. And finally, she's speaking of cultural crossover, of two seemingly disparate faiths joining forces to help the vulnerable. I know that this is the world Ephraim dreams of, misses, wishes for when he considers our fractious, divided planet.

I ask Sister Cletus what skill is most important in pastoral care.

'The main one is to be a listener. And, you know, there aren't a lot of good listeners in the world. People, especially at the end of their days, need to reminisce and talk. And it's not for us to be judgemental, or even to tell them what they could have done better. It's our job to let them spill it all out. And so, I'd say the bottom and the top line of being a good pastoral carer would be just to keep quiet, let them tell their story.'

Ephraim and I are smiling at Sister Cletus's voice, chiming into his dining room from the banks of the Murray River. I find myself thinking I could listen to her all day.

The life and deathwork of Ephraim Finch

'And then, if they're comfortable, they'll fill it in a bit, and you can give some little hints,' she says, referring to spiritual guidance or traditional wisdom. 'But in Bethlehem, there wasn't much time for that. You might only meet them the one day and they'd be beyond talking the next. And so, you had to be very, very diplomatic.' I think of the way Ephraim has practised this in the mourning space, the many examples of him simply observing, moving out of the way but not out of the frame.

'And that's where Mr Finch ...' She pauses, as though catching my thought, before continuing: '... he's non-judgemental. He didn't come to fix it all up. He listened. I picked all that up'.

'Thank you,' Ephraim says, almost inaudibly. Now he is not giggling, but rather sombre. His gaze grows cloudy, misty almost, in that way it does when he is remembering deceased individuals. Again, I can see him seeing.

'People wanted him. People asked for him. They won't ask for you if you're going to make a judgement on them. So, they asked for him,' she says.

Sister Cletus confirms that while the hospital loved having Jewish patients, the Jews did not necessarily love being in a Catholic hospital. Most were transferred from the Alfred, a large tertiary hospital three suburbs away. 'And, probably, some of them were scared of being sent' to Bethlehem. 'They wouldn't have had a say, they would have just been told. And, you know, it's a very difficult time for the families. A lot of them wouldn't have wanted them to come there,' she says.

I ask Ephraim about his memories of that time. He acknowledges that he was mentored 'by the top teacher in pastoral care'. Then he asks Sister Cletus if she remembers some of the funny stories, the fact that even in this saddest of settings they sometimes saw celebration, joy.

'Oh yes, a lot of funny stories,' she responds. 'I remember one man who had four wives around his bed.'

'Wasn't he lucky?' Ephraim chuckles, not missing a beat.

'And they weren't fighting. They were laughing and talking. And when he died, they came out to have a cuppa. I left them there,' she says, again referring to that need for giving space.

They reminisce about the nurses keeping a special bottle of 'dark lemonade' for Ephraim behind their desk, which he would use to make a *l'chaim*. They concur on the fact that the nurses could anticipate when a person was on the cusp of passing, their sense often sharper than a doctor's. Sister Cletus mentions that the work could be extremely difficult, especially when negotiating between feuding siblings or spouses. She recalls the unique sadness of a partner sitting vigil, 'and you'd just sit by the bed and let them share whatever they wanted to share. And often they'd tell you their life story. And, you know ... all beautiful.'

One day, Ephraim had come to Bethlehem having suffered a loss in his own family. Sister Cletus, seeing something different in his gait as he approached her, knew what he needed. 'The nurses were all there looking stupid and I knew how upset you were and I cuddled you,' she says to Ephraim. They both giggle at this transgression, but knowingly, because it is also a perfection.

'We never asked people what religion they were until they were in the bed,' Sister Cletus continues. 'We didn't want anyone to think they had to be a Catholic to come here.'

'I must admit I miss those years,' Ephraim says.

'I do too. I'm grateful for them. They were the most sacred years of my life. And I left a much better person than when I went there,' she responds. I ask Sister Cletus what she means by 'sacred' here, what made these years so.

'I think when we are coming to the end of our life, that's the most important part of our lives,' she says. She explains that before she worked in pastoral care she was a schoolteacher, and that religious instruction was just half an hour a day. True, she worked hard to teach the kids to read and write, but the rest of the time she was 'teaching them some manners' or dealing with parental complaints. But in pastoral care, 'the whole time you were on duty', she says, her voice easing. 'You've got one thing on your mind and that is to help that person go home, to forget about the past … just helping people to go home to their God. What can be more sacred than that?'

Ephraim and Sister Cletus spend a good hour or so chatting, reinforcing each other's memories, touching on this singular time. When we hang up, Ephraim reopens the letter she has sent him. He reads, out loud, about Sister Cletus's activities, her health, the wellbeing of the nurses and priests they once worked with. Due to 'being a little wobbly on my feet', she doesn't go out, except for her morning visits to aged-care homes and 'shut-in parishioners'. This she does seven days a week.

Then her letter glides from the prosaic to the poignant, moving, like a sermon, towards its philosophical import.

'The years keep going, don't they?' she writes. 'I hope your lovely wife is as well as possible. And all the family coping well in this crazy world. Most of the older people I visit are worrying about their grandchildren. I have to remind them that our own childhood was not easy, in a different way. But we never walk alone. Faith is a wonderful gift, isn't it? I remember sitting with a man in Bethlehem Hospital beside his dying brother. Both were Holocaust survivors. I asked him if he believed his brother would go to heaven soon. His answer was, "No. Because of the Holocaust I have no faith. But I have hope. I hope that what I used to believe in before the Holocaust is true. Without hope you are nothing". That was the first time I differentiated between faith and hope and I have quoted it often to people.' Ephraim sighs softly at this and we let it settle. Then he picks up the light-blue piece of paper again and reads Sister Cletus's last words.

'I hope you can read this letter. It is the only thing about me that hasn't improved over the years,' she writes, humorous to the last. 'Do take care and I'm sure we will meet again soon. Sometime. If

I fall and break something I will be in a Melbourne nursing home. I'll tell Joan to let you know. Give my love to Cas and let us pray for each other and keep in touch. Sister Cletus.'

Ephraim has told me that he dreams of the dead, that he imagines all the people he has buried sleeping, side by side, in an underground city. He is visited by people's faces, their voices. He has described driving around Caulfield and St Kilda, Malvern and Bentleigh, the areas where most Jews have lived in Melbourne, and remembering the houses he has entered to collect a body or assist the bereaved. To me, this sounds like a haunting, a constant intrusion from another realm that would feel untenable. But for Ephraim, this is neither distressing nor frightening; this is not where his panic lives. Ephraim can bear the presence of the deceased. What he cannot bear is disappearance, the notion that once upon a time there was something—a complex, thinking, sensing being, a culture of song and medicine and magic—and then there is nothing. His worst nightmare is not the return of a ghost, or even the finality of death itself; it is of a void, of voices muted.

The stories of this 'very practical man' have followed me to the coast, to this house that is populated with its own kind of silence. There is the wind in the gum trees, the crash of the waves behind the garden and over the dunes. There is the occasional snore from my dog and a neighbour's flyscreen slamming shut. Otherwise, I am cocooned by the dense walls of books, shelves and shelves of them; the many empty bedrooms, in another season occupied by visiting toddlers and teenagers and partners and friends. I hear their summertime shrieks, the thwack of a cricket bat, feet tromping down the stairs and out to the beach. Then I come back to the vast table before me, scanning the stacks of folders Ephraim loaded into my arms before I left for the

The life and deathwork of Ephraim Finch

coast. One stack is humming at me with a particular intensity, vibrating with a story that has wanted telling for decades, that has travelled across the seas and back again.

8

This is a story of a historic Jewish cemetery, of razed earth and archaeologists, of rescue and restoration. It unfolds like something from a Steven Spielberg script. It takes many turns. But let's begin with the layers, with the nipaluna land and the muwinina people, who walked on this story's soil long before it became Hobart. Today, the Indigenous people of this Country call themselves palawa; their language is palawa kani. For tens of millennia their ancestors have camped and hunted here, sung their songs and told their stories.

Even before the Black War and introduced disease devastated the Tasmanian Aboriginal population, colonialism rent a violent gash in the Indigenous culture. The dispossession from Country occurred as soon as the first ships landed, in 1803, catastrophically impairing kinship networks and the transmission of traditional knowledge. Settlers set about clearing the bushland for sheep farming and wheat cultivation, destroying hunting grounds and engaging in active combat with the palawa wherever they saw fit.

Of course, the other colonial imperative was to administer a penal settlement, and among those banished to Van Diemen's Land were Jews. Seventeen Jewish convicts were brought to Van practice, intermarriage, physical isolation, public anti-Semitism and the inability to assert basic cultural freedoms.

Historian John S. Levi writes, 'Nearly all chose to remain Jewish in the face of a harsh Anglican hegemony. The fact that they had been born within tight-knit and deprived urban communities gave them a strong sense of identity, and enabled them to survive and sometimes to thrive in the new hostile environment.' In other words, the early Jews of Van Diemen's Land had to hold tight to their tradition lest it disappear.

The shul gave the Jews space to pray, but also served a civic purpose, providing Shabbat meals for the incarcerated, and allocating specific benches for the poor. In the 1880s the congregation grew with an influx of Russian immigrants fleeing the pogroms; in the 1930s the community swelled with European Jews fleeing Nazism. It would continue to be a safe harbour; it would grow and diversify, eventually welcoming both Orthodox and reform members.

A visitor pamphlet opens with this gorgeously ecumenical statement: 'The members of the Hobart Hebrew Congregation extend a warm welcome—to those who feel themselves to be Jewish and those who consider themselves friends of the Jewish people—to worship in this place'. Further down, the author highlights the crucial bond between visibility and preservation: 'This Synagogue was built to defy the passage of time. It was built to be a monument. It was built to be noticed and to remind the most casual passer-by that here was an ancient faith in a new old land.'

Reading through the folders of Ephraim's documents, I consider this 'new old' land to which the Jews came, their painful freedom-getting. Inscribed into the synagogue's lintel is a passage from Exodus, a book synonymous with the Jews' escape from slavery and genocide.

And I can't help but imagine those bodies and voices absent from the history page, who at this very time were battling their own erasure. A deep enquiry into Tasmania's Indigenous history is, of course, beyond this story's reach. Still, it feels unconscionable—in a book about a man aflame with the need for cultural preservation—to

Diemen's Land between 1803 and 1818. One convict was a Viennese man named Bernard Walford, who was residing in England when he was sentenced to transportation for life for 'stealing a basket of laundry in Petticoat Lane'. Upon arrival in the colony, Walford worked as a baker and tavern keeper, becoming such 'a successful member of the community' that he could persuade the lieutenant governor to demarcate some land for a Jewish cemetery. A 1.5-acre allotment at Harrington Street, these days in the centre of Hobart, was granted. In 1828 Bernard Walford was the first person to be interred at the new 'Jews Burial Ground'.

Over the coming decade, emancipated Van Diemen's Jews and a new wave of free European settlers grew the community; the 1841 census records 259 Jewish Hobart residents, a number that would peak at 452 later that decade. To meet this cultural groundswell, a synagogue was built and on 4 July 1845 the Hobart Hebrew Congregation was consecrated. Designed by James Alexander Thompson, a Scottish convict who'd been transported for attempted jewel theft, the shul is a valuable lens into the complex history of Tasmania's early Jews.

Initially, the governor refused to grant the land, as it would be used for an 'Un Christian' purpose. Subsequently, a Jewish community leader by the name of Judah Solomon donated a portion of his private land. As soon as the building was completed, the government directed 'all prisoners of the Jewish persuasion' who were not under a custodial sentence to attend the Shabbat service. (Another source says detained convicts did attend the service, some in shackles.)

The synagogue's website notes that many of the Jews behind its construction 'had been born in Europe into privation and squalor, had arrived in their new home as convicts, and had painfully won their freedom'. Indeed, the fate of early Jews (those arriving as convicts, between 1803 and the 1830s) was precarious. Corporal punishment for resisting Christian worship was common; in addition, they faced severance from their Ashkenazi Orthodox practice, intermarriage, physical isolation, public anti-Semitism and the inability to assert basic cultural freedoms.

Historian John S. Levi writes, 'Nearly all chose to remain Jewish in the face of a harsh Anglican hegemony. The fact that they had been born within tight-knit and deprived urban communities gave them a strong sense of identity, and enabled them to survive and sometimes to thrive in the new hostile environment.' In other words, the early Jews of Van Diemen's Land had to hold tight to their tradition lest it disappear.

The shul gave the Jews space to pray, but also served a civic purpose, providing Shabbat meals for the incarcerated, and allocating specific benches for the poor. In the 1880s the congregation grew with an influx of Russian immigrants fleeing the pogroms; in the 1930s the community swelled with European Jews fleeing Nazism. It would continue to be a safe harbour; it would grow and diversify, eventually welcoming both Orthodox and reform members.

A visitor pamphlet opens with this gorgeously ecumenical statement: 'The members of the Hobart Hebrew Congregation extend a warm welcome—to those who feel themselves to be Jewish and those who consider themselves friends of the Jewish people—to worship in this place'. Further down, the author highlights the crucial bond between visibility and preservation: 'This Synagogue was built to defy the passage of time. It was built to be a monument. It was built to be noticed and to remind the most casual passer-by that here was an ancient faith in a new old land.'

Reading through the folders of Ephraim's documents, I consider this 'new old' land to which the Jews came, their painful freedom-getting. Inscribed into the synagogue's lintel is a passage from Exodus, a book synonymous with the Jews' escape from slavery and genocide.

And I can't help but imagine those bodies and voices absent from the history page, who at this very time were battling their own erasure. A deep enquiry into Tasmania's Indigenous history is, of course, beyond this story's reach. Still, it feels unconscionable—in a book about a man aflame with the need for cultural preservation—to not at least call out the wilful silence, to fortify the acceptance of terra nullius that inflects the records of this time. In my research, I find just two exceptions; this 'new old land' phrase from the Hobart Hebrew Congregation, and one sentence from a 2013 John S. Levi book introduction: 'for thousands of years the inhabitants of the vast Australian continent marked the passage of life by their awareness of an intimate and spiritual identity with their environment'. Aside from this, I find no reference to First Nations people.

When it was established in the early 1800s, the Harrington Street cemetery was laid out along the top western boundary of the allotment, spanning thirty metres. From this elevation, the dead were thought to symbolically 'sleep' while watching over the town. However, this burial practice was soon to be discontinued, as burying remains uphill and upwind from the residential centre of town was thought to encourage the spread of disease. This belief, alongside the issue of poor drainage, eventually resulted in an amalgamation of several small cemeteries in an all-denominational public cemetery outside the city limits.

In 1872 the Cornelian Bay Public Cemetery officially opened, as the Jewish burial grounds at Harrington Street were closed. A Jewish section was created at the new site. Interestingly, in continuing to investigate the health risks of elevated, inner-city cemeteries, the Hobart council noted the exceptionally fine condition of the now-disused Jewish cemetery. In 1901, an inspection covered by a local newspaper found that 'the only closed cemetery in Hobart that remained in a decent condition was the Jews'. Similarly, in 1902 an inspecting officer remarked that 'No effort has been spared to keep ever sacred the memories of those buried there. Tombstones are well cared for, and the ground presents the appearance of a soft green lawn.'

The grounds of Harrington Street remained untouched for the first half of the twentieth century. Then, in 1945, the Education

Department purchased the site from the Hobart Hebrew Congregation, along with its sacred, beautifully maintained contents. Their one request was that the tombstone of Bernard Walford be reinterred at Cornelian Bay. In 1954 the Education Department sold the land to the Housing Department, the former assuring the latter that they could develop the land as they liked. (A memorandum penned by the secretary of the department tells the purchaser that 'the stones at present on the site are of no use to anyone'.) In 1957 the Housing Department proceeded to clear the site of headstones and build a 105-unit housing facility called Windsor Court.

In late 2001, a tender had been put in for a $7.5 million redevelopment of the Windsor Court public housing complex at 214 Harrington Street. I find a set of 'Guidelines to Contractors Working on the Windsor Court Site', on government letterhead, warning of a 'medium to high probability that human remains will be uncovered' and requesting that 'any human remains uncovered are to be treated with dignity' and 'handled only by persons of the Jewish faith'. The authors state that 'No demolition and/or major excavation works will commence ... until such time as this portion of the site has been examined and, if required, all reasonably identifiable human remains have been relocated'.

The developers invited Hobart Synagogue member David Clark onto the site, to aid in the culturally sensitive collection of remains. But upon arrival, David learned that an excavator had crossed the grounds, disrupting the soil and its contents. With the help of the contractors, he collected what he could, carefully driving the bagged remains to the *tahara* house at Cornelian Bay Cemetery. He made sure that everyone wore gloves, which—according to *halacha*—means the remains were not being touched. David worked, without forensic guidance and against time, for a week.

The life and deathwork of Ephraim Finch

A late-January press release from the Tasmanian director of housing celebrated the 'sensitivity with which the issue has been handled'. Malcolm Downie went on to say that 'the location and removal of bones was carried out fully in accordance with the wishes of the Jewish community and in consultation with the Public and Environmental Health Service, the Coroner's Office and Hobart City Council'.

However, not everyone agreed with this round-up. Under pressure from the state's Heritage Committee, the government conceded that more rigorous, methodical removal was required before the next round of works. It is at this stage that David Clark called Ephraim Finch. (In an amazing side-plot, David and Ephraim's acquaintance goes back to 1988, when Ephraim flew down to Hobart to build a *mikveh* for the community. The *mikveh* is in fact attached to David's former residence in Battery Point and is used to this day.)

While Ephraim got organised, the Tasmanian Government engaged an archaeologist, Parry Kostoglou, who spent a week at Harrington Street, horrified by what had transpired. Aside from the disruption to remains, Parry's report notes the egregious lack of documentation. He indicts the developers for their failure 'to show any skeletal remains in all but 1 photograph. Likewise the on-site map showing the location and order of exhumations was hand drawn without any regard to scale or direction ... no notes and field drawings detailing burial attitude, contents, dimensions etc. were kept.' The report also laments that 'In addition to the damage wrought on human remains, the excavator's unchecked movement across the site has damaged several very significant head stone inscriptions'.

The archaeological report contains an historical summary, which conveys, with grim clarity, that this was not the first assault suffered by these burial grounds. Regarding the 1950s Windsor Court development, Parry Kostoglou writes that although no mass exhumations were made, 'some disturbance to remains would have been inevitable given the scale of the construction work'. He notes that garden beds and clotheslines were installed, and that 'the facility served as Hobart's major density public housing complex until its closure in c2001'.

'I can still remember the feeling of opening the doors of the old *tahara* house, the sun streaming in,' reads Ephraim's chronicle of arriving in Cornelian Bay and seeing the hastily salvaged remains for the first time. He describes 'standing in the presence of people who had been laid to rest over a period of sixty years, whose eternal peace had now been disturbed'.

When he recalls the moment now, Ephraim is as upset as if this were a violation of living beings. Of course, there is an understandable distress at the wilful disrespect of human remains and memorial articles—funerary stonework, inscriptions—but there is something else. I am increasingly getting the sense that Ephraim views the burial ground itself as an organism, that for him it is not just a medium for interring bodies but a universe unto itself, a feeling, breathing entity. Just recently he told me about the foxes and fruit bats that make their home at Springvale Cemetery and when I flinched, he said, 'Well, why not? A cemetery is a nature reserve.' In fact, I saw this for myself; when we visited Springvale, he apprehended the tombstones with the same awe as the weeds growing at their edges. He spoke to the humans with the voice of reverence he used for the swallows who 'sweep through' to collect the moths after the rains have passed. As above, so below, seems to be his cosmology, all of it interconnected and in conversation.

After laying eyes on the bagged remains, Ephraim and Parry inspect the excavated Harrington Street area. The archaeologist's report will go on to list what they found: not just bones, but 'assorted physical features', including 'sandstone fragments from numerous headstones, altars and at least one sarcophagus'. Parry lists, among the 'surface scatter', a 'neo-classical sculpted torso of an individual executed in high relief'. There is 'An almost intact child's headstone', headstone fragments inscribed in Hebrew, a headstone 'containing sacred text written in English' and 'fragments of slab with ornately carved "windows"'.

It is hard not to see the lives beneath the academic annotations. Each one of those details would have been the product of someone's care, the fascia of someone's grief. Money would have been spent on the masonry, and an artisan would have focused his touch on the chiselling, dusting, polishing. Eyes would have assessed angles and taken measurements; an inner voice would have pronounced the name of the deceased. It is gutting to read Parry's words: 'At the time of the Windsor Court development in the mid 1950s, numerous grave markers appear to have remained on the site where they were broken up and the stone re-cycled in a variety of ways. One of these uses involved the creation of retaining walls and walkways within the vegetable garden beds complex ... These gardens were tended with decreasing dedication until the flats were decommissioned.'

Parry records that among the broken and mingled remains, forty skeletons were located, interred in coffins, 'which survived as thin dark coloured organic veneers surrounding the remains'. The individuals 'were buried without ... personal effects' and wrapped in a 'plain textile bag'. This suggests that some Jewish custom was maintained. But 'decreasing dedication' rattles around in my mind, a continuum of neglect that somehow bleeds into outright wreckage.

Reading the archaeologist's report, I see how much of a professional comrade Ephraim had in Parry, how invested Parry was in the mitigation of these ruins. He details the headstone inscriptions found among the assorted sandstone piles, inferring what he can about the lives honoured. He lists the words 'an excelle / amiable' on one stone, which he traces back to an inscription for David Lionel Moses, who died in 1845 at the age of eighteen. 'Of an excellent disposition and amiable in manner his sorrowing relatives deeply mourn the loss of one thus prematurely separated from them' reads the full inscription.

He cites 'a lengthy poetic dedication to the deceased', an unidentified person who was, in the words of her mourners, 'young, amiable and dearest'. 'How are thou dear?' they ask, farewelling her as 'hope and joyful treasure of thy parents'.

After visiting the site, Ephraim drives to the Hobart shul, photographing the memorial board that lists fifty-nine of the people interred at Harrington Street. 'My fact-finding trip was now complete and I headed back to Melbourne to plan for the reburials and possible further exhumations,' he records.

It is a bitingly cold morning in Hobart on 20 May 2002. Ephraim surveys the hill upon which the former Harrington Street Jewish burial ground once stood. Gazing up the steep incline, he contemplates the large-scale excavation about to take place, this time under the watchful eye of the Chevra. By his side are archaeologist Parry Kostoglou, forensic pathologist Lititia Carter, the Hobart shul's David Clark, 'a labourer with a shovel', an excavator and two representatives from the Adass burial society in Melbourne. Ephraim wants 'the whole area done' and Parry promises to stay until all remaining burials and significant stonework are safely removed.

'The first layer of soil did not show any evidence of a burial, but the second layer showed the "ghosting" of a grave,' Ephraim notes in his diary. 'The third layer was carefully dug up until it revealed a skull, then the archaeologist brushed away the soil to reveal a complete skeleton.' Placing the remains in their individual coffins, Ephraim is reminded of the vision of Ezekiel, of a valley of dry bones that symbolised the people of Israel in exile. In the Bible story, Ezekiel watches the bones turn into fleshed beings, a portent of the Jews' future homecoming. Unfortunately, while Ephraim is doing everything in his power to re-home these particular Jews, he and his team discover more desecration.

The life and deathwork of Ephraim Finch

Along the southern boundary wall, Parry finds rubbish pits from the 1880s, 'an 8 x 5 metre wide scatter of assorted historic domestic refuse' that includes medicine tincture bottles, 'fragments of a Dutch case gin bottle', food storage containers, 'several mutton bones with marks from butchering' and 'one section of barrel hoop iron'.

The team dig and brush and document for two days straight. On the third day, thinking the process is over, the team begins to pack up. But Ephraim feels a niggle and requests one last excavation, at the left corner of the site. Three more sets of skeletal remains are found, hidden under the neighbour's fence.

Lititia Carter must work fast to glean information about the people buried at Harrington Street. Ephraim recalls that the Tasmanian Government granted her only one day of on-site work, which would have given her a maddeningly small window. Still, she confirms that of the fifty-one sets of human remains, there are seven babies under one year of age, five children under sixteen, seven adults under sixty and seven adults over sixty. The rest are of unspecified age.

Lititia assesses bones to determine ailments such as osteomyelitis and osteoarthritis. Inquest records also indicate that individuals interred at Harrington Street had died from illnesses such as dysentery, 'enlargement and disease of the heart', and 'various fevers'. One individual, a Jonathan Mocatta, died at the age of fifty-two from delirium tremens, or severe alcohol withdrawal.

Parry Kostoglou's report estimates that seventy-six persons were interred at Harrington Street over the years of its use. In doing this, he relies on the archival information kept by local bodies, foremost the Hobart synagogue and the State Archives Office of Tasmania. There are also Cornelian Bay Cemetery records and the Register of Tombstone and Memorial Inscriptions of Tasmania, as well as headstone transcriptions collected by a community-minded 'private individual' by the name of William Henry Dawson in 1895.

In other words, the work that he and the Chevra have done on the ground is vital, but this passion for conservation is not exclusive to them. A quick look at the current website of the Hobart shul shows an extensive digital record of media articles, books, artworks and civic records; there is even a recording of the musical score performed at the consecration of the synagogue in 1845. I also encounter a weighty tome titled *These Are the Names: Jewish Lives in Australia 1788–1850*, by John S. Levi, which provides the biographical details of over sixteen hundred Jews in the Australian colonies, including Tasmania. (It is this book that acknowledges an Indigenous population in its preface.) It is reassuring to visualise this great number of formal and informal archivists, across two centuries, assiduously gathering and storing precious data.

Parry also records the 'unusually good state' of the remains exhumed in 2002. After acknowledging preservative factors (such as the 'limey and alkaline' soil chemistry) he makes this remarkable statement: 'This opinion was a unanimous one shared by the archaeologist, pathologist, Jewish funeral directors and Cornelian Bay cemetery staff who collectively have extensive experience in the handling of human remains. Anecdotal information from the Cornelian Bay cemetery staff would suggest that the bones of persons interred there degenerate fairly rapidly and cannot be readily identified beyond 15 years after interment. In contrast to this the bones at the Harrington Street former Jewish cemetery are perfectly preserved after a period of between 130–180 years.'

The day after the exhumation, ten small coffins are taken to Cornelian Bay and buried in the Jewish section, alongside the remains that David Clark had brought across a few months earlier. Next to them rest the Jewish individuals who had lived and died in Hobart since the formation of the Harrington Street cemetery. Among these is Bernard Walford, who had the notion

The life and deathwork of Ephraim Finch

to petition for a Jewish burial ground almost two centuries earlier. There is Judah Solomon, who donated a portion of his garden for the establishment of the Hobart Hebrew Congregation. Beneath the sweep of eucalypts and pines, there are octogenarians; there are infants and the mothers who'd mourned them. There are publicans, paupers, teachers, librarians, jewellers and thieves. There are people here who came in shackles and never lived to experience life without them.

They lie on the hill overlooking the river and facing the misted mountain, known by the palawa as kunanyi. Long before it was named Mount Wellington, kunanyi played a part in Indigenous creation stories. In an interview with the ABC, palawa woman Sharnie Read describes it as a 'pathway to our ancestors and to the spirit world, a doorway … to the next stage of who we are'.

At Cornelian Bay, the four men—Ephraim, David Clark and two Adass staff—intone 'El Maleh Rachamim', a prayer for the soul of the deceased. Normally, the deceased person's Hebrew name is said, and their parents' names. On this occasion, it is not possible. Still, there is a salvaging, a pulling back from a brink. The men know this—their limits and the power of their attempt, the importance of doing one's best. Just as they might have done if they were performing *tahara* on bodies at the Chevra, the men who had overseen the exhumation say a final prayer. Under their breath, each man asks for forgiveness for any suffering they may have inadvertently caused the deceased.

Today, the Harrington Street site contains no trace of its Jewish past save two memorial walls. The housing estate, renamed Walford Terraces in the 2002 redevelopment, snakes up the hill, punctuated by curvaceous driveways and concrete paths. There is a community centre, and an oblong accessibility ramp covering the steepest part of the hill. It is bordered by flourishing, established fruit trees; plum, cherry, mulberry.

I know this because I fly down for the day to see Harrington Street for myself. While I am there, Ephraim calls me.

'Have you taken photos?' he asks, somewhat anxiously. I assure him I have.

'Did you see the retaining wall?' he asks and I say I'm not sure. 'Are there any stones left? Did you see any of the old monuments?' I say no, the boundary is just a garden fence, as far as I can see. I take a video for him, panning around the front section of the estate, slowing for the memorial walls.

The first is at the entry to the estate and features six panels that summarise the history of the site. Three panels acknowledge the traditional owners of the land, as well as Bernard Walford, who petitioned for this allotment. The remaining panels swiftly move to civic concerns, the tone buoyant with the argot of an enthusiastic copywriter. 'The Windsor Court complex was considered particularly innovative in both its approach and modernist architectural style,' reads one panel. Another explains, 'Living in flats suited many residents and a sense of community developed. Over time, however, demand for housing for the elderly and young families increased … In 2000 the decision was made to demolish the flats and redevelop the site.'

Over the road is the second memorial wall, installed by the synagogue. Eight square pavers are mounted in a grid, inlaid with images from the original burial ground. Several are inscribed with scraps of Hebrew and English text. 'Thou hast raised her', 'Aged thirteen Year, Pious', 'reposeth', they say.

Meanwhile, those reburied at Cornelian Bay have been commemorated in their own section. I am taken around by David Clark and Moshe Herst, a member of the synagogue who participated in the 2002 rescue mission, but at a different juncture. This Harrington memorial is the product of Moshe's labour; once the bones were interred, he and David built this new memorial space. The headstones are assembled in an oval, interspersed with sandstone pavers and a shrub named, remarkably, 'breath of heaven'. They are adorned with bronze Stars of David, some in constellations and some solitary, each star holding the name of a person reinterred.

'The idea was, at least in my thoughts, that these stars are gonna last longer than anything else,' says Moshe, pointing to the grander headstones around us. The larger Jewish section is walled off by a Mediterranean cypress hedge, and these Harrington headstones are walled off once again, by a knee-high sandstone border. The border also incorporates the rubble and badly broken headstones that Moshe collected from the desecrated site. It's a double reinforcement, a soothing closure after so much disturbance. The stone border has a wrought-iron gate featuring a *menorah*, a sacred candelabra, and it sits like a latch on an antique bracelet.

Moshe is a bright-eyed, slender man, likely in his seventies, in a baseball cap and jeans. He speaks with a mellow American accent, giving me the momentary sensation that I am with Paul Simon or Bob Dylan. 'The big monuments that went to the big bucks out there, they're beautiful, but ultimately, they're going to fall apart. And so these people who are left behind, so to speak, will stay behind. You know, there'll be some recording, for whatever that's worth. And ultimately, that'll go away as well. But they'll be here longer. The stars will be here the longest,' he says, with casual, heart-twisting poetry, as we proceed through the stone garden.

Isaac 'Ikey' Solomon is here, the man thought to be Dickens' inspiration for the *Oliver Twist* character of Fagin. Henrietta Moses is here too, and the fullness of her stone is revealed: it is she who is referenced at Walford Terraces who is 'pious' and 'reposeth'. Henrietta Rachel Moses, aged thirteen years and eight months, 'departed to Eternal Happiness' on the eve of Shabbat in December 1853. Near Henrietta is a stone for a double burial: 'Frances Nathan, 35 y & Infant, d. 1844'.

Next to the *menorah* gate there is a black-marble tablet inscribed, in gold, with the following words: 'Remember the days of old / Consider the years of ages past'. This is not a passage from Exodus but Deuteronomy, the fifth book of the Torah. This book documents the Jews' forty years of wandering, shortly before they reach the Promised Land. It contains perhaps the most widely intoned and universally identifying Jewish prayer, the Shema, which is recited twice daily, as well as on Yom Kippur and on the cusp of death. The rest of the Cornelian Bay monument reads, 'In this sacred place are re-interred the remains of pioneer Jewish settlers who were buried in Hobart's first Jewish cemetery in Harrington Street. May their souls be bound up in the bond of life.'

'This sacred place.' The words echo inside me. Both the notion of 'sacredness' and 'place' are self-evident to those who hold them as such. Both have so often needed defending, protection against active nullification and gradual forgetting, which moment by silent moment culminates in disappearance. I think of the Wendell Berry poem 'How to Be a Poet'. 'There are no unsacred places,' Berry says. 'There are only sacred places and desecrated places.'

I fly back from Hobart and complete this chapter in my friend's surf-coast house, on Wadawurrung Country, where I first began to write it. As a matter of ritual upon arrival, I throw open the doors and windows and stand on the wooden deck overlooking the estuary. I close my eyes and listen to the crashing tide, which is around the bend and out of view. This airy 1970s house, piled with kids' toys, snorkels, well-loved couches sequestering the odd sock or sun hat, is the comfiest home away from home, the warmest nest for unborn ideas.

As I tidy the colossal stack of documents about the Harrington chapter, I find a letter from David Clark, asking Ephraim for advice on the commemorative panels. Among other things, David undertakes to collect and deposit 'all the relevant documents with the Tasmanian Archives Office'. A layer of memory, sealed. I turn back to the start of Parry Kostoglou's report, now also on public record. Before the lengthy inventory of negligence and ruin, on the very first page, Parry makes his acknowledgements: 'Ephraim Finch, Executive Director of the Melbourne Chevra Kadisha, kindly prepared several documents'. Then he adds, 'but far more importantly, saw the potential opportunity to help give the deceased back their identities', adding yet another layer, sealing it again.

Once I have packed up, ready to relocate myself and the stories once more, this time to my home in Melbourne, I look around. This house belongs to my friend's mother. She is the child of Holocaust survivors, herself born in a Munich refugee camp. Among the posters of coastal fauna and photos of kids on their boogie boards, I notice a black-and-white photo of Ashkenazi ancestors. Three men and three women. Two of the men are in black *kapotas* and hats; the third is in a dinner jacket and bow tie. The women, in high-collared blouses and neatly folded hair, cross three generations; one is a young adult, one is in middle age, one is elderly. Each of them is staring into the distance, neither smiling nor frowning. If anything, they look resigned.

The image hovers imposingly by the balcony door. Or maybe it's not imposing, and what is imposed is my imagining of their plight, of the family members missing from that group portrait. I greet them as I pass, I tell them why I am here. I lock the back door, then the balcony door, trapping the last gulp of ocean air in the house. I pass by the ancestors one final time. I thank them for letting me write my stories around theirs, silent though they are. I do this without speaking.

PART III: THE RETURN

9

Almost every Jewish festival has a joyous component, but Shavuot is one of the sweetest. It marks the receiving of the Torah at Mount Sinai—that lynchpin narrative Jews return to time and again as a marker of our tribal identity. It is also known as The Feast of First Fruits, marking the ancient pilgrimages to Jerusalem, when the harvest was brought to the temple as an offering. Like all Jewish holidays, it begins at sunset, when a table is laid with fresh flowers and dairy foods. In Israel, the streets fill with children dressed in white, hair garlanded with spring greenery. At synagogue, we stay up all night reading the Torah and other religious texts, absorbed in thought and discourse.

By the time this year's Shavuot rolls around it is almost June, and I have been meeting with Cas and Ephraim, every week or two, for seven months. Our dialogue has radiated out beyond the official meeting times and often we will send each other poems and illuminating quotes; Ephraim will text me a 'Shabbat Shalom' meme or an interview with an inspiring thinker. There is also a growing mutual care; I am genuinely concerned when Cas isn't feeling well, and she is equally worried, calling me one evening, when my son is admitted to hospital.

So I am not surprised when they invite me to the impending Shavuot dinner, and not just me but my parents and my children and the publisher of this book and her adult son. The Finches' hospitality is abundant and relaxed and I can never reverse-engineer it. Is it that they live in a community where an open door is intrinsic to being? Is it a generational thing or just their nature as humans?

In fact, it doesn't really matter.

What matters is the graciousness they exhibit around the entire event. I spend the week leading up to Shavuot trying to 'get it right'; I learn that I can deliver flowers, but not on the day, because the high holiday has already begun and transport of goods is forbidden. When I arrive the day before with a potted orchid, Cas accepts it with gasps of delight. My mum asks what she can bring, and Cas warmly replies that nothing is required, but if we wanted to bring something, a kosher wine or cake would be most appreciated. Even in the instruction there is hospitality, a wish to uphold dignity for all involved.

On the night, I arrive first, my nine-year-old daughter in tow. Immediately, she is taken in by the band of grandchildren, ranging in age from three to twenty-five, and they disappear to the back of the house and the shelves of toys. The way the kids intermingle is also remarkable, crossing generations and levels of religiosity. They chat and laugh and poke each other in the ribs. I see a teenager resolving disputes between the toddlers, the tweens conspiratorially whispering about some incident at school. Of course, I know virtually nothing about their personalities and relational dynamics; I am observing a moment. But what I see in the kids, and in Ephraim and Cas's adult children, as they bustle about the kitchen, is unremitting cohesion, a current of warmth beneath and between. It feels familiar to me, this atmosphere: the noise, the jostle, the bumping and the laughing and the talking over each other. It feels, remarkably, like home.

Then my parents arrive. They enter the crowd timidly, politely greeting people as they go. Because they are my flesh and blood, I know the subtle signs of their discomfort. My mother's posture, my father's lowered voice, their eyes unsure of where to land. I sense they would like to be invisible until they've gotten their bearings, until they've been accepted. But they also know that this is not the way acceptance operates. They know—as immigrants, as Soviet Jews who came to the tradition late in life—that to even have a chance at being included, one must show up.

Fortunately, it turns out I am not the only one reading their shyness. As soon as Ephraim clocks them, he makes his way over, shaking my father's hand, smiling at my mother's smile. He calls Cas over and before I know it the four of them are looking at the paintings on the living-room wall. Then they are down the hallway, looking at more art. I see them silhouetted in the doorway, talking, nodding, laughing.

When it is time to sit down, my parents look momentarily lost again. As dozens of bodies fill the dining area, they take themselves to the furthest edge of the long table, perhaps hoping to escape visibility again, or a religious task such as saying a blessing. And again, Ephraim is on them. Only this time, he doesn't take them for a walk. He calls them over, by name, waving them in towards him. They approach along the table slowly, trying to sit down a couple of times. But each time he waves them closer, until they are by his side at the head of the table. He pours them a drink, then he blesses the bread, asking nothing of them. When all the food is on the table, he turns to them and asks about their life in Odesa, a topic that requires no prior learning. As they discuss their work, their kids, their passions, I see my parents grow gregarious, charming. I see them wanting to share, excited to show. They will remain here, under his wing, chatting, listening, laughing, for the rest of the night, long after the food is cleared and the others have gone home.

Ephraim's empathy for the outsider has shown itself over and over in the short time I have been learning his story. I see it in his recollections of the deceased, but also as one of his own foundational experiences: he knows the sensation of being on the periphery. In the early days, as the Finches were stepping into Judaism, this sensation was prominent, following the family from Canberra to Sydney to Melbourne.

When they arrived in Melbourne, they were warmly embraced by many families in the community. But the outsider sensation did not miraculously disappear. They tell me two stories to illustrate this.

The first one centres on Rabbi Ben Tov, a renowned kabbalist mystic with a special gift. About three years after the Finches settled in Melbourne, Rabbi Ben Tov was visiting from overseas. Cas explains his gift like this: 'If there is something happening in the family, an illness, a worry, whatever it is … there are people who believe, and I happen to be one of them, that something happens to the actual writing of the *mezuzah*'. The *mezuzah* is a tiny scroll containing a prayer, enclosed in a casing, hung on the door of a Jewish home. It is thought to protect the home, as well as reminding its residents of their religious obligation.

'Sometimes, even though it's encased in plastic, glass or metal, there is something wrong … a letter half-taken out, or a word missing, even though it had been a perfectly complete *mezuzah* when you put it up on the door. And Rabbi Ben Tov was somebody who had the ability to read what was wrong. So we went to him.'

The Finches handed him one of their *mezuzah*s. The rabbi took it out of its casing, and without knowing anything about this couple, began to say, in Hebrew, 'What is wrong? What is wrong?' Cas and Ephraim waited for him to elaborate. Then he explained that in the text, the word 'Israel' was missing. Then, focusing on the writing again, he said, 'Has somebody in this marriage converted? Why is somebody in this marriage so upset about having converted?' As he spoke, he looked at Ephraim.

'I am upset,' Ephraim said. The rabbi asked him to say more.

'Why couldn't I have been born Jewish?' Ephraim pleaded.

The life and deathwork of Ephraim Finch

Recalling this, his voice wavers. It is still, seemingly, so fresh. 'And he looked at me like I'm stupid. And he said, "Don't you realise Rabbi Akiva, one of the greatest rabbis, his father wasn't Jewish?"' Rabbi Akiva, a first-century sage, was famously executed by the Romans for defying their prohibition on Torah study. Some traditions hold that his father was, indeed, a convert, making him a fascinating confluence of identities. On the one hand, he was not of an exclusively Jewish lineage; on the other, he was the paragon of Jewish faith and devotion. This, like the story of King Solomon that his old teacher Mr Rieder had once told Ephraim, brought Ephraim comfort.

'It was just illuminating to me. I didn't realise that that's how Ephraim was feeling. He had never said anything to me about that,' Cas adds, illustrating that this question visited them separately, privately as well as together. After the visit, they immediately corrected the *mezuzah*, and took all their others to the rabbi. Ben asked if he could see the rabbi himself and went in privately. Cas and Ephraim had no idea what the rabbi said to their son, but when Ben came out, Cas recalls, 'he was red in the face and he said, "I can't tell you what he said, but he knew everything"'.

The second story also features a visiting rabbi, Rabbi Nissen Mangel, a renowned scholar, author and community leader who'd come out to Melbourne from America in the early 1990s. Rabbi Nissen Mangel was a child of the Holocaust, having survived multiple death and labour camps as well as the infamous Death March. At age ten, he had a direct encounter with Josef Mengele while interned at Auschwitz. (When Ephraim tells me this, the words tremble out of him: 'He'd been in front of the Angel of Death and got through'. 'The Angel of Death' was a pseudonym given to Josef Mengele, and when Ephraim speaks of him the terror that passes through his face is far greater than any I have ever seen him exhibit in talking about actual death.) Nissen Mangel not only survived but went on to cultivate a life of illustrious scholarship, speaking far and wide on topics such as the endurance of the human spirit and the intersections between faith and survival.

Cas attended his sessions in Melbourne, 'dwelling' on the rabbi's every word. But his words had also unsettled her; just like her husband, she couldn't understand why she wasn't born into Judaism. 'Why was it?' she recalls asking, her voice still freighted with pain all these years later.

After one session, Rabbi Mangel went out to the back quadrangle of the building. Tentatively, Cas approached him, hoping to ask a question.

'Of course, of course,' the rabbi replied. Watching the rabbi speak online, I am struck by his warmth, the intensity of life in his dark eyes, the vast radiance that comes from his tiny, elderly frame. His voice is resonant but patient, like a teacher addressing his favourite class. I watch a talk he gives on the miracle of surviving Auschwitz, showing an uncommon expansiveness in the face of abject horror. It is easy to imagine how comforting his presence must have been to Cas on this evening.

Cas spilled out her deepest sadness. 'And I was crying, and I was turning around because I was so embarrassed. And he turned around with me and I think we turned around in almost a complete circle. And he said to me, "The only thing in life that is eternal is the soul. And only God knows what certain moment of a certain day of a certain year, your body is to become one with your soul. And only God knows why".'

In this moment, Cas understood that 'I had always had a Jewish soul. It was just that I had been born into a body that belonged in a different family.'

I am touched by Cas's willingness to share this vulnerable story and I imagine her enthusiasm in sharing with others over the years. I notice how bound her courage and her enthusiasm are to each other, how willingly she gives of herself so that others may feel less alone.

The life and deathwork of Ephraim Finch

By way of wrapping up our conversation I ask about her work for the Beth Din, preparing people for conversion, which she does to this day. 'What do you think those people need most? When you're teaching them, what's the one thing you always feel you need to give them?' I ask, knowing she knows I am not speaking to technicalities. I am asking about sentiment, values.

'To give over my love of Judaism,' she says at first. Then she pauses, adding, 'and to give them the understanding that they are not a second-class citizen'.

For most Jews, attending synagogue and observing the rabbi in a public capacity—at the *bimah*, speaking to a congregation, instructing the community on the Torah portion or officiating at life-cycle events—is the extent of the relationship. But for some, especially in the Hasidic tradition, there is a more intimate dimension, one where the individual seeks life advice from the rabbi and learns at their foot directly. And such is the relationship between Ephraim and Rabbi Yisroel Sufrin, who is the head of the congregation that Ephraim attends, but also, a figure I can't help but call 'Ephraim's beloved rabbi', such is Ephraim's affection for the man, and the reverence.

'Go and have a chat with Rabbi Sufrin,' Ephraim has said on many occasions, sometimes offering this as a shortcut to knowing him better. This has included the times I have prodded into this sensitive area of conversion. 'Go and see Rabbi Sufrin,' he has said when I've circled around and around the same questions: 'But what is a Jewish soul?' and 'What do you mean there are five parts to it?' and 'If a Jewish person is always Jewish, doesn't that make the word "conversion" inaccurate, even redundant?'

And so I go to see the rabbi, at his office in the synagogue in East St Kilda. Before we get to the conversion questions, I ask Rabbi Sufrin about this very thing: the role of the rabbi as a personal guide. He opens his reply with a wonderfully humane phrase, one of my favourites in the vast Jewish catalogue: 'The Torah wasn't given to angels'.

This notion unfolds in two directions: ordinary humans are fraught with imperfection and wondering, many of us living with a low-level hum of uncertainty, idling somewhere around our solar plexus. We guess, we mess up, we do our best with the information we've got. The second level is that even the learned among us, including rabbis, are not immune to vulnerability, to the uncertainty that accompanies being human.

'The way God has set up our religion is that if you're not sure about anything, check with a human being. That's a leader that has certain credentials; that's all you need to do,' Rabbi Sufrin says, clarifying. Moreover, that's all the rabbi can do. 'Is their advice a hundred per cent certain? That's irrelevant. You go to a doctor for medical advice. Do you know a hundred per cent? No. You have to follow medical protocol, you can't do more than that,' he says. I like this very much, this humility across the board, this acknowledgement of our limitations regardless of where we sit in the hierarchy of expertise and even wisdom. (The rabbi underscores this with something that makes us both laugh: 'My previous boss, Mr Gurewicz, who was the principal at Beth Rivkah, used to say, "No one is perfect besides you and me, and you I'm not so sure about."')

But the upshot is, when one is stuck in an ethical quandary, the Torah prescribes asking, in Rabbi Sufrin's words, 'the leaders in your generation for advice'.

Then, the rabbi expounds on my question again, with a fascinating question of his own: 'Can you have an AI rabbi?' When I respond with a vehement 'No!' he gives a more measured response, and a more sophisticated one: 'The answer, at least which some people give, is, you can't, because it's not about just the information. So maybe certain things the AI can help you with, but to have that rabbi relationship, you need a soul.' We pause there, and I start to see why Ephraim feels such affinity with this teacher, how their idioms align. 'You know, the Torah was given as the written Torah and the oral Torah. Why couldn't everything be written? There are many reasons given but one is because you need that soul-to-soul connection,' he says, deftly tying up several threads in one bundle.

Rabbi Sufrin has known Ephraim for close to thirty years. He taught some of the Finch daughters when they were at Beth Rivkah and officiated at two Finch weddings. The two men intersected professionally in the early 2000s, when Rabbi Sufrin was a rabbi for a branch of the Mizrachi community. A lot of his work involved counselling families through challenging situations, including death, and sometimes, this felt beyond him. He cites an example of a bereaved mother of twins asking him to come to hospital and to officiate at the funeral, and Ephraim helping him to find the words for this darkest occasion.

In trying to understand Ephraim, I ask my prepared questions about conversion, about the anatomy of the Jewish soul. Rabbi Sufrin answers me with examples from the Torah, runs through the many names for the soul in the Kabbalah. But none of it coalesces, none of it comes from the ether to the ground, until I simply ask him to speak about Ephraim as a human being. It turns out that only in abandoning the formal agenda can we begin to apprehend Ephraim's drive, and inside that drive, his wrestle with place and belonging and tribal obligation.

'Is there such a thing as "the key" to Ephraim, some crucial understanding that might illuminate him to the world?' I ask.

'You may have this already, but what's incredible about Ephraim is that he is not just liked, but loved, by all walks of life. He's loved in the Chabad community. Adass. Mizrachi. The non-religious. The anti-religious. Reform. Conservative. I'm not going to say everyone, because he's a human being. But he is held in such high regard, just in the world in general, by so many of the human beings out there. *Loved*,' he emphasises, to distinguish it from 'liked' or 'respected'. 'Religious leaders, mortuaries, hospitals ... he's at home everywhere,' says the rabbi.

'And to what do you attribute that?' I ask.

'He's just genuine. He doesn't beat around the bush. Just says it as it is. And he's caring. A quote I heard: "People don't care how much you know, until they know how much you care". And Ephraim is a caring man,' the rabbi replies.

Rabbi Sufrin recalls visiting Bethlehem Hospital and meeting Sister Cletus, who spoke emphatically of this care, of Ephraim's broad-spectrum compassion. These days, he sees Ephraim's involvement with his shul as an example of this warmth, and also of adaptability. The synagogue is known as the Jewish Russian Centre, set up by Rabbi Chaim Elozor Gorelik in the mid-1980s. The shul provided an entry point into Judaism to the Soviet immigrants who arrived in Melbourne in droves at that time. My family was part of this wave. And my grandfather was a part of this shul until he passed in 2022, just as I was on the cusp of writing Ephraim's story. Ephraim doesn't speak Russian, nor is he a Russian immigrant. But he is at home in this place, and bonds effortlessly with its members.

'It's interesting. He kisses people and hugs them,' Rabbi Sufrin tells me. 'And he tells me, "People are not being hugged. People need a good hug." And that's what he does. And you see it; when people receive, they love it.' I tell the rabbi that I think about this a lot, this nexus between the physical and the spiritual in Ephraim's work. 'Handling the dead, it's very manual work,' I say, revisiting my conversation with Ben. 'But it's very spiritual work too. You have to be an open portal to do it in any sustainable way. You can't be spiritually shut down.'

At this, Rabbi Sufrin jumps in, apologising for interrupting. He has a careful, gracious manner and a rich British diction. This, combined with his willingness to answer all and any manner of question, makes him a pleasure to converse with.

'Something just came to mind, which really personifies Ephraim,' he says. I look at him eagerly as he speaks. 'For decades he's been dealing with dead people. You think it would become automatic. Yet, he always showed unbelievable dignity and respect.

The life and deathwork of Ephraim Finch

Each deceased was a human being with a history. And to still have that enthusiasm and respect, as if it's his first week at being an undertaker—that was something which I picked up.'

Here, the rabbi is referring to the fact that he and Ephraim performed *tahara* together. And I recall that one of the first things Ephraim told me about Rabbi Sufrin was that he is especially gentle with deceased babies and children. Briefly, we move into this harrowing terrain. Rabbi Sufrin names this as the most difficult work, saying, 'They are the faces you never forget.' Then he tells me he has recently completed a course with Kenafayim, an organisation that supports families who've experienced stillbirth, miscarriage or early baby loss. 'And one of the reasons why I did the course is very much inspired by Ephraim and the cases that we dealt with,' he says.

Rabbi Sufrin is a tall man, of course bearded, and with large tortoise-shell glasses. His voice would be booming were he to raise it. But throughout our chat he is calm and gentle, with an anchoring presence that is not dissimilar to Ephraim's. Perhaps it is this steadiness that allows me to raise something that has been churning in my mind, something I rarely raise with Ephraim for my own struggle to bear it. It is the subject of suicide.

Traditionally, Orthodox Judaism has had separate rules for people who have taken their own lives; according to Maurice Lamm they are 'buried near the cemetery gate, or at least eight feet from other Jewish dead'. In addition, they are not to be eulogised. The reasoning behind this baffles and disturbs me, as it compares suicide to murder. I also know that it baffled Ephraim. One of the first things I learned about Ephraim, from an earlier interview, is that he lifted these injunctions when he became director of the Chevra. When we visited Springvale Cemetery I saw the graves of several people who had died by their own hand, all buried alongside their next of kin. I am relieved when Rabbi Sufrin concurs with me, and

Ephraim, on this. 'They are bodies with souls, who struggled,' he says, 'and we take care of them'.

Rabbi Sufrin has been performing *tahara* for some fifteen years, and it seems that he is also unable to take it for granted. He tells me that every single time is confronting, not because it is shocking but because it is precious. 'This is an individual that's had a whole life, a whole history, a whole family, and we are putting them to bed,' he says, mirroring both Ephraim and Ben in his imagery. 'I always have a little bit of trepidation before I start, which I think is a good thing,' he says.

At this moment, the sound of children's voices starts to drift through the window. We have been sitting at the front of the building, down the hall from the body of the synagogue. Between the synagogue and us is a middle room used for a *cheder*, a religious school, where kids come to learn outside school hours. Their voices sound like birdsong, indistinct vocal leaps and whoops, arcing into the sky and back down to land on our windowsill. It instantly opens my chest, shifts my breath, which I realise I have been stilling. The noise of the children is nothing less than a resuscitation. I also read it as my cue to leave the rabbi to his next task. I thank him for his time, and he looks at his watch.

'*Ah! Ne rano i ne pozno*,' he says, in Russian. The sentence means, 'Not too early, not too late', and acknowledges that, without even timing ourselves, we spoke for the exact duration planned. I notice that although his Russian comes effortlessly, there is a very slight accent. This is, of course, to be expected—it's not his mother tongue, and Russian is a notoriously difficult language in which to sound native. The fact that Rabbi Sufrin has acquired some Russian so that he may better serve his congregation makes this moment even more touching. It also illustrates, so beautifully, something he said at the very start of our chat, when I asked him about conversion.

'The Torah is full of making sure that the converts are taken care of. And why does the Torah make an emphasis on converts? Because it's not easy. When your family came from the Soviet

Union to Australia, it wasn't easy, but that's life. Therefore, we need to be sensitive. If somebody's in an environment that they weren't brought up with, you need to make them feel at home. That's what God asked us to do.'

It is not news that the major religions preach compassion; the holy texts are replete with entreaties to care for the newcomer, to practise tolerance. But talking to Rabbi Sufrin it occurs to me that the newcomer plays an active role in the process; it is a mutual exchange. The gift of those outside the status quo—if we have the wisdom to notice—is showing us something important about ourselves. We are shown our rigidity, our narrow straits.

'It also says, "*ger shehitgayer*", which means "a convert that converts",' he adds. 'It doesn't say "a gentile that converts".'

'Which, to me, sounds like someone coming home,' I reply. I have been thinking of the notion of *teshuvah*, or return, which is so central to Jewish philosophy. The idea of returning to wholeness, to oneness with the divine, is the deepest-held wish in the Jewish soul, perhaps in any soul. It is a concept central to Yom Kippur, when we invite twenty-five hours of introspection through fasting, prayer, the wearing of white shrouds and abstinence from worldly pleasures. (The crossover with funereal imagery is not accidental; our appearance on the day is supposed to mirror this holy transition, as we contemplate our morality and our mortality. We dress, as Leonard Cohen puts it, 'in these rags of light', to strip away daily artifice and distraction, as we stand before the divine.)

We discuss the notion of Baal Teshuvah, a lapsed Jew who has returned to the faith, or a secular Jew who has decided to become more religious. Again, the notion of effort and intention is commended—'Baal' means master, and so a person who makes this choice (wilfully, with agency), is a Master of the Return.

But Baal Teshuvah doesn't apply to those who have converted. And Rabbi Sufrin indicates as much, shaking his head slightly when I ask about the crossover, too thoughtful (and perhaps too polite) to give me a concrete 'no'. When he settles on it, he says,

'There is something about their soul. The soul belongs to Judaism.' Of course, this presupposes not only a belief in the soul, but a belief in the soul's wanting, some kind of inner knowing that guides it towards actualisation.

The Kabbalah talks of reincarnation, of the soul splitting in order to learn more and more from successive lifetimes. I don't hold to a definitive schema this way or that, nor an interest in proving the soul empirically. What I do have is a felt sense of this inner knowing, a drive towards home that is more wilful and insistent than language. So when Rabbi Sufrin talks of the soul's belonging, I know where to put the idea; it is a statement of shape, a description of movement. He is pointing to a circle rather than a line, to the idea that home is always waiting, that our lives are an ongoing loop between the body and the spirit, one chasing the other like children around a garden.

10

Researching pre-existing publications on Ephraim, it is impossible to see him as simply an undertaker. The National Library of Australia's digital database contains eighty-nine listings (1986–2008) with the words 'Ephraim Finch'. I print them off and see not only a portrait of a deeply involved community figure, but of the community itself.

Many of the listings are classifieds in the *Australian Jewish News* for talks and community get-togethers. In September 1992 he discusses 'Jewish burial, mourning customs and reasons' with university students participating in a Life Cycle Seminar. He is recorded as training *tahara* volunteers in the ACT in 1996, while September 1997 sees him addressing a group by the name of Second Generation of the Holocaust Inc., with a discussion enigmatically titled 'Last Stop before Heaven: Don't Take It with You'. He speaks to the Bentleigh Progressive Synagogue about mourning customs and the history of the Chevra, and takes Year Eight students from King David School on a tour of Springvale Cemetery. 'Students were given maps with the location of graves of their relatives and friends, and then visited these graves … with Mr Finch as their guide,' says the article.

His appearances cross denomination, gender and age, and all of them demonstrate his efforts to demystify death,to open the conversation and bring the beauty of tradition to a wider public.

Much of this record shows his on-the-ground advocacy, fuelled by a pragmatic compassion for people of all backgrounds. Through a 1998 article I learn that Ephraim volunteered for Jewish Chaplaincy Services, visiting prisoners in Melbourne and country Victoria, arranging food parcels for the High Holy Days. A piece from 1995 reports on the Chevra's decision to conduct more free or minimum-charge funerals due to the harsh economic climate. In the piece, Ephraim points specifically to the high rates of penniless Russian elderly individuals needing burial. Another article, discussing the halachic prohibition against euthanasia, doesn't mention where Ephraim sits on the debate but does quote him saying that 'the manner of a person's death' makes 'no difference to the treatment of a dead person and the performance of Jewish burial rites'.

There is a preponderance of articles documenting the spike in fatal heroin overdoses in the Melbourne Jewish community in 1999, an increase mirrored in wider Victoria at this time. In July of that year, the Chevra reports burying, on average, one individual a month who has died from a heroin overdose. It is clear from the articles that Ephraim was instrumental in shifting the consciousness around drug use in the community. He attended a panel on harm reduction in August of that year, alongside a clinician from the government's Turning Point initiative, school students and police representatives. The panel discussed not just heroin but the rising prevalence of other street drugs, broadly critiquing both zero-tolerance and the head-in-the-sand attitude.

In June 1999, a symposium held by the Jewish Community Council of Victoria leads to the establishment of a confidential support group for families of Jewish addicts. Parents are bolstered by meeting others with similar challenges, grateful to lift their silence, to name the sensation of guilt that shadows them. Meanwhile, a naltrexone program, Pegasus, has been established in Melbourne's north, and shows a no-relapse rate of 60–70 per cent. Momentarily, it seems things are changing for the better.

Then, in December 1999, three members of the Melbourne Jewish community die of a heroin overdose within a fortnight. They are three men, aged twenty, twenty-one and thirty-one. Ephraim expresses his distress publicly. 'It's shocking,' he says. Some of the people he has buried 'are hanging on by their toenails and one day catch a hot load. Others have been dry for some time and then start up again using the old dose. They forget that the body can't take it and that they need to take smaller doses to restart.' Steadfast in his belief in harm minimisation, and his fight against denial, Ephraim also suggests a dedicated bricks-and-mortar facility where intravenous-drug addicts from the community can be 'slowly taken off their drugs while receiving constant care, supervision and counselling'.

Ephraim's concern for the individuals who had died during this dark period is not just documented in the newspaper clippings; it lives on in his bank of memories. Earlier this year, I came across an interview he gave that shows how these stories lodged in his heart, how stubbornly he bore the sudden losses. Even though it happened decades earlier, Ephraim recalls the name of a man who died of an overdose, the street he died in, his age. 'I used to take him to his job as a taxi driver,' Ephraim says in the transcript, providing a seemingly odd detail that with just a moment's consideration shows something plain and enduring about Ephraim Finch: people in the community asked all sorts of things of him, and he gave, simply because they asked.

Now, in among the reportage, I find a story about this very person, a man by the name of Stephen Black, who died on 4 February 1999, 'alone in an old, unregistered unroadworthy car' parked in a residential street in North Caulfield. He was thirty-six years of age. In the piece, his mother mentions that he knew Ephraim, as well as 'many rabbis from the community'. She and Stephen had an open dialogue about his heroin use and her heart remained open to her son throughout his years-long addiction: 'I have never rejected my son. We as a family used to say, "We love you dearly, but we are not very accepting of the lifestyle you lead". They are two separate issues.'

Stephen had been clean for nine days before his overdose; when the police found him in his car, they also found a *tefillin*, a *tallit* and three prayer books. His yarmulke was in his pocket. These particulars make no difference, of course, to the weight of Stephen's story or the preciousness of his memory. Moreover, the fact that a person is religiously observant is no buffer against harmful drug addiction. Where it comes to bear is in Stephen's mother's attitude, her plea to the community that her son was part of. She speaks of a rehabilitation centre akin to the one Ephraim envisioned. 'There needs to be safe houses,' she says. 'I believe that if you can keep a heroin addict alive long enough you may be able to rehabilitate them. But once they die they are lost.'

It is no surprise to find Ephraim's name listed in the Queen's Birthday Honours in 2018, where he is awarded an OAM for his service to the community. The archive heaves with community voices; letters to the opinion section, editorials, feature stories, declarations of grief or gratitude that—as a corollary—refract Ephraim's reach.

There is a feature article from a journalist called David Langsam, who discusses how he, as 'an atheist Orthodox Jew', experienced the passing of his mother. Born to Jewish parents, Langsam was circumcised and underwent bar mitzvah. He attended a Jewish school. However, he is unequivocal that 'my Judaism—an anathema to the holier-than-thou sects—does not require a God'. This seemingly contradictory identity reconciles itself in the moment of his mother's death, whereupon he consults 'the Chevra Kadisha's ever-helpful Ephraim'. Hearing that Langsam's mother requested a Jewish burial, Ephraim refers him to Maurice

The life and deathwork of Ephraim Finch

Lamm's *The Jewish Way in Death and Mourning*, and it is in its pages that Langsam finds meaning, what he calls 'the psychological and environmental appropriateness of our way of death'.

He is comforted by the simplicity of funereal dress ('our shrouds have no pockets and carry no material wealth. This trip needs no ticket'); the finality of a quick, communal burial ('We had seen her in death and confirmed her passing through participation in the physical act of burial. There was no confusion that ... she was not really dead. It was done. We knew it. We buried her. Full stop.'). He describes noticing, three days after the burial, that life goes on; while walking the dog, he appreciates 'carrying my mother's walking stick with the scent of her hand still upon it'. He mentions that although he does not say kaddish for his mother regularly, hearing it in shul 'confirms that grief is shared and universal. The ritualised acknowledgement eases the pain.'

I do not wish to overstate Ephraim's role in Langsam's journey; clearly, Langsam made his own matrix of observance, drawing out the cultural and psychological connections for himself. But I can't help but wonder what would have happened if the Chevra had been managed by a 'holier-than-thou' individual rather than Ephraim Finch when Langsam needed support. I can't help but think of Langsam's fortuitous timing, picturing this grieving son calling the Chevra on the landline and explaining, 'I might not need a God, but I understand the place of ritual' to the undertaker on the other end.

A 1995 article on the Jewish Secular Humanist Society discusses the tricky area of funerals for secular and atheist Jews. The president of the society, Julie Ruth, is quoted as saying, 'Many people, particularly in the older Yiddish speaking community, were avowed atheists, and it made a mockery of all their values and beliefs if a rabbi recited kaddish over them'. However, she acknowledges that while people wish to be buried in the manner in which they live, 'many secular Jews still wanted to be buried in a Jewish cemetery for spiritual or family reasons'. Ephraim responds to this by reiterating that while everyone buried through the Chevra Kadisha undergoes *tahara,* the funeral can be conducted without a rabbi. If a person is Jewish, and there is a *minyan*, any of its members can lead the service. 'The truth is the role of the rabbi in Judaism has always been that of a teacher. The role as religious functionary or clergyman is a relatively modern one,' he says. But before he gets to the rabbis, he addresses the precious subjects at the centre of the conversation: 'People who do not want a religious ceremony are often Holocaust survivors and after the *gehenom* (hell) they have been through, I do not feel we have a right to dictate anything to them'.

'Among the guests at yesterday's unveiling was funeral director Ephraim Finch, of Melbourne Chevra Kadisha, a familiar figure at the institute after 20 years brokering the most sensitive of territory—the demands of coronial investigations versus the cultural aversion of many people in the Jewish community to autopsy procedures.' This is a passage from a 2005 article in *The Age,* reporting on the unveiling of a $2 million CT scanner at the Victorian Institute of Forensic Medicine. The scanner would allow pathologists to investigate cause of death without making an incision, in many cases forestalling a full autopsy. This is a coup for the Melbourne Chevra Kadisha, whose compliance with religious law has historically clashed with the imperatives of the Coroners Court. Specifically, the Torah commands *kavod hamet*: honouring the sanctity of a dead body, which in effect translates to a prohibition on any surgical procedure post-mortem unless it saves another life.

Of course, Jewish custom functions inside the framework of Australia's legal system, and it acknowledges as much. Jewish law contains within it the concept of *dina demalchuta dina*—the law of the land is the law. The one area where this seems to cause perennial tension is that of autopsy and swift burial. Listening to

The life and deathwork of Ephraim Finch

Ephraim's stories, I can see how, over the years, negotiating these tensions became an essential part of his toolkit.

It was not until 1988 that the *Coroners Act* formally enshrined Jewish religious requirements and, even then, the Chevra had to liaise with the court on behalf of the deceased's next-of-kin. It provided pro bono legal advice to those wishing to object to an autopsy, and where possible, Ephraim advocated in person.

In the course of his work, Ephraim cultivated relationships with morticians, the court's reception staff, even the coroner himself. He stayed on good terms with police and with the contractors from various funeral parlours.

'The thing was, in most cases it was me that was on the line for the family. I had to do the right thing. I had to be there. I had to make sure that it was right,' he says, remembering what it meant to juggle the various parties and their needs.

'It felt like we were the front row of a rugby game. The ball was kicked, you have to follow,' he says. By 'we', he means the Hatzolah Jewish ambulance service, as well as lawyers who worked on autopsy cases with the Chevra.

He shares the story of a teenager who died in an accident on the eve of a public holiday. In order to bury the boy ahead of the long weekend, a great many people had to cooperate. The nurses helped to carefully collect the life-carrying blood, to be buried with the body. An administrator at the Coroners Court organised a police report so that all would be ready for the pathologist. As Ephraim outlines the practical details—which plastic bags held which remains, which form must be signed by which official, the names of hospital staff, the words of the police—I can see his heart imploding at this life cut short. I am struck by his coordination of all the parties, but also the teamwork, the synergy of goodwill.

'It sounds like many people in that world have a very strong conscience,' I say.

'Yeah,' Ephraim replies, his palms upturned in a gesture I am now familiar with. Once again, I am reading his hands like subtitles, and in this case, they say 'Of course', and 'People are mostly good', and 'If you model kindness, you will be met with the same'.

'And I love saying to everybody, "You've done a true and loving kindness to someone who can't thank you",' he says, visibly satisfied by the transmission of care from one being to another. 'And they can't help themselves. They want to do it. It's one way to make it a bit lighter for the family.'

It is a Tuesday afternoon when Ephraim receives a phone call about a seventeen-year-old girl who has been fatally hit by a car outside her school.

'It's like a painting in my mind,' he says, twenty-six years later. 'Every time, I see myself going up this lonely road at dusk. There are no cars, even though it's peak hour. And on every corner, there is a policeman.' He recalls arriving at the scene of the catastrophe. 'I had to take control. I had to calm everybody down, even the police … then the contractor coming.' By this he means someone from the Coroners Court, coming to take the body to the morgue.

'And how he wished he could take her home,' Ephraim suddenly says, in a seeming non sequitur. In fact, he is making perfect sense. He is describing the child's father, amidst all the chaos, struggling to let his girl go. Ephraim can see the father's distress at the slippage of time, is himself dreading the arrival of the contractor.

'In certain cases, I could intervene and say to the court, "Look, I'll bring the body in". But in this case, the police were there. They said, "We've rung the contractor, he is coming very soon". So when he drove up the road, I could see he was a guy I knew from Mulqueen. They used to do our Shabbos collection.' Ephraim watches the man park his car and approaches him calmly, steadily. He greets the contractor, who greets him back. Then he says, under his breath, 'When you get out of the van, I'll cuddle and kiss you, just go with me. I want the coppers to know I'm friendly with you. I'll help you put her onto the trolley. I'll wrap her properly. We'll put

The life and deathwork of Ephraim Finch

her into the vehicle.' While the contractor waits, Ephraim carefully attends to the body.

'When we were all ready, I said to the mother and father, "I'm now following him into the Coroners Court. And I will stay with her all night",' he says. And so he does, driving behind the contractor's van to the building in Southbank. I ask him how he managed to spend the night at the court, who facilitated this. He explains that thanks to an amenable colleague, he was allowed to sleep on a bench in the vestibule, just outside the morgue.

'I asked for a lot in my time. And they accommodated me,' he replies. At this point, Cas joins in the conversation, for she too recalls this devastating incident.

'I think that Ephraim was deeply aware of making people feel at ease with Jewish bodies and death and the fact of who he was,' she says, adding, '… his relationship towards his community, the things that he asked for. They were not just, you know, "Do this" or "Do that for me". These were from the depths … these were of a tradition, these were important. And in order to do that he spoke to nurses, to doctors, to anaesthetists, to whoever could be involved in any way.' This brings to mind Sister Cletus's portrait of Ephraim, his role as intermediary between the Jewish and the non-Jewish world.

'I knew everybody there. It was lovely,' he says, softening at the recollection of this time, this world. 'They're salt of the earth, these people. They've worked in the funeral industry. They know what it is. They're not just clerks. They're people with understanding.'

I continue to see the layers that make up Ephraim's work ethic, woven tight like muscle. There is the fight for cultural respect, but all through it is his ache for the outsider. His stories, and this pile of newspaper clippings, show his preoccupation with those dwelling alone, those shunned by their family, those who might slip through the cracks.

I recall our visit to Springvale Cemetery, when we chanced upon the headstone of a woman who had died in the late 1980s. I noticed that next to the name of the deceased sat another woman's name, in the place where a spouse would be listed. Reading my mind, Ephraim waved his hand in front of his torso, as if shooing something away. 'Some people said to me …'—he made a face to indicate disapproval from more conservative members of the community—'… and I said to them, "It was her partner! What do you expect?"'

I think about Ephraim's uncommon ability to relate to such a wide cross-section of humanity, to meet people just where they are. Sometimes, this involves people outside the Jewish community, or the Orthodox one. But sometimes it is people in Ephraim's cultural inner circle that highlight his unique approach.

Namely, Ephraim has shared numerous accounts of supporting extremely religious families who are reluctant to bury their stillborn baby.

'In some cases, people don't bury a baby in the coffin. It's buried in the ground. They don't tell anybody where it's buried,' he tells me one time. 'I think exactly the opposite: it should be buried in a box. And the family should know.' He has met people at the cemetery looking for the unmarked grave of their baby, years after the loss. Often, these parents were woven into an older generation's thinking, one that, according to Ephraim, might have suggested, 'Don't worry about it. You're young, go on and live your life.'

'I don't think it should be shunned and I don't think it should be pushed away,' he says to me, and I agree. But I wonder how on earth he would have spoken to these parents, freshly shattered, in these moments. He cites one example.

'I got the husband to carry the coffin to the grave. Then, I'd say to him, "Give me your baby", so I could place it in the ground.

The life and deathwork of Ephraim Finch

I use *loshen* like that to get him to understand that he's losing. He is losing like she lost.' *Loshen* is a Yiddish word that translates directly to 'language', but also means something deeper and more nuanced. *Loshen* is the heart's idiom, the words that live in our cells and our earliest memories. In this case, Ephraim is describing the importance of not just speaking *at* a person but into them, of reaching their deepest self.

'Her body knows that,' he says of the bereaved mother. 'So she doesn't need words.'

'That's right,' I respond, feeling my own maternal heart grow heavy.

'So she's carrying, then he's got to give over. It's important,' he says, raw with anguish.

It takes me several days to order and read the printed articles and classifieds. Coming to the end of the pile, I find a 1995 newsletter from the Australian Jewish Genealogical Society that excerpts a talk Ephraim gave at their inaugural Victorian meeting. The talk, entitled 'The Tapestry of Life', shares some of his Chevra experiences around history-taking and the unlocking of revelatory family details.

'As in all tapestries, the patterns vary and so does human existence,' says Ephraim in the speech. He describes an interview with a widower and his son that led to the discovery of a great rabbinic lineage. Another story tells of a woman searching for her great-great-grandfather's grave. She had a surname and a year of birth but nothing else. Ephraim was able to determine, through the database he'd been building of Jewish Victorian burials, that the man was buried in St Kilda Cemetery. The woman then asked if he had details for the man's deceased baby daughter. Ephraim had nothing, but promised to investigate. Via the microfiche for Carlton Cemetery he located the child's name and date of death. He added her to the database.

I have worked on this book in multiple locations. I have read and thought at the local library, at the house on the coast, in a cavernous office block slated for demolition. Today, I am seated at my mother's kitchen table as I sift the articles. The walls of her living area are covered in her artwork, mostly portraits, oils on canvas. They feature men's faces and women's bodies; figurative, sometimes abstract. Even in repose, they convey movement, as though the subject is saying, 'I am always thinking, I am always breathing'. They pull you in with their contradictions, by a twist in the story—for every splash of saffron there are underworlds of inky blue; smiling mouths are watched by melancholy eyes, a tiny mother embraces a giant child, a girl is at once running and sleeping, a winged man takes flight through the bars of a gilded cage.

I am aware that my portrait of Ephraim is mutable, but with any luck, faithful to his complexity. I am mapping his ethical contours as I go, listening to his words and the reverberations of his actions. It is a relief to know that in some foundational way, I am limited; I will never capture him entirely or definitively. But I would like to capture the bits that collide, the facets of his being that butt up against each other to make sparks. It is these sparks that seem to hold his essence, this lifelong agitator who reveres tradition, this once-outsider who has fought so hard to bring others home, to enfold them in their belonging.

I turn back to the pile of newspaper clippings, to Ephraim's 'Tapestry' speech. 'As I listen and observe the vast tapestry of life which is spun in our office, I am always amazed at what a vibrant, pulsating people we are, and what has happened to the wandering Jew,' he says, revealing more about his drive—and his dreams—than my words ever could.

11

A king once told his prime minister, who was also his good friend, 'I see in the stars that whoever eats any grain that grows this year will go mad. What is your advice?'

The prime minister replied, 'We must put aside enough grain so that we will not have to eat from this year's harvest.'

The king objected, 'But then we will be the only ones who will be sane. Everyone else will be mad. Therefore, they will think that we are the mad ones. It is impossible for us to put aside enough grain for everyone. Therefore, we too must eat this year's grain. But we will make a mark on our foreheads, so that at least we will know that we are mad. I will look at your forehead, and you will look at mine, and when we see this sign, we will know that we are both mad.'

— *'The Tainted Grain', Rabbi Nachman's Stories: The Stories of Rabbi Nachman of Breslov, trans. Rabbi Aryeh Kaplan*

'I'm trying to find my books,' Ephraim says one morning when I have come for a chat. He points to two rows assembled on the dining table, mid-century hardcovers in glossy dust jackets. I am embarrassed to admit that I only recognise some of the authors, though to Ephraim they are as familiar as blood relatives. Rabbi Nachman of Breslov. Avrohom Ben Avrohom. Rabbi Aryeh Kaplan. Here is *The Legend of the Baal-Shem* by Martin Buber. *Souls on Fire* by Elie Wiesel. I know that these books portray Hasidic rabbis but are also filled with the rabbis' own writings; spiritual lessons embedded in mystical vignettes; folktales and legends; parables that illuminate the Torah. All of them braid quotidian life (harvests, brides, elderly parents, illness, school) with the grandly magical (fallen angels who marry human women, laughing trees, werewolves, a 'melancholy saint', a blazing cave).

'It will let you know exactly how my mind works,' Ephraim says, handing me *Rabbi Nachman's Stories*. I know why he says this, why he uses the word 'mind'; there is something in the stories' structure that demands a particular way of thinking—in their riddle-like nature, in the way that they invite infinite, tangled, self-referential discourse. The very pages are structured in a way that forces a pause, then interpretation: one or two lines of the story run across the top in a larger font, the rest is commentary, questions, unpicking of etymology, references to the Talmud or the Zohar or the musings of the Sages.

In addition, there seems to be a clear moral import, but never the same one on any given day. 'Maybe it's better if we are all mad' you think, reading 'The Tainted Grain' one day. 'No, none of us is mad, no matter what happens, and that's the point!' you think on another. Each reading requires a bending and flexing of the mind, a willingness to grasp and promptly let go.

But not only. For although Ephraim uses the word 'mind', I sense that what he also (and even rather) means is 'heart'; these stories—of cosmic chaos and justice, reason and nonsense, melancholy and transcendent joy—capture what matters to him, his deepest values. These are stories of people wrestling with their most primal sensations: fear, jealousy, anger, bliss.

'Tell me about Rabbi Nachman,' I say as a jumping-off point. Ephraim picks up a collection and reads the introduction: 'Rabbi

The life and deathwork of Ephraim Finch

Nachman's stories are among the great classics of Jewish literature. They've been recognised by Jews and non-Jews alike, for their depth and insight into both the human condition and the realm of the mysterious.'

'Are they parables from the Torah or stories he made up?' I ask. Ephraim says nothing, gently defying my need for categories. He gives me a quizzical smile.

'See these stories … "The Lost Princess", "The King and the Emperor", "The Cripple" … so much in it,' he replies, evading me.

'But are they reflections or inventions? What is their genre? And when are they from? Is he dipping into a canon that pre-dates Hasidism?' I forge ahead, stubborn like a little ox. Now he is looking at me mischievously, somewhat enjoying my frustration, the beating of my forehead against my own intellectual enclosure.

'Hhhhhmmmmmmm …' he responds, humming a shapeless tune. Mercifully, he follows up with something of an explanation.

'See, Nachman was the great-grandson of the Baal Shem Tov. When you're a descendent of the Baal Shem Tov, it goes without saying. He relies on him for inspiration.' I love this response so much. Not because I am a devotee of the Baal Shem Tov, the eighteenth-century mystic and founder of Hasidism, but because it speaks so richly to Ephraim's apprehension of storytelling. I am gathering that in his mind, all our stories are a gift from someone, from somewhere else. Even when they are invented, they are a gift 'from the sky', as my late grandfather, himself an author, would have said. As such, stories function like an inheritance or a fever; whether we are channelling an invisible higher wisdom or our observable environment is irrelevant. The point is that storytellers are vessels—this is what Ephraim's enigmatic clowning is saying. Good storytellers are envoys for ideas that help us grow. The best storytellers turn our heads and open our eyes. What does it matter if they are from the visions of a wandering sage or from the records of the town scribe? What matters is who you become in the reading, what you do with the new knowledge.

And this makes me realise that there is yet another aspect of engagement here: the spirit. Ephraim is reading these tales with his mind and feeling them with his heart. But what he does with them is spiritual: he takes every simile, every Hebrew cognate, every Midrashic extrapolation, as an opportunity to grow himself, to stretch to his higher self, to find his place in the great wheel. These narratives, like a man in the belly of a whale, like the burning bush, like ten holy vessels filled with primordial light, are no weaker for being metaphors. They are his spiritual dialectic, his wrestle with something beyond the material realm.

I also know that stories have been his comfort, his solace in the face of deep daily sorrow. 'Friday nights, even though I was starved of sleep, I would stay up and read books,' he says, referring to the only night of the week when he wasn't serving the Chevra.

Friday nights were for personal reading, but the rest of the week was for the stories of others. Cas shares an image of Ephraim sitting at this very table in the evenings after work, after the children had gone to bed, surrounded by books, folders of documents. He would be completing records, filling in histories. Even when he was officially off the clock, he was communing with the deceased.

'He used to sit there late at night and I knew there was nothing to be gained from saying, "When are you coming to bed?"' Cas tells me.

'So this is what he would do in the intervals. He would attend to the people by way of writing their stories,' I say.

'That's exactly right. And I would see him and sometimes he would be crying. I used to just go in there and stand behind him, beside him, and just touch his head,' she responds. She is solemn in the telling; the past is in the room with us. 'He was with these people that he knew were gone. You know, the remnants of extraordinary people.' And so, Cas would leave her husband to his stories—the reading, the recording, the channelling.

'And, of course, Elie is the centre of it,' he says to me today, as I scan the blurbs of his books. 'The man who is the centre of my life,' he says, without apology for the superlative. Ephraim is talking about Elie Wiesel, whom he has mentioned almost every time we've met. He has told me about meeting Wiesel, about reading his memoirs and his novels and retellings of these Hasidic tales that sit before us. He also told me of an astonishing synchronicity that occurred between him and the great author, Nobel Peace Prize laureate, activist and journalist. And each time I have stalled the moment, promising that we would come back to this important figure in his life, sensing perhaps, that it would overtake everything once we got started.

But when he says this today, when he opens with, 'I didn't realise how he took over,' it lands with a new urgency. It seems now is the time.

Elie Wiesel has authored fifty-seven books, and taught humanities at Boston University for nearly forty years. He is hardly obscure. Still, the fervour with which Ephraim describes his discovery of Wiesel belies a deeper kinship between the two men.

'Cassie and I would go into a Jewish bookstore and fossick around,' he tells me, 'and he would surface.'

'And why him? Do you think his personal story speaks to you as much as the stories he wrote?'

'Oh, geez yeah!' Ephraim exclaims.

'And something about him as a young boy,' Cas adds. 'The way he wrote about lining up outside with his parents and his sister, and their suitcases. And then looking at their house and knowing they would never see it again.' Here, Cas is referring to a scene from Wiesel's memoir *All Rivers Run to the Sea*, where he tracks—among other things—his childhood in Romania and deportation to Auschwitz aged fifteen. Volume One (1928–69) describes life in Sighet, the Carpathian shtetl where he grew up; his nascent love of Torah scholarship, of language; his relationship to mystery and to the divine. It is also achingly poetic, which I know is a shortcut to Ephraim's deepest heart.

'Our turn came on Tuesday, May 16. "All Jews out!" the gendarmes screamed, and we found ourselves in the street.' So begins the passage that both Cas and Ephraim often reference: 'There was another heat wave. My little sister was thirsty, and my grandmother too ... As in the presence of death, I didn't dare raise my voice ... Wherever life took me, a part of me would aways remain in that street, in front of my empty house, awaiting the order to depart.'

I ask Ephraim what his entry point into Wiesel was, if he recalls the first book.

'It wasn't *Night*. It was one of the stories ... *Legends of Our Time* or *Souls on Fire*.' By 'stories', Ephraim means works of fiction, but of the type we have just been discussing—stories steeped in the Torah's wisdom and filtered through the Hasidic prism. He picks up a book and opens it to 'The Tainted Grain', passes it to me wordlessly.

'But we will make a mark on our foreheads, so that at least we will know that we are mad,' I read out loud.

'See, he played on madness so much. And he was always talking about the madman in the village,' Ephraim says of Elie. And it's true; most famously, there is the opening of *Night*, which describes Moishe, the penurious caretaker of the synagogue in Elie's village, 'awkward as a clown', prone to speaking in song, who is deported from Sighet in 1942. He is taken by train, along with numerous other Jews, to Galicia, in Poland. There, the Gestapo forces them to dig trenches, then approach the pits one by one to be shot. Moishe, taken for dead and ignored, miraculously survives. He returns to his village and tells of the horrors, but no one is willing to believe him. 'They think I'm mad,' he whispers to the young Elie, who has offered him a sympathetic ear. And Elie—budding poet, aching empath, carer of exiles—notes that 'tears, like drops of wax, flowed from his eyes'.

'How could this be happening in our civilised world?' the Jews of Sighet think. How could the people who have had Jews in their midst for centuries, who bore Goethe and Schiller and Remarque, be responsible for such barbarism? And so Moishe is branded a madman by his own community, despite the reader knowing he is right. Moishe reads the tea leaves, while the reader has already seen them turn to ash.

In *All Rivers Run to the Sea*, Wiesel makes multiple references to the vocal pariah figures in his village, the outcasts who spoke a forbidden truth. He also describes the mental breakdown of his two close friends, with whom he studied the Kabbalah from the extremely young age of thirteen. In a preface to the 2006 edition of *Night*, translated from the original Yiddish by Wiesel's wife Marion, he wonders how the writing of the story impacted his sanity after the war. 'Why did I write it?' he asks, 'Did I write it so as not to go mad or, on the contrary, to go mad in order to understand the nature of madness, the immense, terrifying madness that had erupted in history and in the conscience of mankind?'

Wiesel's preoccupation with madness is also contextualised in *Witness: Lessons from Elie Wiesel's Classroom*, Ariel Burger's account of working with Wiesel at Boston University. Burger notes that 'For Wiesel, madness was not simply a literal, clinical dysfunction. It was a motif, a metaphor, a moral circumstance, one that briefly attracted him as an alternative to human community.'

'The madman has a wise side. We know this from the literary archetype of the jester, right?' I suggest to Cas and Ephraim. I am thinking of Shakespeare's Fool in *King Lear*, or Feste in *Twelfth Night*. 'And I guess if society has written the mad person off as irrational, they have permission to say whatever they want. As a result, sometimes they are the only ones who tell the truth,' I say.

'That's why my rabbis like me,' Ephraim says, somewhat jokingly. He is referring to the cheekiness he brings to shul, the wordplay in which he engages his friends, the importance of leavening the moment. He is also, perhaps unwittingly, referring to the need for rebellion. Something I see continually, as I read my way through Elie Wiesel's work, is the way both he and Ephraim challenge the status quo.

'He was concerned with the weak and vulnerable, the outsiders and the endangered, in life and in literature. Human rights, freedom of speech and religion, the plight of the oppressed and of refugees—all were at the centre of his attention,' writes Burger. Ephraim, of course, is driven by a similar imperative.

'See, I just get so worked up doing all these things and I hate it when I have a barrier that stops me. Because my intention is honourable. And I hate it when I get this attitude, "You can't do this". Shit yes, you can. You have to! This has got to be recorded. Why was I put in this place? I'm not saying I'm great, but I saw what had to be done. Like, I've gone berserk trying to learn ... When they come into my office, I've changed into their clothes to learn what they've been through. And then when they left, I'd change back into my clothes.' This is a tract of dialogue I find from an earlier interview, where Ephraim is audibly distressed at the stories of the deceased going undocumented now that he is no longer at the Chevra. 'They' are the secular families of deceased individuals, those who might feel intimidated by the undertaker's religious garb, and hence less likely to open up.

'So you would change in order to look at bit less *frum*?' I say in response.

'Yeah. And bit more mad,' he says, without a hint of humour.

I recall another time, on an autumn morning early in our encounters. Ephraim is waiting for me with *All Rivers Run to the Sea*, the thick hardcover volume open, ready to be shared.

'So important, so bloody important,' he says, stabbing his finger at a passage underlined in red pen. He begins to read.

'For years I dreamed of returning to my native town. It was an obsession. It took two decades, and that trip has now been added to my obsessions. It was night. There was a sleeping town and a sleeping house which hadn't changed: the same gate, same garden, same well. Choked with fear, as though caught in a whirlwind of hallucinations, I wondered whether it had all been a dream ... I waited for a window to open and for a boy who looks like the child I had been to call out to me: Hey, mister, what are you doing in my dream? But strangers were living in my house. They had never heard my name.'

I find this passage confusing, the way Wiesel elides his waking life with his dreamworld, the way he slides across time and vantage point. But before I have a chance to ask Ephraim, he speaks, in a voice of surprising distress. 'See, unfortunately, sometimes I make more than what the writer has written. In my mind I add things to it,' he says.

'But surely that's your right as a reader,' I respond. 'We all do that, we all interpret.' Ephraim looks unimpressed at my suggestion, or at least unplacated by it. He is not bothered by the shifting vantage point, or the lack of temporal anchor. He seems to be wrestling with his own florid imagination, and perhaps his needy heart. The sensation I collect is that Elie is already giving him so much, but he wants more. This storytelling is all the more torturous for being so vivid, so precise; the empathy Elie elicits appears to be driving Ephraim crazy, the writing is too good. I sense that he wants nothing short of jumping into the page—Mary Poppins style—and standing with Elie, shoulder to shoulder, by the little house in Sighet on that silent night.

He skips a few pages, continues reading: 'Meanwhile, our world contracted steadily. The country became a city, the city a street, the street a house, the house a room, the room a sealed cattle car, the cattle car a concrete cellar where ... No, let us go no further. Decency and custom forbid it. I said it earlier, when speaking of my grandfather: in Jewish tradition a man's death belongs to him alone. Let the gas chambers remain closed to prying eyes, and to the imagination.'

Ephraim finally met Elie in August 1988. Wiesel gave a public lecture at the Melbourne Town Hall, but Ephraim was invited to meet him at a smaller gathering at a community centre.

'I was entranced by him, the way he spoke. Such a voice, and the eyes were so dark,' Ephraim says. At the same time, he didn't feel it was appropriate to rush to the front of the line. 'I thought, I can't go up, there's a lot of old people here. They must want to ask him some deep questions.' But what he heard was people making banal chit-chat, asking if Elie knew their cousin in New York and so on. This waste of a titan's mind galvanised Ephraim to get out of his chair and walk over to Elie Wiesel.

'He looked at me and saw me,' he says, in a beautiful description of overlapping actions, layered intimacies. 'And our eyes were fixed on one another. And I put my hand out and said, "*Shalom Aleichem*"'. '*Aleichem Shalom*,' replied Elie Wiesel.

'I knew you before I knew you,' Ephraim continued. 'Your books are you.' The great author thanked him. Then Ephraim said, 'I've come to ask a *shayla*.' A *shayla* simply means 'question' in Hebrew, but in the context of Torah study it refers to a moral or philosophical conundrum a student might bring to a rabbi. 'How did you mourn the loss of your father in the death camp?' Ephraim asked.

Elie Wiesel writes, with agonising spareness, the final separation from his mother and little sister at Auschwitz, but reading his memoirs, it seems his father is his primary psychological fixation. His father's ghostly visitation of Elie in his dreams brackets the chapters of his memoir; in fact, the book opens with the lament that Elie 'knew little of the man I loved most in the world'. He notes his father's scholarly brilliance, his charity, his affection for the paupers and misfits of the town. Moreover, Wiesel conveys how instrumental his father was to his survival in the camps. He describes the Nazis encouraging inmates to forget their perished families, a strategy designed to weaken their chances of survival by giving them less to live for. 'Those who retreated to a universe limited to their own bodies had less chance of getting out alive,' he writes, 'while to live for a brother, a friend, an ideal, helped you hold out longer. As for me, I could cope thanks to my father ... I would see him coming with his heavy gait, seeking a smile, and I would give it to him. He was my support and my oxygen, as I was his.'

Back at the community centre, Ephraim waited eagerly for Elie's reply to his question. Could they mourn their dead? Was there a way to consecrate the names, to honour the bodies merging with the smoking sky?

'There's no *halacha* on how to mourn in a death camp,' Elie replied, 'but when we were liberated, we walked out through the gates and turned around and said kaddish together.' As he said this, he took Ephraim's hand. When Ephraim describes this moment to me, neither of us wants to move on. We linger in its transcendence, the many strands of healing it gathers.

As I read Elie Wiesel, I see how many devotions he and Ephraim share: the love of storytelling, the examination of faith, the absolute necessity of marking a life and a death, the fervent need to speak up in a landscape of oppression, the belief in art as resistance, the ethical value of beauty. But all these preoccupations are underpinned by anxiety about one notion, what Ariel Burger describes as 'the radical separation of ethics from knowledge'. Specifically, he is talking about the apathetic muteness that preceded so much twentieth-century genocide. How is it that educated, humane people could allow such a thing as the Holocaust to occur? According to Wiesel, the answer is not that people lacked knowledge, but that people lacked memory. If memory is not retained, it cannot be shared, and not only does a world disappear but a bridge cannot be made into another's heart. Transmission of memory is the cornerstone of empathy, a redemptive outcome of suffering. 'You must tell your story,' says Elie Wiesel to a Boston University student, a Zimbabwean woman whose brother was murdered by the Mugabe regime. 'This is because, if even one person learns from it how to be more human, you will have made your memories into a blessing.'

Listening to Ephraim describe his encounter with Elie Wiesel, I think of one statement in particular, which runs like a plumbline through both men: 'My goal is always the same: to invoke the past as a shield for the future.' I can see that for both Elie and Ephraim, memory is the thing that stops catastrophic cruelty from being repeated, not just for its recording of facts but for its deeply personal component. It is a siren from the heart, one that forces us to look each other in the eye. As the signs-on-heads in 'The Tainted Grain' signal, memory is the thing that allows us to register our own madness.

We come back to the story of their meeting, the moment where Elie took Ephraim's hand. After some time, Ephraim introduced his daughter Sarah, who had been standing by his side. Then Elie asked Ephraim why he was particularly interested in this topic of mourning in the death camps.

'I work for the Chevra Kadisha,' Ephraim said, to which Elie replied, 'You do a *groyse mitzvah*,' a great deed. 'I said, "Elie, I didn't come for praise, I just wanted to ask you that question"', Ephraim recalls. And then it was time to go, as the organisers tried to usher Ephraim away.

Cas describes the wrench of their separation, the 'sinew and power' between the men's interconnected arms. Elie was leaning on an upright piano with one arm, while his other hand held Ephraim at the wrist.

'Elie wouldn't let me go. He just wanted to talk,' Ephraim says. And I wonder if this too was wishful remembering, a longing to be near this man he had admired and imagined for so long. But of course, there is no way to know, as all we have is Ephraim's memory of an encounter that occurred thirty-five years ago.

Elie Wiesel died in 2016.

Ariel Burger's account of saying goodbye to his mentor, his friend, his intellectual inspiration, is one of the most moving things

The life and deathwork of Ephraim Finch

I have read in all my research for Ephraim's biography. It mirrors so much of what I have learned from Ephraim and about Ephraim; foremost, what it means to farewell a human being with dignity and from the faultlines of your broken heart. Burger sits by Elie's coffin at the chapel, speaking with him and reciting psalms. He has already cut the breast pocket of his favourite shirt, a custom that signals the cut over the mourner's heart. Then he recalls the importance, in Jewish tradition, of speaking a deceased person's name to them: 'According to legend, a person who has just died must remember his or her name in order for the soul to ascend—the name is the key. But with the trauma of death, it is easy to forget. I don't know if I believe it literally, but I remember Professor Wiesel discussing it in class ... I quietly lean down and whisper, "Remember your name. You are Eliezer, son of Shlomo the Levite." Then I take my seat.'

Ephraim's fabric is woven with longing, specifically for a bygone Hasidic world. This is a world of Talmudic contemplation, of Yiddish-speaking village life where multiple generations live under one roof, of a calendar year garlanded by festivals and a week concluded by the Sabbath's queenly peace. He longs for the early-Hasidic veneration of nature, for esoteric storytelling, for the *nigun*, a song spiralling away from the pogroms and into transcendence, to 'the celestial sanctuary where words become song'.

This is a phrase from Elie Wiesel's grandfather Dodye Feig, a man whose company Wiesel describes as 'a festival for the heart and mind'. By Elie's account, he was a marvellous singer, a captivating raconteur, a scholar who worked the land—a fusion of worldly and spiritual traits: 'A cultured and erudite man, an avid reader of the Bible and of the Rashi and Rambam commentaries ... my grandfather was fascinated with the Midrash ... and with Hasidic literature. He maintained a perfect balance between his quest for the sacred and the exigencies of daily life. He was a whole being.'

Although Dodye Feig was not a rabbi, he commanded immense respect in his community. He inculcated the young Elie into a world where, 'in the House of Study filled with the flickering shadows of yellow candles', the elders 'spoke of the great Masters as though they had known them personally. Each had his favourite Rebbe and a legend he liked above all others.' This cosy communion drew Elie in and held him, and its resonance holds Ephraim.

As Ephraim reveals his literary and religious inspirations—from Sholem Aleichem to Rabbi Lau, from Isaac Bashevis Singer to the Ribnitzeh Rabbi—I am forming a picture. I am starting to understand, that for individuals like Ephraim, there is a difference between a rabbi and a rebbe. What I am gathering, what I circled around with Rabbi Sufrin, is encapsulated beautifully by Ariel Burger in *Witness*: 'The word *rebbe* is translated variously as "teacher", "saint", and "guru", but the rebbe is something else; he is simultaneously traditional and creative; rooted in Jewish text and practice, yet wild and iconoclastic ... a rebbe, unlike a rabbi, is more than an authority figure—he is a friend, a guide, a supporter of each student's spiritual journey. Where a rabbi builds community and emphasizes its norms, a rebbe builds souls and nurtures individuality.'

Of course, here I think of the relationship between Ephraim and Rabbi Sufrin.

Hasidic lore also imbues the rebbe with prophetic powers—he knows an individual across their incarnations, holding their soul's evolution in his line of sight. As such, he has a long-range vision of the past, present and future, often knowing when catastrophe is imminent. Over our months together, Ephraim has relayed many stories from his Chevra work that speak to a rebbe's mystical capacities. One particular tale has stayed with him, and in turn, with me.

Edek (Edward) Retman's eulogy is given in November 2011 by a longtime friend. It begins with a quote from Dante's *Divine*

The life and deathwork of Ephraim Finch

Comedy: '... *nessun maggior dolore / che ricordarsi del tempo felice / nella miseria*'. 'There is no greater sorrow than remembering happy times in the midst of misery.' But happy times the eulogy does recall, including Edek's vast love of literature, his ability to quote poetry from memory in any of the languages he spoke (Polish, Yiddish, German, English, Italian), the special affection he had for the people and language of Italy. 'This largely self-educated man loved browsing among the thoughts and utterances of learned essayists, wise philosophers and elder statesmen,' reads the tribute, before describing Edek's tremendous personality: He 'harboured a genuine curiosity about the great world' and 'was keen to involve others in his excitements'. My favourite line in the tribute is that Edek 'was a man who understood the place and the value of joy'.

Each of these traits is confirmed by Edek's son David, whom I meet at Ephraim's table one evening around a bottle of whisky and piles of records.

'He loved to garden, he loved to be around people. He had lots of one-liners, and they were just hilarious,' says David. I am forming an image of a magnetic individual, and this is precisely how Ephraim describes the late Edek when he recalls their friendship.

'Well, I'm a person that goes up to older people and starts talking to them, and with him, it was like a magnet and a piece of metal, it was so comfortable,' he says.

'But he was certainly far from being an Orthodox person, I can tell you that,' David adds, pivoting into an interesting facet of his father's story. Edek Retman, born in 1921 in the Polish town of Sosnowiec, had an enduring connection with the Chentshin Rebbe, a Hasidic master who happened to reside in the nearby town of Olkusz. Despite not being particularly religious, Edek felt a great trust in this rabbi and sought his advice at important moments.

'We were traditional Jews,' Edek says, in his video testimony for the Melbourne Holocaust Museum, dated 22 January 1995. He is almost seventy-four when he gives this interview, but appears much younger. I notice his healthy bronze complexion, his dancing eyes, the clarity of his diction. And then there is his smile, which opens out across his face like a river delta. I witness this opening several times over the ninety-minute recording, despite his sharing of much devastation.

'I never saw my father putting on *tefillin* but he went to the shul on the High Holidays, and so did we,' he elaborates. He was one of five children, but early in the testimony he shares that two of his sisters (the youngest and the eldest) perished at Auschwitz. When he says this, he takes an extra gulp of air, and lingers, just for a moment. But I do not see him dissolving at the memory; he forges ahead with a solid bearing, a lucid and specific recall.

Although he knew about Hitler's ascent in Germany (the household purchased three newspapers in three languages every day), the young Edek did not personally experience racist persecution in his hometown. It was through the anti-Jewish propaganda filling Polish streets in the late 1930s—Jews being 'ostracised', stores being boycotted—that he noticed a seepage.

German army units entered Sosnowiec on 4 September 1939. The Great Synagogue of Będzin, located seven kilometres from Sosnowiec, was burned down five days later. It was a few days after this that he said to his father, 'It's time to go.'

The Retmans were one of the few Jewish families in the town to own a car, and Edek could drive it. So the family proceeded east towards the Soviet border. Over the course of September–October 1939 they moved from city to city, avoiding bombardment, heeding the cries of local people about the German invasion.

Edek's testimony is replete with remarkable events, both wondrous and tragic. Upon arrival in a small town over the Russian border, Edek immediately found employment as a personal driver for the mayor. This not only kept his family fed, it also afforded them some protection. Although he had to leave them in Russia in 1940, his parents survived the war, moving further and further from Poland; first to Siberia, then Central Asia. Edek would reunite with them in Israel in 1951.

He narrowly escaped deportation to Auschwitz, although his first wife, Frimet, did not. (His second wife, Dora, whom he would meet in Australia, also went to Auschwitz and survived.) Achingly, he tells the story of this in his interview. Although he does not give the date, his surrounding narration suggests that Edek is referring to a mass deportation that occurred in Sosnowiec in August 1942. Standing on the train platform awaiting transport, Edek made eye contact with a German colleague who was walking past.

'Take off your star and follow me,' the man said under his breath. 'And your wife, too.' Edek discreetly removed his yellow star and instructed Frimet to follow, but not immediately. When they had crossed to the opposite platform, Edek heard people screaming, *'Jude!' 'Jude!'* His wife, who was some two hundred metres behind him, was apprehended and taken back to the deportation train. Approximately eight thousand Jews would be transported over the coming days, among them Edek's younger sister, his older sister, his brother-in-law and five-year-old niece. He and Frimet had been married less than a year. He would never see her, or those family members, again.

Amidst the rubble of his shattered world, he continued to see goodness. For the first half of 1943 Edek worked in a store called Rosner, in Będzin. The German owner of this store employed and sheltered as many Jews as he could.

'He was a *tzaddik*, he was all our hope,' Edek says, looking straight to camera. A *tzaddik* is a label reserved for the most righteous of individuals, saintly in their giving. Tragically, righteousness was not enough to save this German man, who was eventually arrested and executed.

Not long after this, Edek was transported to Blechhammer, a forced-labour camp which would become a subcamp of Auschwitz. He speaks of three men coming into the compound to tattoo the inmates. He recalls it was Easter. The interviewer asks him if he has a number. Edek's voice is calm. 'Oh yes, I have,' he says, rolling up his left sleeve. The interviewer asks him to read it out, but of course he does not need to read. '178450,' Edek says, rotating his arm towards the camera.

Then, in June 1944, a momentous event. While working as a mechanic at a compound outside Blechhammer, Edek made friends with a German worker. The man would bring him food parcels and even a suit, which he had procured from another large-hearted gentile. One day, he told Edek he would help him escape, outlining a strategy. He would accompany Edek out of the building, whereupon Edek would hide in a public toilet. (Although he doesn't spell this out in his testimonial, I assume that it was here that he would put on the suit.) Meanwhile, the colleague would buy him a train ticket and knock on the toilet door three times to let him know it was time. Edek would exit, grab the ticket and run.

'And so it happened,' says Edek, another smile gliding across his eyes. The German friend not only facilitated his escape, he found him shelter with a Polish woman in Będzin; she was the very woman who had provided the suit. She would harbour Edek, on and off, until January 1945, when Russia liberated Poland.

There is a pause at the end of the escape story, the first sustained pause in the interview.

'There's a lot to tell,' Edek eventually says. The interviewer remains silent, holding the door open. 'You know, faith comes into it as well,' he continues. And I know that this is going to be the Chentshin Rebbe moment, because the interview is almost over and it's too great a thing for Edek to have forgotten. It is the fulcrum of Ephraim's account, and of Edek's son David's. I have been wondering when he will speak of this, where it is shelved in his massive storehouse of recollections.

'During the war, when my mother was in Russia, there was a saintly man called the Chentshin Rebbe in Olkusz,' he says. 'And my grandmother said, "Go to the rabbi and give a *kvitl*, so that he prays for your mother".' A *kvitl* is a note written by a Hasidic devotee to a rabbi, petitioning for a blessing.

'I went to the rabbi. And he says, "Whenever you will be in danger, repeat the ninety-first psalm". And I did. And I knew it by heart and I know it to this very day.' Edek then proceeds to recite the psalm, in a stunningly natural flow of Hebrew. I notice that whatever non-English language he speaks—Polish, Yiddish, Hebrew—he speaks with utter ease, a melodic richness usually possessed by native speakers.

Reciting a verse, Edek says, 'I was so sure that there were thousands of angels carrying me'. He is referring to this line: 'For he will command his angels concerning you to guard you in all your ways / they will lift you up in their hands so that you will not strike your foot against a stone'. Recalling the psalm, or perhaps taking in its import, he shakes his head incredulously.

'I arrived in Będzin, it was a beautiful day. The sun was shining. I didn't see one person in the street as I went to that lady. They called her "The Jewish Aunt". So as long as I was in Będzin, she used to bring parcels with food, although she worked for a German upstairs and I was downstairs.'

Edek Retman's testimony tracks other miraculous events of his life—being nursed back to health by two families in Italy immediately after the war, a relative locating his parents, sister and brother in Haifa in 1950, a Silesian Jehovah's Witness finding him shelter just before the 1945 liberation, a Polish woman taking care of him after he jumped out of a window in Będzin while on the run.

But none of this is conveyed without the wider context of catastrophe; he is not a blunt optimist.

'What do you attribute your survival to?' asks the interviewer.

'The will to live. And kismet, destiny,' responds Edek. 'But my faith, in all circumstances. Of course, I know it is really profane to think that way, that I survived and all the others went.' Here he pauses, again. He doesn't seem to have an easy answer. In fact, he seems steeped in the opposite, the belief that so much of the universe, the workings of our personal and collective history, is not just unknown but unknowable. 'But that's what it was,' he says, looking at the interviewer, not looking away.

When Ephraim met Edek at the home of mutual friends in 2007, he knelt beside the elderly man and listened to his stories. One of the things Edek related was that he still dreamt of the rebbe, that he missed him terribly. 'I don't see him anymore,' he said to Ephraim sadly. 'I can't see him. I loved him. I could discuss anything with him, all my sins. He had such an understanding of human nature.' These words are captured in Ephraim's journal.

As David pointed out, Edek had never been a religious man. And his experiences in the war did not change that; in Australia he continued to live a traditional rather than Orthodox life. His wife would have liked him to attend shul on the Jewish New Year, but instead he went to the Dandenong Livestock Market. For the most part, as David relays it, 'he was proudly Jewish. But he had no interest in religion per se'.

Across the decades of his life, Edek continued to feel the rebbe's presence.

'He used to speak of the rebbe quite often ... what an amazing man he was,' David says. As he says this, he pulls out two laminated black-and-white photos of the Chentshin Rebbe, whose full name is Yehoshua Heshel Horowitz. He is an extremely slender man, with a curved posture and deep-set, dark eyes. In one photo, he is dressed in a voluminous black *kapota* and appears deep in thought even as he is walking down the street. The second image shows his face quite literally buried in a book. He is holding it so close he could be kissing the page; his white beard rests on his hands, which are almost at his chin. Most likely the close holding is due to his age and poor eyesight. But the impression is of a man utterly unified with the text, a circuit between his mind and the words; one can't help but wonder what is being transmitted, what state of consciousness he is in and who—or what—else is there with him.

The life and deathwork of Ephraim Finch

The photo belonged to Edek, but when it was taken or how he procured it is not known. Ephraim tells us that the rabbi was in hiding prior to the German invasion of Poland and that Edek would go to visit him, sitting with him and touching his arm. When he shares this image, it seems Ephraim misses the rabbi as much as Mr Retman did. I can see it's deeper than a spiritual admiration; it seems that Mr Retman provided Ephraim with a physical link to a lost world.

'And I know you have a very deep and full feeling of that world, in your heart and in your imagination, but this is physical. This is like he's touched the thing and then touched you. That's a very, very important thread,' I say, to which Ephraim nods, clutching the photos of the rabbi with both hands.

'The Rebbe said that he would see his parents again, they were in Siberia, but he had to say Tehillim [Psalm] 91,' reads the passage at the bottom of Mr Retman's Chevra Kadisha form, in Ephraim's emphatic block lettering. He has squeezed it in, alongside Edek's marriage details, and directly beneath a large inscription of his tattoo number. Now Ephraim is passing the form to David and David is examining it as though with fresh eyes, despite having undersigned it twelve years ago.

David concedes that he didn't know about his father's link to the rabbi or to this psalm, but that Edek would often quote from it. It was not until his father's funeral that David connected the dots: 'All our lives we kept hearing him say this particular thing. I never put two and two together as to where it was from or what it was. But it was actually Psalm 91.'

It is comforting to see the return of such an important story to its family. But I feel restless with questions as David continues to speak. I want us to talk about faith, about unwavering belief in a person or a force. I am troubled by the ad hoc blurring of fact and fiction, which is ironic given how drawn I am to metaphor, how heavily I lean on figurative frameworks in my work and in my wider life. As a writer I am a sniffer dog for symbols, I look for the parallels, for masks and the promise they cover.

Of course, we all do it, from the moment we can understand language. We bind ourselves to a story and then use it as a lesson, an ideological anchor, a compass. In fact, faith, this most common and confounding thing, is reliant on us trusting what we cannot know. Without this suspension of criticism, without a momentary dalliance not just with the improbable but with the impossible, we cannot reap its gifts. This, when I read it back, sounds like madness. And yet, I cannot fathom a sincere and fulsome life without it. A life without faith—faith in the unknown, or indeed the unknowable—feels like a wasteland, a desiccated march towards a solitary end.

Over the coming days, I turn to the stack of books Ephraim has lent me. I skim the pages I've tabbed, the bits that reveal my anxieties on questions of belief. There is so much there, and Wiesel addresses this dissonance head on: 'The Baal Shem's call was a call to subjectivity, to passionate involvement; the tales he told and those told about him appeal to the imagination rather than to reason. They try to prove that man is more than he appears to be and that he is capable of giving more than he appears to possess. To dissect them, therefore, is to diminish them. To judge them is to detach oneself and taint their candour—in so doing, one loses more than one could gain.'

At the same time, Wiesel insists on an ethical application of holy texts, acknowledges that 'the Torah itself can be either an elixir of life or a poison, depending on how it is used. If it is made into a weapon, it is the worst weapon of all.' He insists that a reading of any scripture must turn on courage and compassion and—at all costs—avoid dehumanisation.

Ephraim does not yet know this chapter's contents—as a rule, I write a draft and then read it to him. But sometimes he will intercept my process in mid-air, and so it is on this day. As though to remind me that he is not only interested in the candle-flicker of ye-olde Hasidism, Ephraim sends me a YouTube recording of thirteen-year-old Cormac Thompson singing 'Empty Chairs at Empty Tables' from *Les Misérables*.

The child carries, in a celestial falsetto, an elegy for fallen comrades. He is accompanied by a piano only, and the minor-key melody rises and falls with the melancholy of a Russian folk song, which of course is only a breath away from a *nigun*. If you trace the rise and fall of the notes with your hand, it outlines a steep hill that gradually takes you down to a valley, where you must linger for a moment. Here the wood smoke surrounds you, the distant clang of a cowbell, the shudder of trees, laden with snow. You can take a breath of the crisp Carpathian air before ascending. He sings of a 'grief that can't be spoken', of a 'pain that goes on and on'. The image of the empty chairs, of course, commemorates the friends who lit a flame, who gathered to envision a tomorrow that would never come. Perhaps it's not such a departure from what I know of Ephraim, either emotionally or imagistically.

I close the messaging app and continue scrolling the dishevelled catalogue of folders on my phone: 'Ephraim Finch Photos', 'conclusions/thoughts', 'Still to interview'; 'Finch books and movies'. In an album titled 'Ephraim Finch Saved', I find a photo I recently took of him. He is standing in the entryway to his house, the grove of books. It is not unusual for him to stop me in the doorway, text at the ready, sentence in mid-flight. '… just look at it, look at what he is saying,' he'll plead, then point to the marks on the page. In the photo, he is showing me Shakespeare's famous passage from *As You Like It*, the one that opens with 'all the world's a stage'. But I recall that on that day, Ephraim was not getting worked up about the iconic opening, the notion that we are 'merely players'. He wanted me to notice the way Shakespeare divides the 'acts' of our lives into seven ages, and specifically the sixth:

The sixth age shifts
Into the lean and slipper'd pantaloon,
With spectacles on nose and pouch on side;
His youthful hose, well sav'd, a world too wide
For his shrunk shank; and his big manly voice,
Turning again toward childish treble, pipes
And whistles in his sound.

Ephraim was saying, without saying, which is so often his way, his elusive, whimsical, indirect way: 'This is me now. This once-robust body is again feeling small in the world.' Standing in the hallway, I had to look away, concealing the arrow to my heart, my ache for his growing fragility.

Now, looking at this passage, my eye is riveted to its conclusion, the 'Last scene of all / That ends this strange eventful history / Is second childishness and mere oblivion / Sans teeth, sans eyes, sans taste, sans everything'. I want to ask Ephraim what he makes of this oblivion; I know he does not really accept that once the body goes, everything goes.

As though to conjure him, I look at the printed matter that has gathered since I started to chronicle Ephraim's life. Boxes of books, hundreds of pages of photocopied articles, forms, reports, interviews. Paper underlined and highlighted, all evidence of an attempt to grab something, retain it. One day all of this will be distant, perhaps disappeared. And yet, to leave the story untold is a soundless surrender I cannot bear. I open the topmost book, the chronicle of Elie Wiesel's early years. On the cover, Elie stares directly at the reader. His fingers are steepled in front of his chin, two of them resting on his lower lip. His hair is greying at the sides, but his skin is taut and golden. He was sixty-six when he sat down to pen this volume, had lived a thousand incarnations inside this one, and yet, was somehow still that quick-to-tears child from the Romanian shtetl.

The life and deathwork of Ephraim Finch

'Sometimes we must try because it is for nothing,' he writes in *All Rivers Run to the Sea*. 'Precisely because death awaits us in the end, we must live fully. Precisely because an event seems devoid of meaning, we must give it one. Precisely because the future eludes us, we must create it.'

12

Our darling and precious Simi. We understand that you are about to go to Poland, to visit Auschwitz. Remember that Zaidy and I, Sharona and Sascha and Chali, have walked in the same places as you're about to ... Apart from the very empathic guide there were only seven of us walking through the museum section. And there were only our footsteps in the heavy snow. We saw no signs of anyone else there the whole day. Frank's driver parked the small bus that Frank had leased for our trip. And then we walked through the 'Arbeit Macht Frei'. It was an extremely powerful place to be, we were all very solemn and aware of the souls that we had lost in that living hell. I found that I was almost struck dumb with emotion as we went around, nearly all separately, seeing the huge number of prostheses, glasses, shoes and hair. I just stood at that window imagining the mother plaiting her daughter's hair. Did she fear that it would be the last time? It was the blonde plait that kept me glued to the window ...

So begins a letter from Cas to her granddaughter Simi. It is dated July 2021 but speaks to events that took place some fifteen years earlier. 'Zaidy' is an affectionate form of *zeida*, which is 'grandfather'. 'Chali' is Michal, the youngest of the Finch children. Sharona is the middle child and Sascha is her husband.

The life and deathwork of Ephraim Finch

The family is travelling with Frank Dobia, a Melbourne-based friend of the Finches who is a child survivor of Buchenwald. He is their guide across Poland's death camps, synagogues, cemeteries and museums. Auschwitz is the central leg of their journey; they will also travel through the Czech Republic and Belarus, enlisting guides and helpers, meeting angels and monsters, and eventually answers, as they go.

I first interviewed Cas and Ephraim about this trip in early 2023, and we sat around their dining table with Sharona, who came full of energy for the story, a palpable wish to get it down and get it right. Ephraim had arranged stacks of photo albums along the table and Cas had the letter to Simi ready.

The evening, as it barrelled through me, felt both epic and unfinished. I wanted ten more such occasions, though the stories shared on this evening cracked something in me, revealed a brutal poetry I was not prepared for. And while it would be nice to say Ephraim's words brought repair, that's not exactly the truth. The stories of the Finches' trip to the death camps of Europe filled a fracture rather than healing it. Its volcanic churn, its laboured breath, still goes where I go.

It is almost November, and I am only now able to approach this part of the story. I revisit the transcripts from March, looking for footprints in the snow.

I begin the interview by asking how the notion for the trip came to be, who had the first dream. 'It was 2005 and Sascha and I were living in London. And it came about because my parents were going to come and visit us,' says Sharona. I ask if the younger generation pushed for the Holocaust-memorial component (their own 'March of the Living') or if the idea was mutual.

'Mutual. It just felt inevitable,' she replies, using that word that comes up time and again in the story of her father's life.

It may have been inevitable, but it was also complicated. A few weeks before dates were set, Sascha and Sharona called Ephraim to discuss the trip. Specifically, they wanted him to guide them through the camps. He had heard so many stories, borne witness to so much detail.

'And I said, "I don't want to go, because I've already been",' Ephraim says. At this point Cas interjects. The Finches rarely talk over each other, but in delivering this story they have woven and spliced their recall, a mounting song of urgency.

'No, you said, "I don't want to go back there",' Cas corrects.

I notice how loaded these memories are for them, how profoundly each person still shudders. But to me, Ephraim's specific wording seems of secondary importance. I am more interested in his blurring of what he has and has not lived through, his over-identification with the traumatic experiences of others.

'But Aba, you've never been there. What do you mean you don't want to go back?' Sharona recalls saying to him.

'I have been there,' he replies, 'I'm sort of there every day.' I am relieved to hear the 'sort of', to hear Ephraim making some logical separation from the experiences of the Holocaust survivors he knew and his own. Still, there is clearly a merging of stories, the thinnest membrane between worlds. At my fingertips is a printout of a previous conversation, with another interviewer. 'Everybody takes me there,' Ephraim says to the interviewer. 'Who's born in Częstochowa, who's born in Chęciny, who's born in Katowice ... I'm like blotting paper, I have Poland sucked into me.'

The family decides to leave in the first week of January 2006. When friends ask Ephraim why he is going to Poland in this freezing season, he replies, 'Well, two reasons—Cas is a teacher, she can only get this time off, and Poland does not deserve to be seen in colour as all the blood's been taken out of the place. I want to see it in black and white.'

The life and deathwork of Ephraim Finch

A journal entry from October 2005 reads, 'I know this idea sounds outlandish, but it has been nagging me for some time that I (we) would go to Poland ... I really want to find where the Chentshin Rebbe is buried in Sosnowiec. And while we are there, let's go to Rostok, Mecklenberg, my family's home in Altona Hamburg, Prague, Sighet—Elie Wiesel's home in the Carpathians, very mystical. I would like to write to Elie Wiesel to find his house so I can press my body against the wall under his childhood window and see if that little boy could see me. I wonder if Dodye Feig, the madmen and all those of his village would watch over us and smile to one another as we from Australia, a new generation of Jews, come to honour our past!'

Another entry, dated 31 October 2005, reads, 'Now reality kicks in. Booking flights, possible destinations, some ruled out because of access. I look at the atlas and see all the names of Jewish Europe. I would love to walk those shtetls, down a lane, visit the cemeteries, photo everything. I wish I could record the previous generation, their places, where they lived, worked and if lucky buried there.'

During our interview Ephraim tells me that several of his acquaintances had given their histories, folded bits of paper with place names into his hand, so that he may visit their lost times and places. This adds another layer to the mission; he isn't just going for the sake of the past. He is going for the sake of the present.

Their first stop, after flying into London, is Prague. After a couple of days settling in, they go to Terezín, which is sixty kilometres from the Czech capital. Everywhere they go—and they are mostly travelling overland, getting about in vans and taxis—Cas observes the countryside. She sketches the roadside huts and houses, the trees and monuments, even a funeral procession. They also talk to their drivers, collecting the unofficial histories of a place. On this occasion, travelling to Terezín, their driver explains that he can take them to the edge of the compound but cannot follow them inside. He has lost grandparents here. He waits while the Finches visit the various parts of the camp, including the museum that screens a ten-minute propaganda film made by the Nazis in 1944 to disguise the camp's true purpose.

In 1941 the Bohemian town of Terezín was renamed 'Theresienstadt' by the Germans and became a camp-ghetto, a holding pen for German, Austrian, Czech, Dutch, Danish and Belgian Jews who were eventually deported to Auschwitz. It was also a labour camp and a crucial prop in the infamous fiction performed for the rest of Europe, which was now beginning to question where the deportations were ending. The US Holocaust Memorial Museum summarises the deception as follows:

> *Succumbing to pressure following the deportation of Danish Jews to Theresienstadt, the Germans permitted the International Red Cross to visit in June 1944. It was all an elaborate hoax. The Germans intensified deportations from the ghetto shortly before the visit, and the ghetto itself was 'beautified'. Gardens were planted, houses painted, and barracks renovated. The Nazis staged social and cultural events for the visiting dignitaries. Once the visit was over, the Germans resumed deportations, which did not end until October 1944.*

'It was strange driving into this town of squares of parkland, which the Jews could not walk into,' writes Ephraim in his journal, which he has been lugging from place to place. It sits before us now, as we revisit this part of his life, the leather-bound colossus I was shown at the start of the year. His entries cover a lot of ground. He lists the names of bridges and churches, the distances between villages, what was on the breakfast buffet table at various hotels, being called to the Torah at various synagogues. One entry records the temperature in the Prague hotel room and the need to open windows. When I comment on this intense specificity, all three Finches recall Ephraim's fanatical scribbling.

The life and deathwork of Ephraim Finch

They remember Michal and Sharona asking him if it was really necessary. At the end of one day, about a week into the trip, he said, 'What did we do yesterday?' and they were not able to recall. 'Well then,' Ephraim had said in a rebuttal to their question, continuing to write.

'The main building is very white and austere, almost clinical,' one entry says of Theresienstadt. 'Then you go around the other exhibits, such as the drawings from children (average age eleven years), and poetry, which moved me to tears.' Theresienstadt is infamous for the art made inside its walls, a horrific cultural moment that existed along two planes. The Nazis brought artists into the camp as part of their hoax; at the same time, the inmates of the camp wrote, sang and painted in secret, as an act of resistance.

Christopher Latham, former violinist with the Australian Chamber Orchestra and the Australian War Memorial's first musical artist-in-residence, writes that 'the Nazis brought artistic talent to Terezín to create a showcase Jewish city, so as to fool the Red Cross and international observers'. Once the propaganda film had been recorded, the musicians were transported to Auschwitz.

The camp saw some fifteen thousand children pass through, ninety per cent of them eventually exterminated. But while they lived, many attended a school on the labour-camp grounds; an extraordinary number of them created art. The Jewish Museum in Prague houses 4387 children's drawings from the Terezín Ghetto, made between 1942 and 1944. The drawings in this collection are the fruits of Friedl Dicker-Brandeis's pedagogy, from the clandestine lessons she gave to the imprisoned children. Dicker-Brandeis not only provided a therapeutic outlet for them, she also archived their visions. She collected their works in two suitcases, which she managed to hide in the children's dormitories before she was transported to Auschwitz, in the autumn of 1944. After the war, the pictures were found and taken to Prague's Jewish Museum, where they have resided ever since.

The journal continues to track the Finches' remarkable day: 'We got back into our taxi and drove around the corner to a tenement building. We walked through to a courtyard. I was wondering where we were going to. At the back is a garage ... to the right is a workshop. We go into the room and to our surprise it is a hidden synagogue.' Cas recalls how 'prosaic' the entryway was; a fence lined with weeds and geraniums. When they pull up to the gate, the driver toots the horn and an elderly woman steps out, guiding them deep into the courtyard. Inside the small building—in fact, a single room—they see paintings of candles aflame, a large, encircled Star of David. The ceiling is domed, creating a theatrical effect; the walls are inscribed, in red paint, with prayers. The text is in ancient Hebrew, adding a layer of antiquity to this distinctly twentieth-century moment.

'But despite all this, we have not forgotten Your name. We beg You not to forget us,' reads an arc of text, quoting a daily prayer known as Tachanun. Below it, in smaller writing, the text reads, 'Hear, our King, our prayer, and from our foes rescue us. Hear, our King, our prayer, and from every distress and woe rescue us.'

This building is one of several 'secret synagogues' of Terezín, where Jews gathered when they could during the German occupation. Formerly a storage space, it was converted by a German Jew called Artur (Asher) Berlinger. Berlinger was an artist who perished at Auschwitz in 1944, and who used his last years to provide a religious space for the inmates of the Theresienstadt Ghetto.

Ephraim's entry ends on these words: 'The synagogue was damaged by the flood in 2002 but is still okay above the waterline'. It is tempting to read this as metaphor, a mosaic of signals from the past about our fragility and our resilience both. But to place it on the metaphoric plane, to attach too fondly to symbol is a risky endeavour. It threatens to efface the facts on the ground, the very real lives that were terminated right in this place, the blood—not paint—that stained this very earth.

The life and deathwork of Ephraim Finch

When they return to Prague they visit the Altneuschul (Old-New Synagogue), which is Europe's oldest active synagogue. The building, completed in 1270, is bound up in Eastern European lore, specifically the tale of the Golem, a mythical creature said to reside in the attic above the shul. In fact, this is no ordinary attic. It is a *genizah*, a temporary storage area for damaged or worn-out religious texts, Hebrew books, anything containing the name of God. Here, the books sleep until it's time for them to be interred in the *shaimos*, the special cemetery plot reserved for sacred objects.

I don't know much about the Golem prior to this evening's conversation, and in trying to establish the narrative basics I am once again met with Ephraim's mystic prism.

'The Maharal made the Golem from clay,' he says. 'He put God's name on the forehead. And the Golem couldn't speak but he could carry out what the rabbi was telling him to do.' The Maharal is another name for Judah Loew ben Bezalel, the late sixteenth-century Rabbi of Prague, whose seat remains in the synagogue, cordoned off by a rope. I ask Ephraim what the Golem represents to him.

'When you come to Prague ... when you come through at night, it's a mystical place,' he says, once again, ambiguously. 'And he would go out at night, not the daytime.'

'And he made everyone so afraid,' Cas adds. I wait for more clarification; I still don't have a sense of whether the Golem is a hero or a villain.

'Well, he made them afraid and stopped them attacking the Jews,' Ephraim says, resolving my question. 'The blood libels were so bad, around Passover and Easter, and when a Christian child would disappear, the Jews were blamed for taking the child's blood,' he adds. And so the Golem was created to protect; a malleable giant, brought to life by incantation, to fight accusations of blood libel. When I read about the Golem later, I learn that he has been a guardian of imperilled Jewish communities across the centuries. In the words of the Jewish Museum of Berlin, the Golem 'symbolizes each era's dreaded dangers and hopes for redemption'.

The other feature of the Golem is its capacity to go rogue. Like dybbuks of any culture, like a sorcerer's apprentice, he speaks to an ancient human anxiety: that of a creation turning on its creator. This is supposedly what led Rabbi Loew to eventually destroy him and lock his remains in the attic of the synagogue. Today, the attic is off-limits to the public and apocrypha surrounds those who have dared to enter.

But Ephraim could not have gone to Prague without visiting the Maharal's cordoned seat, without gazing at the Altneuschul attic. Although Prague was a stepping stone to visiting the camps, Ephraim centres it in his account. The first thing he chronicles is walking the Charles Bridge, Prague's foremost landmark. The medieval bridge, which connects the Old Town to Prague Castle, is punctuated by thirty statues of saints. It also features a black metal statue of Jesus on the crucifix, his head encircled by gold Hebrew letters. The letters, installed in 1696, spell '*Kadosh, Kadosh, Kadosh, Adonai Tzva'ot*' ('Holy, Holy, Holy is the Lord of Hosts'), taken from a central Jewish prayer, the Kedushah. Jewish community leader Elias Backoffen was forced to pay for the installation of the gold-plated Hebrew letters as a punishment for alleged blasphemy, compounding the humiliation to the city's Jews.

'You could imagine the Jews walking this sinister, dark bridge,' Ephraim writes, lamenting how it must have felt for them to 'acknowledge the crucifix' every time they crossed the bridge. Now he is not dealing in abstractions; he is not conjuring a fantastical creature. Ephraim is setting the tone for what is to come, for the way that history will burst through mist, the way that all the Finches on this trip will need to forge an inner giant, to keep them safe and sane in the dark night ahead.

After Prague the family drive to Kraków. There they visit Oskar Schindler's factory, which each of them has seen in *Schindler's List*. Although they have just been to Theresienstadt, something about the familiar visual cues—Schindler's office, the factory floor—pushes the moment into their bodies.

'I'm trying to put an unfused thought into words,' says Sharona, recalling the moment, her eyes closed, her thumb and forefinger pinching together. 'It was like, my God, we are really here. This is real.'

In Kraków, their old friend and tour guide Frank Dobia—who walked out the gates of Buchenwald with Elie Wiesel, who lost his parents and two siblings at Treblinka, who has spent years restoring the desecrated Jewish cemeteries of Poland, a lifetime collecting and preserving lost-world Jewish memorabilia—has a watershed experience. At the Eden Hotel, where he and the Finches are staying, Frank finds himself at a long, crowded trestle table one night after dinner. The guests are 'benching', singing a cycle of blessings for the meal they have just shared. Although he has not sung the prayers since he was fourteen, is not even sure he remembers, something pushes Frank to sing. Something in the familiar childhood setting, in the Polish land itself, perhaps in the captive audience (it is Shabbat, and no one is rushing anywhere) unlocks him. And he sings this song, followed by a *nigun* from his perished Dobrzyn ancestors, drawing from a well he had taken for dry.

This story mirrors one from David Retman, about his father Edek's return to Poland. It was mid-2006 and Edek was by then frail, less mobile. At home he had been using a walking stick and when the family (he, his two sons, his wife Dora) arrived at the airport, he requested the use of a wheelchair.

'And we get to Poland, suddenly, the stick goes under his arm and he's off and running. It was like he just got a new lease on life. We couldn't work it out,' says David, astonished. 'I remember we went walking that afternoon. He wasn't using the stick. He was walking, you know? It was almost like something just clicked inside, and said, "Back to our childhood!"'

It feels vital to write these exultant moments as I am weaving the horrors of the wider story. It is especially powerful to imagine that for some survivors, returning to the land of loss is not automatically traumatic; that, in fact, it can be the opposite. I am looking for these glimpses of redemption, transient sunshowers of grace upon a scorched earth. Sometimes they come clear, and sometimes they are flickering, elusive.

In some cases, such as the photos of the Ghetto Heroes Square in Kraków, I find myself unable to extricate the beauty from the pain.

As the Finches are describing their time in Kraków, Cas passes around a photo of this memorial space. It is a town square, covered in snow, interrupted only by a grid of ordinary house chairs, spaced a few metres apart. Because it is winter, the seats are covered in snow too, creating an eerie tranquillity, as though the snow is a blanket keeping them warm for the night, for the season. Formerly known as Plac Zgody, the square became part of the Kraków Ghetto in 1941 and referred to as the *Umschlagplatz* ('collection point') by the Nazis. Over the course of two years, as waves of Jews were made to assemble in the square, as they passed through the ghetto and onto Płaszów or Auschwitz, the area collected their everyday articles—not just chairs but suitcases, tables, bundles of clothes and precious heirlooms. It became a repository of abandoned things.

In 2006 the installation received a Special Mention in the European Prize for Urban Public Space, an initiative of the Centre of Contemporary Culture of Barcelona. In awarding the commendation, the centre describes the project that came six decades later to memorialise this period:

Instead of installing a singular monument, the intervention set out to use the square itself as a channel for passing on the memory. And so it was deliberately conceived as a poetic container which transformed the place into a sign of the past.

As the authors of the project explain, it was impossible to talk about that tragedy literally. Written documents, photographs and direct testimonies of the survivors describe the history of the Ghetto as a succession of removals. In one photograph we can see a line of children filing along the pavement, each carrying a chair on his head. In another a little girl carries her bundle between the legs of a chair with the back sticking up. The choice, then, was to tell the story of the place through the configuration of the urban space itself...

As we pass the photo around, we talk about the power of such an offering. A statement of truth in the face of denial, a claim of responsibility decades down the track. Woven through this is our anguish for the dashed hope—these people's realisation that things were so much worse than they had fathomed. We imagine what it must have been like for these Jewish people of Kraków to see their fellow humans turn on them like this. The artists behind this installation were wise in acknowledging the limits of language. Their statement is clear: some betrayal is so great, no plaque or pamphlet can do it justice. The chairs are dark, their bronze spines stark against the soft white snow. 'A poetic container' is a beautiful gesture, perhaps the only possible one.

Sharona grabs her phone and scrolls through her emails until she finds the exact date. Then she reads out loud to us: 'We visited Auschwitz today. 12 January 2006'.

Ephraim picks up the narration: 'As we walked through the gates, I kept on looking back because there was no one else there with us. And I felt ... I wanted to make sure the gates didn't close.' These chilling words leave all of us silent for a time.

Sharona collects the thread again: 'It was the most intense, devoid sensation being there. And it was the perfect time to visit because it's just so incomprehensible how anyone could survive living in those conditions in that weather. Here we were with socks and waterproof shoes, and coats and beanies. But the sense of being there, it was like a deafening silence. Nothing was living there. No birds …'

'… surrounded by death, death,' Cas says, layering on Sharona's words like snow.

'It was death. That physical feeling of nothing … It didn't even feel like a spirit was there. It was like nothing wanted to have anything to do with that space,' Sharona says.

The family wanders amidst the bunkers and barracks. The snow is ankle-high and crackles beneath their boots as their eyes take in gallows, watchtowers, the Camp Orchestra Site, the 'Black Wall' Execution Site. They pass a building labelled on the map as 'Medical Experiments', each of them filling the hollow space with their own imaginings. For hours they don't see another being. There are no official tour guides and so they walk unaccompanied, cutting through the sleet, sheltering in each other's gaze when the silence grows too strong. It's minus twenty-three degrees Celsius.

'And because we had the snow clouds over us, when the trains were blowing their whistles down further, it felt like the train was coming into Auschwitz,' Ephraim says. At this point, he is also hearing the bark of German Shepherds.

In the wandering, they find themselves at a museum building, and a guide appears. Cas and Ephraim peel off to one area, looking at piles of glasses, mounds of shoes, when they hear a scream. It's Sharona, in front of a display cabinet housing suitcases.

'Aba! Aba!' she is calling, her pitch high, unstable.

She is pointing at a suitcase that is slightly separated from the others, leaning on the front of the pile. She is shaking. When Ephraim and Cas approach, they read the inscription, in white paint, on the brown leather: 'L. BERMANN. 26.12.1886. No. 2019. HAMBURG. VI/11.42.'

They know they are not allowed to take photos, but Cas asks the museum attendant anyway. I know the attendant said yes, because Cas is holding the photo as we speak.

'And she grabbed our hands,' Cas tells me, 'and she said, "This case has been waiting for you".'

Reeling, the family lumbers across the camp to the extermination blocks of Birkenau. As they are scraping a path through the snow, they do not talk about the suitcase, but each of them is imagining possibilities. Ephraim's gut is telling him that none of this is a coincidence, that he is being shown his past. He feels the inklings of new ghosts in him, a rush of questions that might well defeat him, especially now that Nana Behrmann is no longer around. He continues to trudge through the snow, suddenly deafening in its crystalline crunch, a new past strapped to his back, heavy and unyielding.

Beyond the crematoria, they stop at a frozen pond. Recounting this, Ephraim holds up a photo of a clearing, rows of dark thin trees. Then of four black marble gravestones, marking the bodies that had been cremated and submerged in this very pond.

'When we got there, Frank went straight up to the headstones and started saying kaddish,' Ephraim says. Normally chanted at funerals, the communal prayer is recited as a call and response. Traditionally, it requires a quorum of ten adult Jews. Still, Frank goes ahead and those by his side answer him, their voices trailing his. They agree—in a silent pact—that on this occasion they will be forgiven for breaking with tradition.

'And we were standing in a desert of snow,' Ephraim says. 'I had to go there because I was told so much by so many people. I had to go there so I could come back with the knowledge.'

'Darling, I felt full of awe for all our people who were murdered there. I felt that we all have a huge responsibility to always be aware of being alive, to live out our passions and create our own story when so many had that privilege taken from them simply because they were Jews.' So continues Cas's letter to Simi, who is eighteen years old, on the cusp of seeing these things for herself.

I ask how the evenings felt after days like these, how each of them processed such immensity.

'Well, that's it,' says Cas. 'At the end of the days we used to just say a simple goodnight and go. Nobody said anything.'

They keep moving.

'When we got to Treblinka, we were the only ones there. Our footprints were the only ones in the snow,' says Ephraim of the next leg. Treblinka is where Sascha's paternal family perished, his grandmother being the sole survivor, who eventually made her way out of Europe to settle in Shepparton, Victoria. Recalling the day trip to Treblinka, Ephraim says, 'It's bloody hard to find'. The Finches and Frank Dobia are navigating their way through forest, guided only by a row of train sleepers that lead into the camp. In fact, the 'sleepers' are concrete slabs that commemorate the trains that delivered people to the camp. Unlike the Auschwitz grounds that they have just visited, Treblinka has no original buildings. There are no crematoria or gas chambers, though of course both once existed here. When the Finches arrive in the winter of 2006, they are met with a clearing in a forest, marked only with paved paths and various memorials for those who died here between 1941 and 1944.

Inside the forest of birches and moss, there is a forest of stone. There is a row of eleven stones, listing the countries from which inmates were brought. Other stones mark the undressing areas. The central monument, built on a hill, is made of large granite blocks. Their warm sandy colour resembles the Wailing Wall, but unlike the wall, it has a crack down the middle. In front of it sits a smaller rock, inscribed with 'Never Again' in seven languages. It is surrounded by seventeen thousand pieces of quarry stones, jagged and varying in size.

The life and deathwork of Ephraim Finch

The Finches take a photo in front of this structure, all of them bunched together, eyes heavy under their winter hats. Ephraim's beard, longer and darker than it is now, is billowing in the breeze. Right behind the family, at the back of the granite monument, is a rectangular hollow filled with black basalt. It is a memorial of the crematorium, which the Treblinka Museum describes, hauntingly, as 'forming irregular clots and icicles'.

'And you can see hoofmarks from the deer,' says Ephraim, ever-observant of the natural world, of what continues.

'So, it's kind of wild?' I ask.

'Wild yet …'

'Dead,' Sharona and Cas answer together.

The women speak of a 'continuation of flatness'. Both agree that Auschwitz was 'as low as it could go', that 'everything from there on was a little higher'.

Interview transcript, 13 March 2023

Katia: 'Did you have your questions answered? You know, when you went there … what you wanted to know about it? Did you see what you wanted to see?'

Sharona: 'I think it was more than that. I think it was a feeling and a sense rather than having word questions answered.'

Katia: 'Right. You touched the thing that you had, somewhere in you, hoped to touch even though it was so, so dark.'

Sharona: 'Exactly.'

It feels painful to abbreviate any of this accounting, to truncate even one stretch of this trip. Reductiveness, the fact that I am actively omitting details (no need for modifiers here, they are all 'crucial'), feels physically unbearable. Writing the stories in a contracted fashion feels dangerous. And yet, there is no way to say it all, to memorialise all the memorialising.

So, a brutally reduced summary. After Treblinka the family travels to Belarus, where they visit the childhood home of Sascha's paternal ancestors. There, they encounter a past that has been largely extinguished. Still, they find the house where his grandfather was born; they stand at the memorial in his childhood village of Kletsk, and with their sheer presence, they say '*hineni*', the ancient Hebrew phrase meaning 'I am here'. The memorial honours the victims of a massacre that took four thousand Jewish lives in one day, on 30 October 1941. Sharona passes me a photo of the memorial plaque and I read its Russian text out loud, a shudder going through me. '*Yama*', the word for 'pit', goes to my core with its familiarity, its banality turned sinister.

After visiting Sascha's grandmother's hometown of Wysokie, then Minsk, the family leave Belarus. Via Warsaw, they head to Hamburg, where they know Ephraim's ancestors owned a hotel. They locate the Hotel Behrmann, in the centre of town, and show up at reception. Ephraim tells the receptionist that he is a descendent of the original owners. Do they have any history, any names? No, says the receptionist, indifferent. The sadness I see in Ephraim as he recalls that indifference is palpable, a dark mist entering the room that will not exit no matter how many windows we open.

In Hamburg Ephraim begins to really process what he saw in that museum cabinet, the possibility that it was his paternal ancestor's name he just glimpsed. He is aware that the spelling on the suitcase is 'Bermann', not 'Behrmann', but he also knows, from decades of compiling personal history forms at the Chevra, how flimsy spelling is in times of war and internment. He has heard too many instances of border guards writing names as they hear them, spellings morphing according to the dialect of a given location.

He takes his mind back to Summer Hill, to the conversation above the butcher shop, his father saying, 'You know, son, my mother's got Jewish blood.' He recalls Nana's refusal to talk further, her eerie statement that if there were European-Jewish relatives, 'they lived happily ever after'. Then a new memory surfaces. He recalls asking Nana why she never told him, how she could have spent years watching him and Cas circling the mountain of Judaism and not say anything.

'You were doing such a good job by yourself, I didn't want to disturb you,' she replied calmly, a calm Ephraim has never quite understood.

After Hamburg, the family flies to London and then home. The trip, so vast in its breadth and depth, has taken just eighteen days. For better or worse, the minute they get back, everyone is flung into their daily responsibilities, and there is not much time to unpack the stories. Then, one night, a few months after their return, Ephraim is at work when he receives a call from Cas. She tells him to come home, it's urgent. When he walks into the house he sees Cas at the television, and without taking her eyes off the screen she is waving him over.

On the screen, he sees Oprah Winfrey walking though Auschwitz in the snow, tracing his very steps. Next to Oprah is Elie Wiesel, showing her the grounds on which over a million people perished.

'The immensity of the place. It's a universe,' Wiesel says slowly, in his rich Carpathian diction. 'I come here and I try to see the invisible and try to hear the inaudible.'

Oprah asks him if he believes the ground there speaks, carries the voices of the dead.

'Absolutely,' he replies. 'I think the souls are here. I think that they listen, they cry, they warn. Look, this is the largest cemetery in recorded history, and what do you see? Nothing.'

Ephraim finds the discovery of this interview painful but heartening. To have his hero visit this place, to see him walking the same ground, articulating the past, brings Ephraim deep comfort. Then he learns that Elie was there in early 2006, either just before or just after he and Cas and the children. They missed each other by a few days, by a heartbeat.

It seems fitting that the postscript to this epic journey involves Elie Wiesel, Ephraim's dearest guide into a vanished world, his bard of ineffable sorrows. Having immersed myself in these transcripts for even a few months, I can see how the stories could make you mad, how easy it is to lose your footing in such abject darkness.

I am starting to understand why this chapter took me eight months to begin, why I had to walk the shore of it, multiple times, before diving in. I know I'm not physically going to the death camps of Europe, and to the best of my knowledge, my immediate family was not interned in the places Ephraim visited. But I also know—from growing up in the anti-Semitic, locked coolroom of the Soviet Union—the sensation of being hated, hunted, for my heritage.

In my cells is a memory not just of a war, the 'Final Solution' of which was the complete eradication of Jews from our planet. It is older than that, and wider. My epigenetic map features the hillocks of Ukraine that saw my maternal ancestors burnt alive in their hut after a neighbour dobbed them into the authorities during a pogrom. It tracks a great-uncle bolting across the tundra after ten years in a Siberian labour camp. I know *yama*, the Russian word for 'pit', as well as I know the word for 'bread' and 'mother' and 'house'. I hear the pejorative version of 'Jew', as it is said in Russian, and every time it is a metallic prison door slamming loud and hard in my ear.

Maybe Ephraim is not mad after all, or maybe I am only as mad as he is. Because I do not want to 'go back there' either.

I do not want to go back there, and yet, in the year of writing this story, the world will show me, and Ephraim, and millions of Jews worldwide, that we are not as far out of the woods as we'd imagined. The largest massacre of Jews since these camps shut, the subsequent warfare, the activation of an ancient wound between the peoples of the Middle East. All these things—while uniquely of this moment—will transform a distant European nightmare into a sudden, global reality.

The life and deathwork of Ephraim Finch

The day I finish writing this chapter, I drop in on Ephraim. He is standing at his dining table of a late afternoon. The late-spring sun is streaming in and over him. He is hunched over his daily prayer book. He cannot see me, doesn't know that I've arrived. Then he looks up, his eyes glazed with tears.

'We're going to need all the prayers we can get right now, my dear girl,' he says. And I feel his words in my bones. The gates aren't closed yet, but we can hear them swinging.

13

'See if you can recognise this fella,' Ephraim says to me, turning up the car stereo. Normally, it is me who drives us on our excursions; to visit the cemetery or the home of the bereaved. But this morning—for reasons he will not explain—Ephraim insists on driving. Akubra, labourer's boots, blazer, pale blue shirt; Ephraim is in his usual attire, but today there is extra fire in him. Refusing the GPS, he is holding and slapping the wheel like he is driving a troika through the Russian countryside.

There is a grind of distorted guitar, then an acoustic strum. A brush drum ushers in the vocals. I instantly know this—this sublimated rage, this lyric bawl—as Nick Cave. He is singing of a train departing, of a butcher's floor, of broken little hearts. Behind him, a choir fills his sails with a gospel wind.

Both Ephraim and I are properly, classically mad by now, a month into the war in Gaza. No one is sleeping. The ground slides beneath our feet like a conveyer belt. Short-term memory shredded, we fixate on the news and the vitriolic megaphones of social media. Today marks thirty days since the massacres in southern Israel, since the brutal deaths of some 1200 Israeli civilians and the disappearance of more than 240 Israeli hostages into a terrorist no-man's-land. Meanwhile, the bodies of Palestinian civilians caught in the crossfire are mounting. They are in their thousands and almost half of them are children. Like many in our midst, Ephraim and I are eternally heartsick.

Thirty days marks *shloshim*, a key moment in the year of Jewish mourning. After *shiva*, the first seven days of mourning, many restrictions are lifted. Mourners may leave their home, return to work, study Torah, attend a *bris* or a bar mitzvah and the ceremonial part of a wedding. In other words, there is something of a return to the world. However, it is a graduated return, because until *shloshim*, one cannot have a haircut or shave, one cannot travel for pleasure, attend dinner parties or concerts, or listen to music.

The world is aflame. There is no end in sight to the bloodshed. And our mourning, which—even in a peaceful setting—is crucial, has not been given due space. We are too keyed up to make the necessary journey inwards, to go slow, to nurse our pain. Ephraim, like most diaspora Jews I know, is breathlessly tracking the rise in global anti-Semitism, lost in a maze of danger old and new. I can see that alongside the loss of lives on both sides of the fence, the brutal scar of terrorism, the existential threat to Israel, it is this—this resurgence in aggressive and globally articulated hatred of Jews—that has cracked Ephraim down the middle.

'I have never seen anti-Semitism like that in Australia,' he says. 'Immediately after Israel has suffered the worst tragedy since the Holocaust, the world flipped.' He rounds a corner out of our neighbourhood and accelerates onto the freeway. 'O Children' has mounted behind him, and Nick Cave's choir, orchestral, swollen, backs his lament.

We talk about my child's Jewish school excusing the kids from wearing uniform because it makes them visible targets for violence. We shudder, in a simultaneous breath, at the menacing chants that echoed off the steps of the Sydney Opera House, just three days after the Hamas attacks. I tell Ephraim about the Sikh gentleman at my local grocery store who let me weep openly at the counter this week and who asked me, rhetorically, 'How much hatred can the world stand?' as I paid for my shopping. Ephraim counters with a story about one of his doctors, a stranger with a 'beautiful soft nature'. This week they talked about his being a funeral director his whole life, what it meant for him to care for the dead. Just as he is about to elaborate, a familiar melody, three piano chords, ascend from the stereo. It is the introduction to 'Into My Arms' and it hushes us. We know, without needing to say, that this is the song for this moment, for this thirtieth day of horror.

'I don't believe in an interventionist God / And I know, darling, that you do,' sings Cave. At the second line, Ephraim joins in. By the time Cave is at the chorus, we are both singing, singing unselfconsciously and with dark joy, like we are crying, like we are clinging and not letting go, side by side in the same tiny boat on a nameless sea.

We are so caught up that Ephraim realises he is lost. In a few minutes he will figure out that we are just around the corner, that he is closer than he knows, that his instinct is serving him well. But right now, he is disoriented and somewhat frustrated at his fading muscle memory.

'Okay, where am I going? Come on, find it, Finch,' he commands, willing himself on.

'It seems fitting that I'm going there today to talk to them,' he says to me. We are driving to visit Yvonne and Felix Sher, whose son Greg died in combat in Afghanistan. It has been fourteen years since the Shers buried their thirty-year-old son.

Ephraim has often told me about Greg's funeral, which was not only a state ceremony, but also one of the first at the new cemetery in Lyndhurst. It would be one of Ephraim's last.

I pull out my phone to enlist the help of a map but am myself disoriented by a white butterfly landing on our windscreen. It hovers and hovers, it won't leave. For a moment, my fatigued brain can't discern which side of the glass it's on. Eventually, after it has drawn a misshapen circle in front of Ephraim's face, the butterfly departs, off the surface of the car and into the flurry of traffic.

'And I don't believe in the existence of angels / But looking at you I wonder if that's true,' continues Cave. Ephraim smiles at the ephemeral visitor. And once again, we cannot help but resume the singing, even though we are lost, even though there is no clear way through this looping, heavily forested neighbourhood. We cross over train tracks. Ephraim looks for a bridge.

'You're gonna have to go with me, girl,' he says after a while.

'Always. That's what I signed up for,' I reply, without hesitation.

'January 5th, 2009. Received a phone call from Rabbi P Heilbrunn that a young Jewish soldier had been killed in Afghanistan on the 4/1/2009, 8th Tevet 5769. On the following day there was a meeting in the parents' home.' So opens Ephraim's journal entry on Greg Sher. It is this meeting that Ephraim recalls most vividly when we sit with Yvonne and Felix in the very same home a decade-and-a-half later. Although he did not know the family previously, he recalls how honoured he felt that 'they brought me into the place. Talked to me. And I talked to the soldiers.'

On this day, Felix describes feeling 'mentally destroyed'. Two nights earlier, he and Yvonne were away in regional Victoria when, in his sleep, he heard the hotel phone ring. He opened his eyes and saw that it was three in the morning. Deciding that it was someone calling the wrong number, he ignored it. But the phone kept ringing.

'And it was my youngest son, Barry. He said, "It's Greg".'

Barry told his father that Greg had been hit by a rocket while on a mission in Afghanistan. He said that he couldn't really talk, that he just needed his parents to come home immediately. Then Felix took the impossible step of sharing Barry's words with Yvonne. As he tells it, I think about the singular void of such a moment, how unfathomable it is for those who have not known it from the inside. I look across at Yvonne, who is listening with her head bowed, her hand over her mouth. Both she and Felix have been incredibly gracious hosts, welcoming Ephraim with an embrace on arrival, showing us around their home, smiling, chatty. But in this moment, they are elsewhere, as Felix recalls his wife's 'gasp of shock' filling the hotel room.

Somehow, they manage to pack their things, check out of the hotel and drive home. When they arrive, they find the house full. There is Steven, who is a mere seventeen months older than Greg. Steven was the first to receive the news of his brother's death, when the military knocked on the door a few hours earlier. There is Barry, Greg's younger brother by five years, and Barry's partner. There is Greg's partner and her parents. Alongside the distraught family, Yvonne and Felix are met with a living room full of strangers: the regimental sergeant major, a Catholic priest, a family liaison member from the military.

When they query the presence of the Catholic priest, they learn that the ADF had attempted to contact their Jewish liaison, a Modern Orthodox rabbi based in Melbourne, but he was unreachable by phone. Subsequently, they went to his house, also knocking on the door. Then, when this failed (the rabbi was in fact overseas at the time), they went to the rabbi's synagogue and rattled the gate.

'In the middle of the night?' I ask, incredulous at this antiquated image.

'Yes. Because they knew that some priests sleep in the church. So they thought maybe the rabbi sleeps in the shul,' Yvonne explains. When there was no response, they called the padre. Of course, he was not of the Shers' faith. But the army personnel decided that something was better than nothing. It was unthinkable that they should come to the home of bereaved parents without chaplaincy support.

We are sitting in the Shers' sunny, spacious front room. I'm trying to picture it full of bodies, heavy faces. A shelf to my left holds a folded flag, Greg's beret, his medals. Around the corner is a photo of the three adult sons together, smiling with the joy of being on holiday. Greg is at the front of the trio, his green eyes radiating, his wide shoulders giving him an air of confidence.

My attention returns to the story, which Felix and Yvonne take turns unspooling, their soft voices enlivened by their melodic South African accents.

The morning of the military's visit, Felix is most concerned with bringing Greg's body home. Through the fog of grief, he manages to find a military chaplain in Sydney who will liaise with the ADF. He explains—to the personnel on the ground in Afghanistan—that being Jews, the Shers need to bury as quickly as possible. Mercifully, they are told that Greg will be home in five days.

It is at this juncture that Ephraim comes on board. He speaks to them many times in the course of the week, as Greg's body is collected from the site of death in Oruzgan Province, loaded onto a RAAF C-17 Globe Master aeroplane and accompanied home by a fellow soldier.

'They had a fellow sitting with him,' Felix recalls. 'And when he was actually killed, they didn't leave him alone for a minute. They all took turns sitting with him.'

Gregory Michael Sher joined the Australian Army in 1998 as an army reserve infantryman. In 2002 he deployed to East Timor, to serve in the peace-keeping mission. For his service in East Timor, he would receive the Australian Active Service Medal, the UN Transitional Authority in East Timor Medal and the Infantry Combat Badge. In 2004 he gained entry into the Special Forces, joining the 1st Commando Regiment.

In November 2008 Greg flew to Afghanistan as part of Operation Slipper, to serve in its Reconstruction Taskforce, which had been there since 2006. On the day of the attack, he was stationed at a forward-operational patrol base near Tarin Kowt. His company was due to go on a mission that evening but was thwarted by inclement weather. That afternoon, Taliban fighters shot two rockets, one of which fell short of their target. The second rocket went through a wall and a container full of water before hitting Greg, who was standing on the other side.

Felix does not go into more detail about what happened. He does, however, describe the final conversation he and Yvonne had with their son.

'He phoned us on Christmas Eve from a satellite phone,' Felix says. Greg told them that the army had provided a beautiful Christmas lunch, amazed at what they could put on in the desert. The family ended the conversation, not knowing it would be their last.

By the time Greg Sher's body arrives at Melbourne International Airport, Ephraim has made two trips there with ADF personnel to see exactly where the RAAF transport plane will touch down. It is to arrive at an undisclosed hangar and Ephraim wants to ensure that the Chevra aligns with this perfectly.

When the plane arrives, the family is invited to step inside and see Greg's coffin. They are left alone for a time. Then Ephraim and Rabbi Heilbrunn (who will officiate at the funeral) join them and Felix reads three short stories from *A Book of Jewish Thoughts*, published in 1941 by Dr Joseph H. Hertz. Each of the stories—mythic vignettes in the style Ephraim adores—speaks to death, to untimely loss, to humans grappling with the incomprehensible. Felix has had this book since his own military service in 1976, when he fought in the Angolan War.

When the family is ready, the coffin is removed from the plane, on the shoulders of soldiers. A member of the unit plays the bagpipes to accompany the procession to the hangar, where a military service takes place. As part of this service Greg is awarded the Afghanistan Campaign Medal, the NATO Medal with ISAF Clasp, the Australian Defence Medal and the Returned from Active Service Badge. Rabbi Heilbrunn, who has known the family since

The life and deathwork of Ephraim Finch

Greg was a boy, sings 'El Maleh Rachamim', his plaintive voice rising through the high-ceilinged hangar.

Ephraim's journal recalls 'The Last Post' being played. Reading this back, I can hear the melancholy notes of the bugle drawing out the pitiful heart of war. Then, 'As his mates peeled off after carrying the coffin, they congregated at the fence and cried,' Ephraim writes. 'We were all crying,' he says, before describing the exigency of getting to the Coroners Court as quickly as possible, because it was the eve of Shabbat.

'When we arrived at the court I started to stir everyone ... we were in a hurry. The coroner came out to see me and said, "Don't worry, Ephraim, everything is organised".' By this the coroner meant that the CT scan and dental x-rays would be performed immediately. Greg would be released to the care of the Chevra Kadisha late that afternoon.

Felix fleshes out this memory, his voice quavering for the first time in our conversation.

'I said to Ephraim, "I want to come to the Chevra and I want to see him".' Felix wanted to see his son, but on the condition that 'his face wasn't an issue'. Ephraim assured him that his son's beautiful face was whole, before accompanying him into the *tahara* room.

'And I saw his face and it was a bit dirty,' says Felix to us now.

'And you cleaned it off,' adds Ephraim. This is the moment that Ephraim has described to me over and over. While he recalls the state funeral, the elaborate ceremony that latticed into the Jewish burial rites, it is this moment that catches him still: a father tenderly wiping dried mud off his son's face. Then, the mother entering, kissing her son's forehead for the final time.

On Sunday 11 January, more than three thousand people attend the state funeral of Greg Sher. The mourners include prime minister Kevin Rudd, future prime minister Julia Gillard, military dignitaries. At the time, Lyndhurst is a brand-new cemetery

(Felix recalls it as 'just a field, or in our home language, a *veldt*'), with no chapel or any other infrastructure. It is an unbearably hot day and the military have set up water stations. The coffin, topped by the Australian flag, Greg's green beret and medals, is driven atop a gun carriage. The procession, which is accompanied by the beating of a drum, includes three contingents: the military, fellow members of the Community Security Group, and family and friends. A guard of honour borders the procession.

Felix recalls saying kaddish in a daze. There is Ephraim cutting Felix's shirt according to mourning custom, then the two men are at the grave, shovelling soil alongside military generals and the Australian prime minister. Many people—including Kevin Rudd, Rabbi Heilbrunn, family and friends—speak at length. The rabbi who had taught Greg for his bar mitzvah sprinkles soil from Jerusalem into the grave. The heat grows so intense that a couple of people faint. At the end of this long, difficult day, the family is escorted home.

As they sit *shiva*, they notice how exhausted they are. Droves of people pass through the house every day, bringing food, bustling about. When the week of *shiva* is over, the house grows quiet.

'When you finish *shiva* you feel a weight off you,' says Ephraim. 'Because you go back to living. Sort of living.' Of course, he doesn't mean the world returns to normal, rather that the world—in its own indifferent way—keeps turning. Yvonne confirms this with her memory of those terrible days: 'After *shiva*, I went to the shop and the world had carried on! I thought, "Oh my God! Everybody is out and about like normal!" That was a shock to me,' she says, capturing the marriage of the real and the unreal that defines the period immediately after loss.

Felix and Yvonne struggle for many years after Greg's death, putting one foot in front of the other, pulled along by the momentum of life, by their surviving children and their growing families. They miss their happy-go-lucky son, their quiet boy who preferred listening to talking. After Greg's passing, Felix takes a good look at his son's bookshelf, finding texts on psychology, astronomy, philosophy. He wonders about some of the actions Greg took immediately before leaving for Afghanistan; he cleared out his room, he grew a beard, he 'packed all his things as if he was never coming back'.

'We were here physically but not mentally,' says Felix.

'We were ... there's a word in Afrikaans but I don't know how to say it in English,' adds Yvonne. She thinks for a moment, her slender fingers combing the air. 'The *dwaal* ... the land of the bewildered. That's how we were. Just bewildered all the time.'

We talk about small mercies, silver linings. Felix describes a Star of David, about a metre in diameter, that a fellow soldier had fashioned out of metal to mark the spot of Greg's death. Normally a cross would be placed there, but Greg's Aussie mate understood that this was not appropriate. Instead, he honoured his friend with a symbol of Jewish identity, an object that Felix was able to have returned home in 2013.

The story of how the Star of David made it home is itself extraordinary. In 2013 Felix contacted the chief of the Defence Force, as the Tarin Kowt base was being closed and Felix didn't like the idea of this sacred object languishing in the desert. The chief of the Defence Force replied that Felix could certainly retrieve the star, but that he didn't know where it was.

'I know where it is,' said Felix. In fact, a few months earlier, Barry had shown Felix a book called *Saving Private Sarbi*. The protagonist was a Labrador-cross named Sarbi, whose handler was wounded in 2008 by rocket-propelled grenades. The blow severed the lead that attached Sarbi to the handler's body armour and the dog was taken by the Taliban. She was held captive for fourteen months, until she was rescued, and identified, by American Special Forces. The book featured a photo of Sarbi in a chapel at Tarin Kowt, and behind her, Greg's Star of David. The star was shipped to Australia and now lives in the *shtiebel* (the chapel) at Lyndhurst Cemetery.

'You know, these are Greg's favourite biscuits—a plain biscuit with jam in the middle,' says Yvonne, passing around a box that Ephraim has brought. 'The shul used to put biscuits out after Shabbos and he would go around to each table and pick off these round jam biscuits.'

Ephraim looks pleased but doesn't say anything. Then I ask the Shers what they recall of Ephraim's contribution at the time of Greg's passing. Yvonne immediately cites the ease with which he dealt with the military.

'He just knew how to work with them, how to handle them. They couldn't understand all our rules and regulations,' she says. She recalls the army liaison didn't understand the 'no flowers' policy, and I know there was so much more besides—the Jewish reticence around autopsies, the fact that a simple pine coffin is not a failure of ceremony but an ancient honouring of equal human preciousness in death. Ephraim oiled all the cogs, ensuring everyone felt heard. On the morning of the funeral he drove out to Lyndhurst to rehearse the procession with the military personnel, to march behind the drum. He wanted to be in the right place, at the right time, when the important moment came.

At the same time, he provided the Shers with tools for bearing grief. Knowing that Felix loved stories, he gave him books: *As a Driven Leaf* by Milton Steinberg, *The Five Stages of Grief* by Elisabeth Kübler-Ross, *Many Lives, Many Masters* by Brian L. Weiss. Over the months following Greg's death, Ephraim drip-fed the family movies, including *Ghost*, which to this day brings Felix to tears.

But there was something above practical resources that Ephraim gave the Shers.

'He was so down to earth. He could understand we weren't ultra-Orthodox Jews. And he could see that and understand that and knew where we were at. He could read us,' says Yvonne.

'He could read us.' This phrase is the kernel. This is what continues to surface in the memories of the mourners Ephraim and

The life and deathwork of Ephraim Finch

I have sat with this year. Inside the vast mosaic of his persona shines his ability to meet people just where they are. I am thinking about this as I look at my watch and realise that—once again—several hours have elapsed in the course of storytelling. I glance at Ephraim. He picks up his Akubra from the chair next to him, indicating that it is time for us to go.

'He helped us cope,' says Felix. And Ephraim reads this too, knowing that we can't possibly bolt out the door after such a statement from a bereaved parent. Slowly, we get up from the kitchen table. We walk to the hallway, passing by the many portraits of Greg's warm, handsome face. We stand at the front door, chatting, saying several goodbyes. At the threshold, we hover some more. We allow the moment to take as long as it takes, all four of us now woven into something new from all the listening and all the telling.

Over the following days I find it impossible to write, as the world escalates in fury and pain. I think of Ephraim's question to Elie Wiesel: how did you mourn your dead in the camps? I wish Elie was here now, to answer a similar question: how do you mourn your dead when they are in a faraway land? How do you mourn all the dead, whether they are of your tribe and not of your tribe, when they are simply of your human family?

I dig up a quote by Primo Levi, who spoke to the need for individual stories amid vast catastrophe: 'One single Anne Frank moves us more than the countless others who suffered just as she did but whose faces have remained in the shadows. Perhaps it is better that way; if we were capable of taking in all the suffering of all those people, we would not be able to live.' Not be able to live, yes. But also struggle to empathise, to build that all-important bridge Wiesel appealed for.

I think of the countless articles and podcasts I have ingested over these suffocating spring weeks. And yet the thing that endures is an image I woke up to on the morning of 7 October, of an Israeli teenager being dragged off the back of a truck by her hair, at gunpoint. Her pants are bloodied, her wrists bound by rope. That image has since been interleaved with a photo of a Palestinian woman kneeling on a body, wrapped in a white sheet. Her face is streaked and stricken. The images are layered, into and over each other; by rubble, by the limbs, by the suffering that lodges like pebbles in my throat.

In the grip of trauma, the pogrom fear awakened, I weave in and out of needing music. Mourning supresses the appetite for song, but the compromised brain wants non-verbal arcs, harmony. I listen to Mendelssohn's 'Rondo Capriccioso in E Minor' on repeat. The piece opens calmly, slow and steady as a beginner's metronome. The speed with which it escalates, doubling into something spiky and erratic, is a weird comfort. It matches my mind.

I send it to Ephraim, but he doesn't reply. It is not until that evening that I receive a message from Sharona that he is in hospital. This is the second time in a fortnight that he is admitted; the first was a dizzy spell the doctors couldn't diagnose and the second for what Sharona describes as 'his heart rate swinging wildly'. 'They are going to restore his sinus rhythm,' says Cas in a voicemail. How can I not over-read these episodes? How can I not see them as a very physical manifestation of Ephraim's breaking heart?

Suddenly it feels physically stressful not to lay eyes on him. I count the minutes until I can call without being intrusive, immersing myself in things I imagine he will appreciate. I read about Leonard Cohen in 1973, when Cohen felt a sudden urge to leave Greece and travel to the Sinai Desert to witness the Yom Kippur War. It was in this period that Cohen wrote the iconic 'Who by Fire', a song that mirrors a central piece of Yom Kippur liturgy, the Unetanneh Tokef. The prayer, which Cohen would have heard in synagogue as a child, conveys the decisions God is making about the fate of every soul in the year to come. 'Who will live and who will die?' is the central question. And for those departing, what will it look like?

The life and deathwork of Ephraim Finch

We chant this prayer as the sun is going down on the Day of Atonement, as the symbolic gates to the kingdom of life are closing. Gates. Again.

I go back to Nick Cave, both on the stereo (*Abattoir Blues/The Lyre of Orpheus* fits this day) and on the page. I return to *Faith, Hope and Carnage*, a book I'd read at the beginning of this year, in some prescient glimpse of the stories to come. 'There is a great deficit of language around grief,' Cave writes, and I exhale. 'It's not something we are practised at as a society ... So many grieving people just remain silent, trapped in their own secret thoughts, trapped in their own minds, with their only form of company being the dead themselves.'

Interview transcript, 2 March 2023

Ephraim: 'It's like a lady I picked up ... it wasn't Springvale but it was close, next to it. It was two o'clock in the morning, the power of the night ... It's so true. Death has a power in the night.'

Katia: 'I love this. Tell me more.'

Ephraim: 'Darkness, it's such a powerful thing. In daytime you have power, life. Nighttime ... things relax.'

Katia: 'I want to know more about this. Can we stay here for a bit? Because this is so beautiful. The poetry of your vision ... What else is special about the nighttime? Everything is quieter, everything is less?'

Ephraim: 'Yeah. And thoughts can come to you in the night. Not bright thoughts. Dark thoughts.'

Katia: 'Sometimes are they useful?'

Ephraim: 'Yeah! But the realisation at night has a power, strong power.'

Katia: 'And what is that specifically? What does it enable us to do that we can't do in the day?'

Ephraim: 'Face it. Go with it.'

FERRYMAN

As I get closer to the end of Ephraim's story, I am clinging. I feel pre-emptive regret at what I haven't covered, either through the exigencies of time or through my own shortcomings. I become married to memory, who goes where I go now, my life-giving bride. Ephraim's stories—early, recent, prophetic, age-old—invade my sleep, they follow me down the street. I dream of shrouds on the bodies of the dead. The wrap of innocence, these rags of light.

One afternoon this week I pull over by the side of the road, sideswiped by more hot tears. I lean my head on the steering wheel, eyes closed. A memory arrives.

'I had that dream again,' he says to me. It must be winter. My feet are cold, even though he has turned up the heater several times. Cas is to my left, knitting. In the dream Ephraim is crossing a river with a barge loaded with souls. He is dressed in white, with a long beard. As soon as he hits the other shore, he offloads the souls. He could moor the barge, step onto solid ground. But some force compels him to turn around. So back he goes. On and on, from one shore to the other.

'This sounds arduous. Is it?' I ask.

'Nah, it's beautiful, calm.'

'You know, someone suggested that we call this book *Ferryman*,' I continue, 'for just that image. You've been telling people about this dream for years, right?'

'Yeah ... yeah.'

'Are you concerned about the crossover with Christian mythology, or the Ancient Greek?' I ask. I am thinking of Charon, the boatman who rowed the bodies over the River Styx. Ephraim says he is not concerned, that the name feels good.

Cas's knitting needles clack along. The grandfather clock keeps its discreet rhythm. Pop's rocking chair occupies the corner, covered in a quilt. I see William Robert George Finch in it, one leg crossed over the other, reading on the back veranda of an evening.

The life and deathwork of Ephraim Finch

'Of course she was a Jew,' Ephraim says, noticing me looking at the chair, somehow perceiving that I'm thinking about Nana Behrmann.

'What makes you say that?' I ask.

'She saw what was happening in families. And she kept an eye on things.' Keeping an eye on families isn't a uniquely Jewish trait, I think. But 'seeing what is happening', when you are one of twelve children, when your family hails from Hamburg, when all you have to say on the matter is 'They lived happily ever after', this makes sense.

I look out the window, mulling over this frustratingly cold lead, this dark tunnel of conjecture. I hear Ephraim get up from the table and shuffle out of the room. I hear him shuffle back, place something on the table in front of me.

'There you are,' he says, pointing to a framed black-and-white photo of a teenage girl in cap and gown, holding a paper scroll. Ephraim is answering me in image, because words are not our ally in this instance. I know, from previous stories, that this is Irene Behrmann, accepting a scholarship at the Royal College of Music in London for her piano playing. She is no more than seventeen years old, all dark hair and dark eyes, her serious gaze fixated on all its future viewers. Perhaps there is a darkness in her countenance, perhaps not. Ephraim will never be able to dig deeper into this particular history because Irene passed away in 1993, her cryptic statement about the Hamburg ancestors going into the earth with her. He looks at me as though to say, 'No point fighting it now.' He is wistful, but he has accepted.

We don't speak. There is nothing more to say. The only comfort comes from the striking resemblance I see in the old man's face before me, his dark eyes and melancholy half-smile a direct copy of the girl's. And one other thing: her hands—her prodigious piano-playing hands—are uncommonly large, her fingers long and smooth, and even in their resting state, somehow assured. I see those hands in the flesh in front of me, and perhaps this is legacy enough.

I return to my interview with Felix and Yvonne. I find a website where they provide a video testimonial to their son. I realise I never asked them what drove Greg to fight in Afghanistan. Felix speaks of Greg's concern for the women and children of the region, of the fundamentalist grip of the Taliban. He doesn't know Greg's precise motivations, because father and son never had that chat. Still, he does his best with the information he has, the thirty years of knowing his boy.

I ask the parents if there was anything they would have liked to say to Greg before he left for the war, anything that slipped through. Yvonne does not reply and my own maternal heart twists at her pain. But Felix's words are even more devastating, because they are so hopeful. They are a prayer for his son, and against the tragedy of war, a hope that something good can come from something terrible. 'I would have liked to wish him well,' he says, tearing up.

The suffocating spring continues and still I haven't heard from Ephraim. The days are intermittently cold, then furiously windy, a hurricane of pollen and plane-tree filaments. This is the longest interval between meetings we have had all year. I am trying to write about our trip to the Shers, but my concentration is at an all-time low. This week a rally in a park by my house saw people throwing rocks across a heavily policed divide, screaming rage.

I talk to Ephraim in my head, willing him to come back. I continue to read Nick Cave on death, on living. 'I think these absences do something to those of us who remain behind,' he says. 'We are like haunted houses, in a way, and our absences can even transform us so that we feel a quiet but urgent love for those who remain, a tenderness to all of humanity, as well as an earned understanding that our time is finite.'

And if I tell you the truth right now, you will think I am inventing for the sake of imagery. But I am inventing nothing.

The life and deathwork of Ephraim Finch

A white butterfly really did accost my car window today, just as I had called Felix to verify a detail. The sun was setting, the road was slick with recent rain. Before talking to Felix, I was listening to Leonard Cohen, greeting his listener 'from the other side, of sorrow and despair'. As Leonard sang on, a cluster of butterflies gathered, a flotilla landing and hovering. 'With a love so vast and shattered, it will reach you everywhere,' sang the old man. The butterflies made it hard to drive, but I couldn't rush them. They stayed as I drove homeward, recounting the vision to Ephraim in my head.

14

Two weeks later, I am sitting with Ephraim in his back room again. He seems well, if tired. Cas is sitting with us and Mishi is coming in and out, bringing his parents lunch, answering Ephraim's questions. Mishi is the continuance of Ephraim's work at the Chevra, building coffins and preparing the *tahara* room. He is, in Ephraim's words, a 'Man Friday'. Mishi is softly spoken and I imagine his gentle presence would be a balm in the halls of mourning. However, his work—and he has chosen it so—is functional; he is not continuing Ephraim's archival passions. Ephraim is no longer there to take the detailed histories, to write the names of the camps, to offer a DVD on the afterlife.

'What do you still want me to write about, Ephraim?' I ask.

'That place, my office at the Chevra,' he replies.

'Would you like to go there? Shall we do a visit together?'

'No, I wouldn't.'

I understand the crack in his voice when he says this. Ephraim doesn't want to visit a room that no longer feels like his old office. He can't bring himself to countenance the evaporated past. Fortunately, not all is evaporated. Early on, Ephraim told me about a poem he had written, called 'The Tapestry of Life'. He has often described his work with this phrase, and I recall the lecture he gave to the Genealogical Society with the very same title. Reading the poem at the first instance, I was struck by his succinct capture of this vast, ineffable subject in verse. But what stuns me now—as he pulls the page out, ready to read out loud—is the poem's age. 'The Tapestry of Life' was written by Ephraim in 1978, the year he and Cas spent in Israel. He wrote it for a beloved friend in Jerusalem, years before starting on the path of deathwork.

'Tapestry of Life'

He weaves us as thread on a weaver's loom
We are individual threads but one pattern
We begin as opposites on the warp
But we pass once or many times
Only the pattern of the weave designed by the
One above—who knows!
We have to follow the length of thread
For He decreed, 'We are only to see behind, never ahead'
The eye of the needle draws us on
The weaver sets the pace
We must go on, our destiny is set
For when we see the pattern, the Master's Hand has left

Ephraim reads the poem with tears streaming down his face. We don't discuss its meaning; by now we don't need to. Instead, I list the stories I will not be able to include in the book, for we are running out of time, out of space. At this he grows silent, looks away. An anguish at my guilty inventory.

'Ask them for my forgiveness,' he eventually says. And I don't question who 'they' are because I know they are everyone and everything he met by that river; the living and the dead, the disappeared and the descended. Besides, I am just an envoy for his stories. Who I am to ask for anything on behalf of Ephraim Finch?

'I will do my best,' I say, but he is still looking away.

This week, Ephraim and I are scheduled to go over the final chapters. But the night before our meeting I receive a text message saying, 'Could you meet me at Beth Rivkah at 10 am tomorrow morning. Rabbi Sufrin and I are giving Sam Recht's family the button from his father. I would appreciate your being there. Ephraim.' I don't know the story of the button or the family in question, but I am grateful to be invited.

The next morning I show up at Empress Street, the central artery of this deeply Hasidic neighbourhood. The narrow street is lined with vans, many of them mounted with a *menorah* on the roof. It is the eve of Hannukah, and the frenzy of preparation for this eight-day festival of light makes parking impossible. Ephraim is on the corner, waving me down to say, 'They're already here, hurry up.' The old fervour is in him, past bolting into present. I take a chance and park in a permit zone, trying desperately not to be late for this family.

Through the heavily patrolled gates (security guard in bullet-proof vest, electronic check-in, photo, visitor pass) I enter a high-walled compound. I must have driven past this school thirty thousand times over the past thirty-five years, so the sensation of being inside is especially bizarre. There is some strange magic in experiencing something from the inside that you have only ever witnessed externally. All around a large basketball court are tiled mosaics and paintings by the students, of the seasons, of the sea, of the world in motion. Girls in navy dresses flit about, giggling, biting their nails, hiding behind their folders in the way that teenage girls do. But these girls are not the meek figures I had (perhaps unfairly) expected them to be. They are chatty and confident. They approach the rabbi and pepper him with questions about what's happening. They say 'Hi' and 'Welcome' to me, as if they're showing me around their house. The air is electric as Ephraim and Rabbi Sufrin, the Recht family and I walk the perimeter of the courtyard and inside for the ceremony.

Three days ago, Sam Recht received a phone call from Rabbi Sufrin, who simply said, 'Sam, I have two things to say to you: 1945 and 1986.' Sam was perplexed.

The life and deathwork of Ephraim Finch

'I've got something incredible to tell you,' continued the rabbi.

'And then it connected, he was about to tell me something pertaining to my father,' Sam tells those of us gathered in the assembly hall—1945 was the end of World War II and 1986 was the year of his father's death.

Rabbi Sufrin said that a button from his father's concentration camp pants—also known as 'striped pyjamas'—had been retrieved by Ephraim Finch, from a filing cabinet at the Chevra Kadisha. Sam had only seen Ephraim intermittently over the four decades since his father's death but had in fact bumped into him just two weeks earlier. Ephraim had always remembered Sam's father, Michael Recht. Every time Sam ran into Ephraim at Rabbi Sufrin's shul, the men would hug, in a silent honouring of Michael's memory. Something about this recent encounter prompted Ephraim to search for the button.

Sam delivers a speech to the Year Ten and Eleven girls, unfolding the story, holding the metal button up for them to see.

'It's very small but I want you all to look at it closely. It doesn't look like anything special, does it?' he asks the room. Then he speaks of 'hope, luck, miracles'. Through his internments, through liberation, through his stay at a Displaced Persons Camp, Michael Recht kept his prisoner pants, and of course the button. The girls are listening. They look sombre, but also tragically au fait with this subject matter, this being their legacy, a strand in their earliest family narratives. I turn to the teacher next to me and whisper, 'Think of the things these girls have heard in their fifteen, sixteen years on this planet.' She nods, her shoulders rising slightly.

'Now you may think, How bizarre is that? Why would anyone in their right mind, after all that he went through to survive, want to keep these pants? Surely you would think the opposite, put these horrors behind you and move on with a new life, a second chance here in faraway Melbourne, a safe haven for him, our mother, and all Holocaust survivors who came here after the Second World War. But no!' Sam continues. Then he explains that the pants were a placeholder for his father's hope, a symbol of survival. His father's wish was to be buried with the garment. I sense that the girls—who have been learning the anatomy of endurance in virtually every subject since kindergarten—had already figured this out.

He then tells the students about the next stage of the button's journey. Ephraim is in the front row, in his black Akubra and tailored coat. He is still with the remembering.

'Now you can imagine, this was no ordinary request when we attended the Chevra Kadisha in October, 1986, and explained our father's wish to Ephraim Finch. Ephraim needed to check if this was permissible because, ordinarily, nothing is allowed in the coffin. I believe Ephraim consulted rabbis to get an answer. With our eternal appreciation, approval was given, due to these very exceptional circumstances. But what we didn't know until three days ago is that a Jewish person cannot be buried with a metal object in the coffin. And so, Ephraim Finch removed this metal button, this apparently small insignificant metal button, from our dad's pants before his funeral and put it his Chevra Kadisha file.'

After the speech, I follow the family into a small office where we, in the delicate words of Michael's granddaughter Gabby, will 'spend some quiet time with the button'. The room is sparse but for a series of mountainous oil landscapes and a large box of Kleenex, placed like an anticipatory gesture by a thoughtful therapist. The family has brought two framed photos of Michael (dark-haired, handsome, sharp-of-eye) and arranged them on the large oak table in the room's centre. A flurry of new photos (Ephraim with Rabbi Sufrin, Rabbi Sufrin with the family, Gabby with Ephraim, Ephraim with the photos of Michael) is then taken.

Once everyone is seated, a hush descends. I notice Ephraim folding his hands into a lattice, lowering his head. As if on silent cue, Michael's daughter Lili begins to recount Michael's internments, her words coruscating with the tragedy and strange fortune of so many Holocaust accounts. She tells us that he had been in several camps, including Treblinka. The first time he was deported, he was twenty years old. In one of the camps, he befriended a boy by the name of Berek Amatenstein, who was the brother of his future wife. Meanwhile, Pola, his wife-to-be, was in Auschwitz, oblivious of his existence.

Later, when Pola had escaped Europe and settled in Australia, she also made a special request ahead of her death. She wanted the Chevra Kadisha to bury her with two bars of soap that she had kept from Auschwitz, soap made from the bodies of murdered Jews. The Chevra honoured her wish; the third bar that she had kept now resides at the Melbourne Holocaust Museum.

Lili shares this story with a calm that, even after months of interviewing Holocaust survivors and their families, stuns me. She is not numb—tears fill her eyes, and her voice trembles when she recalls her mother fanatically showing her, over and over, where the bars were stored so that they may come with her to the grave. But she is steadfast, and this is what stuns me—Lili's willingness to descend to impossible darkness and re-emerge, holding up the vital truth for the world to see.

As the family chats, the phrase 'March of the Living' pops into my mind, a name given to the expedition through the historical camps many people undertake today. But it is clear that the march of the living is also right here, in this small room at a girls' school in Melbourne. It is in Lili's voice, shaking but unstoppable.

'The Holocaust is a strong part of our family,' says Sam, thanking Ephraim for finding the button, for bolstering his father's memory after all these years.

I see how alive Michael and Pola are to their descendants. Gabby recalls walking through Auschwitz with a survivor relative in 2012. In fact, Auschwitz was one of the camps from which Michael was spared, but for Gabby, this soil of annihilation was of a piece with the others. As she is speaking, I am picturing the soulless wasteland that Sharona described, that 'bereft' place where no one and nothing wants to dwell.

'Even though I've never met him, I feel very connected,' Gabby says, referring to her grandfather. Her eyes shift from turquoise to pale green, fighting the film of tears that dances on their surface like rain on a sea. Then she says something that cuts across the wasteland. In fact, it adds a precious new dimension to the raging pain of the world right now, the circular conversations Ephraim and I have been having about the perils of forgetting.

'When we were walking through the gates of Auschwitz, my relative said to me, "Gabby, your *buba* and *zeida* would be so proud of you right now." And two tiger-striped butterflies came past us for just two seconds. There's a significance behind the butterflies with my grandparents. We have always had a story about that in our family. So I believe that they are here with us. And the button is really just a physical reminder.'

The calendar year is coming to an end, and so is my turn around the sun with Ephraim. The strange hot mornings are upon us, pavements burning by schooltime. Cas's beloved pomegranate tree is starting to bud. The eight days of Hannukah are unfolding, and I learn that—aside from being a festival of light and miracle—Hannukah means 're-dedication'. Ephraim sends me a photo of his front gate, a wooden door the height of an adult. Nested inside it, like a picture in a pop-up book, is a lit *menorah*; fire framed by wood. Public and intimate, bold and gentle, it is speaking to the street.

Embarking on this book, Ephraim and I had not planned it this way, had not anticipated a neat circle. But Rabbi Sufrin's Russian phrase surfaces again: *ne rano i ne pozno*—'Not too early not too late'.

I have come to see how the notion of time is specific to grief, and not in the hackneyed conception of 'time heals all wounds'. Yes,

The life and deathwork of Ephraim Finch

I do believe time is, in its own way, the subtle, eventual medicine. But speaking to so many bereaved humans, I see something else. Time lives at the heart of grief because that is precisely what goes when we lose a loved one—those extra years, months, minutes are taken without permission. Time disappears, suddenly, silently, with a finality that leaves us winded.

And yet. 'Death is a night between two days,' writes Maurice Lamm, suggesting that in the Jewish conception it is a season, a portion, rather than an endless oblivion. It may be final in so far as our bodies go, but if you stand back far enough, it is no weightier than our mortal moment. Each is as ephemeral and precious as the other.

Throughout his journal entries, I find Ephraim reiterating this calculus, the equal gravity of both life and death. Interestingly, he is less concerned with 'Where do we go?' than 'What do we leave behind?'. His recurring question seems to be 'What endures?'.

In an entry titled 'Our trip to Wagga', he writes about a trip with Cas through Milbrulong, the countryside of her childhood. In a tiny town called The Rock, they chance upon an antique store where he learns that the shopkeeper's ancestors owned the block that now holds the Great Synagogue in Sydney. He photographs a World War I memorial, then climbs a fence to fossick 'through the ruins of her grandmother's mudbrick cottage'. He notices a vacant spot where Cas's maternal grandmother, Helene Adeline Luhrs, once planted a tree, since cut down by the council.

'It was sad to see an area gradually crumbling, but I should be used to seeing this. The land goes on forever. We pass through, leave a mark, a scratch, then we move on to our crevice in the earth, never to observe what the land, vegetation, does in its cycle of life and slumber,' he writes.

He has told me about walking through the fields at Lyndhurst with an Aboriginal elder before the Chevra formalised its purchase of the land. They looked at the towering eucalypts crossing the field, their roots as vast as their limbs. Ephraim promised they would not be chopped down to make space for burial plots. He wanted the inverse, to 'build the cemetery around the trees'.

What endures after our brief visit, he seems to be asking. What are the forces that do not cease?

Since the attacks of 7 October and the ensuing war, I have found it increasingly hard to be in the world. Not figuratively, but actually; I struggle to leave the house, to socialise in a courteous and ordinary way. A friend recommended a book called *Wintering: The Power of Rest and Retreat in Difficult Times*. The book has been a saviour, mostly because it's given me permission to turn inward while I finish Ephraim's story. I have shrunk my circle to immediate family and the closest friends. Day by day, I distance myself from social media and all but the barest reportage, the occasional piece of long-form writing. I have continued to research Ephraim's life, and to listen to his voice, playing and replaying our interview transcripts. The rest is a tumult outside my door.

The author of *Wintering*, Katherine May, talks about crisis demanding that we adopt an 'unfashionable' life, that our lives will repeatedly require a submergence, a journey precipitated by illness, or catastrophe, or sudden change in circumstance, which will necessarily land us somewhere new when we resurface.

As I contemplate finishing Ephraim's story, as I organise the catalogue of my heart and all its new entries, I remain fixated on notions of time. I wrestle with its slipperiness, the way it holds both immense elasticity and the cruellest restriction. 'Please, time, be kind to me,' I have prayed in the past, dreading the bold line beneath a moment. Now, replete with fresh sorrows, I come across this, deep inside *Wintering*: 'But then, that's what grief is—a yearning for that one last moment of contact that would settle everything'. May is speaking to the suffering inside the miracle, the non-negotiable cost of having an earthly body. This is the lingering ache, the seeming injustice of death. The

The life and deathwork of Ephraim Finch

agony of transience, the waveless last goodbye, the 'what if', the 'if only'.

The Recht family do not see it as a coincidence that Ephraim found Michael's button at this precise time. They believe it is a reminder of survival when we need it most. They appreciate the closure this object brings, such as it is. But I am drawn to something else: its place in the timeline, namely the date with which Rabbi Sufrin opened his call to Sam Recht. 1986. This is the year that Ephraim began at the Melbourne Chevra Kadisha. It is the opening bracket of his tenure, the *shomer* guarding his labours, his loves.

I open one more record, a short documentary about Ephraim made in 2006. The camera follows him around the Chevra building, from parking the hearse, to the *tahara* room, and finally to his office, where he sits at his vast wooden desk. He is surrounded by holy books, records, his map. Down the hall is the filing cabinet with the button in it.

When he begins to speak, I startle. This is not the tremulous voice of elderly and wistful Ephraim; this is the voice of a man at the top of his arc. He speaks quietly, but he is fluent, clear and completely in the moment. He is at home.

'I find that I'm rewarded for this style of life. I couldn't wish for any other style. It's sad, but it makes me aware of where I'm heading and what I'm doing ... Of course, we don't want to die, we want to live. But what we've got to understand is we're here for a specific moment in life, and then we move on to another scene.' He looks directly to camera.

'We say something for someone when they're leaving us,' Ephraim says eventually. 'We say "*Lech le shalom*: go in peace".' Here, he is talking about farewelling the living and the dead; the ancient matriarch, the absent father, the baby that never drew its breath, the wide-eyed grandchild embarking on her travels.

'*Lech le shalom*,' he repeats.

I pause the film and look closely at his face. The timeless gaze of Ephraim Finch. Every moment holds the possibility of repair, it is saying. Go in peace but know the soil from which you come—it is your first and last abode, this dark and silent dreaming. Pay attention to farewells, be alive to the passing. Above all, remember the names. And when the time comes, speak them out loud. Make memory a blessing, turn silence into song.

List of Sources

PART I: The Shore

Chapter 2
Herman Wouk, *This Is My God: The Jewish Way of Life*, 1987, Little Brown & Company, Toronto

Chapter 3
Ralph Waldo Emerson, *Nature*, 1836, James Munroe and Company, Boston

Chapter 4
Francis Weller, *The Wild Edge of Sorrow: Rituals of Renewal and the Sacred Work of Grief*, 2015, North Atlantic Books, Berkeley

PART II: The Crossing

Chapter 5
Maurice Lamm, *The Jewish Way in Death and Mourning*, 2000, Jonathan David Publishers, New York

Chapter 6
Melbourne Holocaust Museum, survivor testimonial: Sally Felzen, 13 June 2017, Melbourne

Larissa Dubecki, 'At last, a place to rest—and grieve—for Holocaust victims', *The Age*, 17 May 2004, p. 6

Anthony Albanese, speech, opening of the Melbourne Holocaust Museum, 22 November 2023, Melbourne

Jewish Care, 'About Holocaust survivor support', 2024, https://www.jewishcare.org.au/services/holocaust-survivor-support/AboutHSSP

Chapter 7

Victor Kleerekoper, 'Chevra Kadisha seeks say in cemeteries review', *Australian Jewish News*, 23 August 1996, p. 5

Melbourne Holocaust Museum, 'Ring of hope', 2016, https://mhm.org.au/2016/05/05/ring-hope/

Chapter 8

Blak Led Tours, Nunami Sculthorpe-Green, First Nations tour of nipaluna, 19 October 2023

Anne Elias and Peter Elias (eds), *A View from Afar: Jewish Lives in Tasmania from 1804*, 2003, The Hobart Hebrew Congregation, Hobart

Parry Kostoglou, 'Archaeological mitigation works, former Jewish Cemetery, Windsor Court Complex, Harrington Street', Housing Tasmania, February 2002

Hobart Synagogue, 'The history of Hobart Synagogue', 2024, https://www.hobartsynagogue.org/history/

Mar I. Pinsky, 'The convict synagogue at the end of the world', *Tablet*, 24 October 2014, https://www.tabletmag.com/sections/news/articles/the-convict-synagogue-at-the-end-of-the-world

John S. Levi, *These Are the Names: Jewish Lives in Australia, 1788–1850*, 2nd edition, 2013, Miegunyah Press, Melbourne

Tasmanian Department of Health and Human Services, 'Windsor Court redevelopment: Guidelines to contractors working on the Windsor Court site', 15 November 2001

Malcolm Downie (Director of Housing), 'Windsor Court site works', Tasmanian Government media release, 23 January 2002

Ephraim Finch, 'Harrington Street Old Jewish Cemetery—Revisiting our past', Ephraim Finch's personal documents

Phoebe Hosier, 'What does Hobart's kunanyi/Mt Wellington mean to Tasmania's First Nations people?', ABC News online, 26 April 2020, https://www.abc.net.au/news/2020-04-26/what-hobarts-mt-wellington-mean-to-tasmanias-indigenous-people/12141266

Wendell Berry, *New Collected Poems*, 2012, Counterpoint, Berkeley

PART III: The Return

Chapter 10

'School briefs; Death and mourning', *Australian Jewish News*, 26 December 1997, p. 6

Bernard Freeman, 'Rabbis say no to euthanasia', *Australian Jewish News*, 7 June 2002, p. 8

Isabelle Oderberg, 'Drugs, fear, another death', *Australian Jewish News*, 6 August 1999, p. 3

Alana Rosenbaum, 'Sharing the struggle of drugs in the family', *Australian Jewish News*, 12 November 1999, p. 4

Victor Kleerekoper, 'A drug death every month', *Australian Jewish News*, 25 June 1999, p. 3

'Naltrexone: Can it save our addicts?', *Australian Jewish News*, 6 August 1999, p. 32

Victor Kleerekoper, 'Heroin deaths shock community', *Australian Jewish News*, 17 December 1999, p. 1

Focus piece, 'The drug crisis: The kid, the addict, the victim', *Australian Jewish News*, 12 March 1999, p. 19

David Langsam, 'A Jewish atheist's way in death and mourning', *Australian Jewish News*, 4 August 1995, p. 18

Maurice Lamm, *The Jewish Way in Death and Mourning*, 2000, Jonathan David Publishers, New York

Margaret Safran, 'Secular humanist marriages now a reality', *Australian Jewish News*, 21 July 1995, p. 3

'Forensic medicine cuts out the scalpel', *The Age*, 9 September 2005, https://www.theage.com.au/national/forensic-medicine-cuts-out-the-scalpel-20050909-ge0uao.html

Chapter 11

'The Tainted Grain', in Rabbi Aryeh Kaplan (trans.), *Rabbi Nachman's Stories: The Stories of Rabbi Nachman of Breslov*, 1983, The Breslov Research Institute, Brooklyn, New York

Martin Buber, *The Legend of the Baal-Shem*, 2002, Routledge, London

Elie Wiesel, *Souls on Fire: Portraits and Legends of Hasidic Masters*, 1972, Simon & Schuster, New York

Elie Wiesel, *All Rivers Run to the Sea: Memoirs, Volume One, 1928–1969*, 1996, Harper Collins, London

Elie Wiesel, *Night*, 1985, Jason Aronson Inc., Northvale, New Jersey

Ariel Burger, *Witness: Lessons from Elie Wiesel's Classroom*, 2019, Houghton Mifflin Harcourt, New York

Melbourne Holocaust Museum, survivor testimonial: Edward Retman, 22 January 1995, Melbourne

William Shakespeare, *As You Like It*, (ed. Albert Gilman), The Signet Classic Shakespeare Series, 1986, Signet, New York

Chapter 12

United Holocaust Memorial Museum, Holocaust Encyclopedia, 'Theresienstadt', https://encyclopedia.ushmm.org/content/en/article/theresienstadt

Carol Saffer, 'Christopher Latham's music of memory', *Australian Jewish News*, 12 October 2023, https://www.australianjewishnews.com/christopher-lathams-music-of-memry/

Jewish Museum in Prague, 'Children's drawings from the Terezín Ghetto', 2024, https://www.jewishmuseum.cz/en/collection-research/collections-funds/visual-arts/children-s-drawings-from-the-terezin-ghetto/

Hana Volavková (ed.), *I Never Saw Another Butterfly: Children's Drawings and Poems from the Terezín Concentration Camp, 1942–1944*, 1994, Schocken Books, New York

Cody Mello-Klein, 'Northeastern student brings new life to powerful history behind secret synagogue of Terezín', States News Service, 30 March 2023, Gale Academic One File, https://go.gale.com/ps/i.do?p=AONE&u=monash&id=GALE%7CA743704609&v=2.1&it=r&sid=bookmark-AONE&asid=321c64c1

Jüdisches Museum Berlin, 'Golem', 2016-17, https://www.jmberlin.de/en/exhibition-golem

Alexandr Putík, 'The Hebrew inscription on the crucifix at Charles Bridge in Prague: The case of Elias Backoffen and Berl Tabor in the Appellation Court', *Judaica Bohemiae*, 1: 26-103, The Central and Eastern European Online Library, Issue 1, 1996

Biuro Projektow Lewicki Latak, Piotr Lewicki i Kazimierz Latak, 'Ghetto Heroes Square Kraków (Poland), 2005: Refurbishment of a square in memory of the victims of the Kraków Ghetto', Public Space, 2018, https://www.publicspace.org/en/web/guest/works/-/project/d019-plac-bohaterow-getta

Muzeum Treblinka, 'Treblinka II—commemoration', https://muzeumtreblinka.eu/en/informacje/commemoration/

'Oprah and Elie Wiesel at the Auschwitz death camp', *Oprah Winfrey Show*, originally broadcast 21 May 2006

Chapter 13

Mostafa Rachwani and AAP, 'Tens of thousands demand Gaza ceasefire at pro-Palestine rallies across Australia', *The Guardian*, 19 November 2023, https://www.theguardian.com/australia-news/2023/nov/19/tens-of-thousands-demand-gaza-ceasefire-at-pro-palestine-rallies-across-australia

Hans Westra, *Inside Anne Frank's House. An Illustrated Journey Through Anne's World*, 2004, Overlook Press, New York

Nick Cave and Seán O'Hagan, *Faith, Hope and Carnage*, 2022, Text Publishing, Melbourne

Nick Cave, 'The Red Hand Files', Issue #6, October 2018

Chapter 14

Maurice Lamm, *The Jewish Way in Death and Mourning, 2000*, Jonathan David Publishers, New York

Katherine May, *Wintering: The Power of Rest and Retreat in Difficult Times*, 2020, Rider, London

The Shomer, director and writer Anton Blajer, producer Jacob Oberman, 2006, Victorian College of the Arts School of Film and Television, Melbourne

Acknowledgments

This book is, in every way, a collaboration. The tapestry could not be woven without the stories of the deceased and the families who graciously shared them. Thank you for your presence of heart, your openness, your willingness to travel the depths.

Huge gratitude to the Finch children, who allowed me into their world and helped me better understand their beloved father.

Thank you to Eva Friedman and Arnold Zable for initiating the project. My preliminary research drew heavily on interviews conducted by Eva and transcribed by Sharon Frankel. Thank you, Eva, for ensuring that these long-ago vignettes did not disappear into the ether and for answering a thousand questions about Ephraim's vast contribution to Melbourne's Jewish community. Arnold—thank you for your intimate capture of Ephraim and for the *ruach* you have brought to the process.

Catherine Lewis, publisher at Wild Dingo Press, is responsible for overseeing this vast endeavour. Thank you, Cathi, for your instinctual and curious nature, for your unswerving commitment to lesser-heard voices and immediate belief in the importance of Ephraim's stories. Lenka Miklos; I was blessed to have your brilliant structural feedback once again. Thank you for feeling each word, each clause and turning point, and for engaging, so deftly, with both the mechanical and the ineffable. Thank you to Paul Smitz for a careful, and caring, line edit.

Kevin Brophy—I continue to be blessed by the gift of your mentorship. Thank you for asking beautiful questions and not letting me write a lesser phrase when there is a finer one hiding in the wings.

Many people gave me technical advice, both as to the accuracy of the text and my portrait of a deathworker. Special thanks to Ben Finch, Rabbi Yisroel Sufrin, Rabbi Ralph Genende, Simon Holloway, Sister Catherine Cletus, Mark Bundy, David Clark, Moshe Herst, Jill Margo and Simon Weinstein. Thank you to the Bundanon Trust for space and resources to revise these chapters on mighty Dharawal Country; the United States Holocaust Memorial Museum; The USC Shoah Foundation; the Jewish Museum of Australia; the Lamm Jewish Library of Australia, for endless expertise and the ideal atmosphere for creating just this text; the Melbourne Holocaust Museum, especially the living treasure that is its librarian, Julia Reichstein.

I am indebted to the *tahara* volunteers who gave me their time and their personal accounts of this holy, quiet work.

This book stands on the shoulders of people who simply believed in it and provided time, practical advice and creative input: Michael Visontay, Gayelene Carbis, Marina Kamenev, Jaye Kranz, Lara Lubitz, Tali Lavi, Isabelle Oderberg, Ilana Faivel, Melissa Weinstein and Rachel Kafka. Special thanks to Miriam Hechtman and Michaela Kalowski for early reading, late-night wisdoms and tireless encouragement. Shoshy Rockman for the wooden deck, the ears, the notes, the dogs and the time we went walking through the estuary and you told me about the Ladder of Giving.

For three years, my family has watched me fall apart and reconfigure around the precious undertaking of *Ferryman*. The work would not have been possible without the loving arms of my parents, siblings and children. You are my home and my reason for reconfiguring after the falling apart.

My enduring gratitude to Cas Finch, who has held my hand and my heart and—with every gesture—shown me the shape of pure love.

Dearest Ephraim—thank you for meeting me with unconditional kindness, for making me less afraid of some things and necessarily frightened by others. Thank you for the *kavod* of our friendship and for showing me that no force is mightier than an open heart.

This book is dedicated to my maternal grandfather, Naum Belogolovksi, son of Froim and Faiga. May his memory be a blessing.

www.ingramcontent.com/pod-product-compliance
Lightning Source LLC
Chambersburg PA
CBHW011420070526
44584CB00026BA/3778